SHAPEDOWN ®

PARENT'S GUIDE

A Guide to Supporting Your Child

Balboa Publishing · San Anselmo, CA

The development of SHAPEDOWN was supported in part by the Department of Family and Community Medicine and the John Tung/American Cancer Society Clinical Nutrition Education Center, School of Medicine, University of California, San Francisco. Developmental testing was facilitated by the Department of Pediatrics of the University. The initial development of the SHAPEDOWN Program was facilitated by the Bureau of Maternal and Child Health Services and the Division of Adolescent Medicine, University of California, San Francisco.

Use of SHAPEDOWN materials is recommended in conjunction with guidance provided by trained health/education professionals following the SHAPEDOWN Instructor's Guide.

Reviewers are requested to obtain complete program materials from Balboa Publishing at the address listed below.

© 2007 Balboa Publishing Corporation

Fifth Edition, Revised

8 7

Library of Congress
Cataloging in Publication Data
Mellin, Laurel M.

SHAPEDOWN Parent's Guide
A Guide to Supporting Your Child

Library of Congress Catalog Card No.: 88-70316
ISBN 0-935902-18-X Paperback

Illustrations: Martha Weston
Graphic Design: Nielsen Graphics
Typography: ProType Graphics, Inc.

Published by:

mybook®

Balboa Publishing Corporation
MYBOOK DIVISION
1323 San Anselmo Avenue
San Anselmo, CA 94960-2244
TEL: 415.453.8886
FAX: 415.453.8888
EMAIL: shapedown@aol.com
WEBSITE: www.shapedown.com

CONTENTS

CONTENTS (Continued)

WELCOME TO SHAPEDOWN!

You have come to the right place. SHAPEDOWN is the nation's leading weight program for children. The program is based on the experience of more than 80,000 graduates and on scientific research showing that family-based interventions like SHAPEDOWN cause weight loss that, on the average, is maintained even ten years later.

What you accomplish with SHAPEDOWN is up to you. However, our hope is that it is not only weight loss. SHAPEDOWN is designed to gently and effectively help your child lose weight. But it also pays attention to the subtle issues that have allowed weight problems to settle into your family's life. SHAPEDOWN is offered as an opportunity to throw open the windows and blow away a few cobwebs - the feelings, ideas, beliefs, and actions that haven't worked well for you - and to consider some new ones. Many families use dealing with their child's overweight as an opportunity to make their parenting more rewarding and to create a more emotionally satisfying family life.

Before you embark on your SHAPEDOWN experience, I want to congratulate you on being one in 250. That's right, even though studies have shown the profound effectiveness of family-based weight programs for the young, most families with overweight children don't find their way into a program. As a mother of three and a person with an oversized commitment to helping the young escape lifelong battles with food and weight, I ask you to go through SHAPEDOWN and, if you find that it helps your child and family, to tell others about your experience. It's a risk to come to SHAPEDOWN, and your encouragement may prompt another parent to take that leap and to get some help, potentially giving rise to their child avoiding the snarl of troubles that obesity can bring.

Let's deal with basics. How does SHAPEDOWN work? It involves three steps:

1. **Assessment** - First, you and your child will participate in an assessment given by a trained pediatric obesity specialist with consultation from a multidisciplinary team of health professionals. This team includes a physician, a registered dietitian, a mental health professional and an exercise specialist. The purpose of your assessment is to give you a clear understanding of the causes and consequences of your child's weight. Then your family can work with your SHAPEDOWN instructor to determine the most effective way to support your child in losing weight.

A computerized assessment, called YES, the Youth Evaluation Scale, is available to families through SHAPEDOWN instructors. YES uses standardized tests to measure many aspects pertaining to weight, such as percentile of body fat, body fat patterning, blood pressure, cholesterol, signs of "gland problems", fitness (flexibility, endurance, strength), lifestyle habits, emotional overeating, knowledge about weight management, self-esteem, anxiety, family lifestyle, parenting practices, family closeness and adaptability, and parent-child communication. YES points out all of the areas in which the child and family are already healthy and those areas on which to focus to get the best results with weight and well-being.

2. **SHAPEDOWN** - Next, you will begin taking care of the weight. The plan you and your SHAPEDOWN instructor develop may or may not involve SHAPEDOWN. Some children require no care. Others benefit from other kinds of counseling before or in addition to participating in SHAPEDOWN. Some families go through SHAPEDOWN in a group; others complete SHAPEDOWN through individual counseling.

SHAPEDOWN is designed to give you the initial support, training, and motivation to start your child and family in the direction of a new way of living. In SHAPEDOWN groups, other parents, facing a child glued to the couch or plaintive pleas for cookies, will give you a chance to laugh, brainstorm and learn. Your child will be with other kids and be comforted by not being the only one up against the teasing of bullies or clothes crises. There will be family time at the beginning and end of the session, too. Your SHAPEDOWN instructor and entire team will be at your disposal when questions arise and to see you successfully through either the group or individual counseling version of the program.

3. MORE SHAPEDOWN - If your child has more than 10 pounds to lose, it is likely that he or she will benefit from additional support after this initial SHAPEDOWN experience. Individual counseling with your SHAPEDOWN instructor is one form of support. Most families benefit more from group programs. There are two that we recommend:

For preadolescents: ADVANCED SHAPEDOWN is the next step if your child is 12 or younger. It gives your family a more secure transition into permanent lifestyle changes. ADVANCED SHAPEDOWN will strengthen you and your child's skills in preventing relapse, keeping boredom at bay, and settling into your new way of living. Moreover, it will gently nudge and generously support you and your child in "cleaning house" of any leftover feelings and behaviors that still concern you.

A unique feature of ADVANCED SHAPEDOWN is that it assists you in anticipating the changes your child will experience in adolescence and lays out clear strategies for dealing effectively with everything from group eating binges to declarations of vegetarianism to uncertainty about what a teen truly requires nutritionally. It is full of ideas, support and stimulation to help you and your child continue your success.

For adolescents: If your child is 13 or older, the TEEN SHAPEDOWN group will keep them on track through the roller coaster of adolescence. In this program, your teen will be with other adolescents and receive peer support to improve their weight. The activities of the group program and the readings and practices in the teen SHAPEDOWN book reinforce their previous SHAPEDOWN training and deepen their understandings of themselves and of their food, activity and weight. In addition, the separate parent sessions available to you will help you shift responsibility for weight to your teen yet feel more comfortable with your parenting during your child's struggle for independence.

Let me assure you that SHAPEDOWN will not tell you how to raise your child or even dictate how to get your child to lose weight. It will present you respectfully with an array of ideas and strategies - some which you will accept, others which you will reject - to shape a style of living that works for you and your child. All of these are very personal matters and I thank you for the chance to dance with you through such sensitive terrain.

Laurel Mellin, M.A., R.D.
Director, The Center for Child and Adolescent Obesity
University of California, San Francisco

THE ACTIONS

Each of us agrees to the following this week:

1. Complete the readings, practices and quizzes for Section 1.

2. Record on my SUPPORT record each day.

3. Meet at least 3 of my 4 SUPPORT goals.

4. If overweight, lose weight: □ ½ + pound **OR** □ 1 + pounds.

THE REWARDS

If **we all** do all of these actions, then **we all** receive our rewards:

_____'s reward:_____
child's name   provided by when?_____

_____'s reward:_____
parent's name   provided by when?_____

_____'s reward:_____
parent's name   provided by when?_____

When the family receives the rewards, _____ will be responsible for
parent's name
rewarding the child. The child will be sure the parents have given themselves their reward.

_____   _____
parent's signature   child's signature

_____   _____
parent's signature   date

PARENT SUPPORT

	MON.	TUES.	WED.	THURS.	FRI.	SAT.	SUN.	TOTAL	MET MY GOAL?
We took FAMILY TIME each day to review these records and to praise each other.	✓	✓	✓	✓	✓	✓	✓	7 days	(YES) NO
I watched no more than 0 2 (4) 6 8 hours of TV	½	½	0	0	0	2	1	4 hours	(YES) NO
I EXERCISED for 50 100 (200) 300 400 minutes or more.[3]	walk 30	aerobics 60	walk 30	aerobics 60	walk 30	swim 20	hike 60	290 minutes	(YES) NO
GOAL OF THE WEEK: Our family ate dinner together on 4 or more days.	✓	✓	✓	✓			✓	5 days	(YES) NO
							TOTAL NUMBER OF GOALS MET ⇒		4

Get your physician's approval before exercising. If you are not now exercising, we suggest walking. Later in the program you will develop a more complete exercise program for yourself.

4

PARENT SUPPORT #1

	MON.	TUES.	WED.	THURS.	FRI.	SAT.	SUN.	TOTAL	MET MY GOAL?
We took FAMILY TIME each day to review these records and to praise each other.								___ days	YES NO
I watched no more than 0 2 4 6 8 hours of TV								___ hours	YES NO
I EXERCISED for 50 100 200 300 400 minutes or more.								___ minutes	YES NO
GOAL OF THE WEEK: Our family ate dinner together on ___ or more days.								___ days	YES NO

TOTAL NUMBER OF GOALS MET ⟹

Get your physician's approval before exercising. If you are not now exercising, we suggest walking. Later in the program you will develop a more complete exercise program for yourself.

5

1. GETTING STARTED

You have an overweight child. You are not alone. Almost one in three children is significantly overweight. And the numbers are growing. Obesity in kids has increased an alarming 54% in the last fifteen years. You and your child are experiencing an increasingly common problem.

You know what it's like to parent an overfat child. It's not easy. Chances are you feel angry, frustrated, perplexed, fearful and guilty.

Amy's weight is all we talk about. I feel like I am constantly glaring at her, thinking, is she going to blow it again? I'm so sick of saying "no"—and watching her pout—that I want to scream!

I really wasn't aware how much fatter than other kids Stacy was until she entered kindergarten. I knew it then, but I didn't do anything about it. Now she's 9 and even fatter. I feel 100% to blame.

We were so afraid that Andrew would look just like his father's dad who is so big and has just awful eating habits. So we put him on diets from the first time we noticed his being chubby. All that effort, and it has been a total failure.

Kristin is such a sensitive kid. She takes care of me as much as I do her. Kristin is wise beyond her years and I find that comforting. I try to put her weight out of my mind. I've always been hopeful that she'll grow into her weight.

My mother has been hounding me that the child weighs too much. The message is that I am a bad mother because my child is fat. I resent her minding my business. But I ignore it. There is too much going on right now to deal with the whole weight thing.

You truly want to help your child. You would like to see your child healthy and happy. It's just that everything you try backfires. Dieting is so negative. Your child ends up hounding you. And finally you give in. You hate to deprive your child. You're fed up with waiting for the weight to come off, so you've decided to give SHAPE-DOWN a try.

Good. It's likely that you'll like SHAPE-DOWN. The program is safe and effective. You'll receive skilled attention from a physician, a registered dietitian, a mental health professional and an exercise specialist. We value the opportunity to guide your child and family toward changes that benefit weight as well as overall well-being.

This guide helps you put into practice the following ten guidelines that have helped other families with overweight children. Please read them. Are they reasonable? Which ones are likely to be important to your child and your family? Which just don't suit your needs?

SHAPEDOWN PARENT GUIDELINES

1. Understand clearly your child's weight, including its medical and psychosocial risks and the factors contributing to it.

2. Become aware of your feelings about your child's weight.

3. Let go of weightism and accept your child's natural body build.

4. Create a light but not depriving food environment at home.

5. Develop a family lifestyle that is physically active.

6. Structure an active and enriching lifestyle for your child that includes daily exercise.

7. Support each family member in openly expressing his or her feelings and needs.

8. Give your child direct messages that you accept and value him or her.

9. Set limits with your child and follow through consistently.

10. Be a good role model by improving your own weight, eating or inactivity problems.

1

What will you gain from SHAPEDOWN?
SHAPEDOWN will start your child on the track to losing weight. In addition, you'll gain some insight into your child's weight problem and strategies for stimulating your child to eat those carrots and take a walk without complaining. You'll probably find yourself nagging and policing less often. Your whole family's health is likely to improve. Parents report that their child's weight prompted them to make changes that they'd been wanting to make for years. What's more, families tell us that they are less tense, closer, and happier after SHAPEDOWN.

What SHAPEDOWN expects from you — You are the conductor that orchestrates changes. SHAPEDOWN won't work unless you give it your full support.

1. Attend all of the sessions. There are so many competing priorities. You are late, tired, overcommitted. Come to the sessions anyway. If you miss a session, the group suffers and so do you. Once a week is minimal help to accomplish the complex changes you and your child are attempting.

2. Come prepared to each session. In SHAPEDOWN there is about 1 hour of reading per week including completing self-assessments and quizzes and about 15 minutes per day of record keeping. In addition, children - especially younger children - need parental help in completing their own readings, practices and quizzes. These activities are central to the effectiveness of the program and are considered required. Therefore, the basic requirement for attending SHAPEDOWN sessions is:

If any participating family member does not bring his or her book and completed practices and records to a session, no members of that family will be admitted to that particular session.

3. Set aside 10 minutes each day for FAMILY TIME. During FAMILY TIME children and parents review their records and practices and praise one another for the positive changes they have made. The nurturing, reinforcement and focus that FAMILY TIME provides is enormously powerful and fuels each person's progress.

4. Address barriers to success before joining the program. SHAPEDOWN will be unlikely to be successful if certain conditions exist in your family. If they do, counseling to resolve them should be undertaken prior to entering SHAPEDOWN. These barriers are:

When parents disagree about the child's weight - If one parent feels that weight loss is important and the other thinks it's a waste of time, the child will be torn between those views. With one parent, the child will diet, with the other, he or she will indulge. This is confusing and potentially destructive to the child. Counseling to resolve this conflict between the parents is a necessary prelude to participating in SHAPEDOWN.

HOW MANY PARENTS TO INVOLVE?

As part of your assessment, you will decide about parental involvement. In general, children benefit from both parents being involved. The risks of only one parent being involved include: exhaustion and overload of the single parent, sabotage - subtle or blatant - from the other parent, or lack of change in the absent parent which results in a dilution or inconsistency of change in the family. Often the success of a child's experience in SHAPEDOWN is due in large part to attention from a parent who previously was less close to the child.

8

Am I ready?

Now Jimmy brings me so much joy. SHAPEDOWN brought us closer.

When the family is too overburdened to participate fully in SHAPEDOWN - Most of us have been there - through custody battles, major illnesses, or crises with kids or work. If your load is too heavy because situations are difficult or family life isn't working well - consider setting aside weight for a while and dealing directly with those difficulties. If you find yourself putting off SHAPEDOWN for more than a year, question whether you are actually receiving the help you need to unload those burdens or to strengthen your family's capacity to cope with problems.

NEW FAMILIES AND SHAPEDOWN

Ozzie and Harriet are no longer the norm and all family types participate in SHAPEDOWN. During your assessment, you will discuss the involvement of step-parents, estranged biologic parents, grandparents, room mates and other adults close to the child with the goal of creating a "coalition" of support for the child. It is particularly important to include in SHAPEDOWN those adults who have authority over the child's food and activity and those who strongly influence the child's emotional well-being.

I feel comfortable with Sandra's weight now. No more guilt trips.

1

When a child doesn't want to participate - Most children are apprehensive about attending SHAPEDOWN, but after the first session, love it. A few children, however, resist participating vehemently. We suggest that parent's require their kids to attend one session to "check it out". If, after the first session, the child still resists strongly, it's often best to back off until he or she is ready. In the meantime, plan visits without your child to your SHAPEDOWN instructor to get support and direction on making behind-the-scenes changes to improve your child's habits and weight.

When a parent will not address his or her own eating problem - We didn't know when we had kids, how much they would make us face our own problems. The truth is, we can't support our child well in eating healthy unless we eat healthy. If we emotionally over-eat, pack away junk food, or won't exercise, our child knows it. There is nowhere to hide. To heal our child, we must heal ourselves.

My own kid helped me get past my weight problem. Bless him!

If you won't commit to acknowledging your problems in these areas and to working toward improving them, we suggest that you do not enter SHAPEDOWN now. Doing so could be enormously confusing to your child and could undercut the intimacy and trust in your relationship. We recommend getting counseling for your own resistances to addressing such problems before entering this program.

When a child's weight loss is too threatening - A person's weight loss can cause serious problems in some families. Although being overweight seems like a disadvantage, it often only persists because of a silent but powerful advantage of the weight. For instance, a child's weight may be a visual sign of loyalty in an obese family. Or intense concern that parents share about their child's weight may hold together an otherwise shaky marriage. In addition, obesity in a spouse has the advantage to an insecure mate of decreasing the chances of being left.

Often these dynamics are buried and parents are unaware of them. If you are aware of an unspoken advantage of maintaining your own or your child's weight, we recommend addressing it prior to entering SHAPEDOWN. If you aren't, yet go through SHAPEDOWN without weight loss, consider thinking through again potential advantages to holding onto the weight.

Brittany was an indulged child. Indulged, at least, by her mother. Father was unhappy in the marriage and coped by withdrawing emotionally and overworking. Mother looked to Brittany for some of what she was missing in her marriage - companionship and acceptance. Mother was overinvolved in the child's life and Father was removed from it. As a "parentified" child, Brittany felt isolated from both her mother and her father and in response developed a huge appetite. She knew she was indulged and felt she was faking it. She missed her father's affection and attention. The family was stuck in this position. SHAPEDOWN would have been unsuccessful in helping this family at this point. Their YES assessment suggested working first on family issues - restoring emotional connection in the marriage which would result in Brittany moving back into the child role. After several months of family counseling, they entered SHAPEDOWN, applied the ideas and watched their daughter slim down.

Before we focus on strategies for helping your child, lets talk about the SHAPEDOWN philosophy and goals.

PHILOSOPHY AND GOALS

The long-term goal of SHAPEDOWN is for your child to become a healthy, normal weight adult who is free from weight and diet concerns.

Our immediate goals are for your child to learn how to take more responsibility for his weight, and to improve his diet and exercise habits, his knowledge about nutrition and exercise and his communication skills. Accomplishing this will require numerous family changes, including lifestyle and communication patterns. SHAPEDOWN works toward these goals with the following methods:

1. SHAPEDOWN avoids high risk techniques. During these pivotal and sensitive childhood years, restrictive or very low calorie diets can slow or stunt growth. They can also cause nutritional deficiencies and rob young bodies of muscle tissue.

Perhaps as disturbing, putting children on diets just makes them feel deprived, punished, wrong and overly focused on weight. Diets just set children up for a life of roller coaster weight and diet/binge cycles. Instead SHAPEDOWN encourages kids and families to eat moderately and nutritiously.

In addition, for some kids dieting earns them a lot of attention. The emphasis on dieting gives children the message that the way to get attention in the family is to perpetually "try to" diet. What child would want to lose weight and give up all that attention?

2. SHAPEDOWN teaches kids to manage their weight independently. Rather than relying on a set diet pattern, SHAPEDOWN teaches them to make decisions about what, when and how much to eat in a broad range of situations. They are not tied to set meals or certain foods. Exercise, too, involves independence. Rather than providing daily exercise sessions, SHAPEDOWN teaches children how to develop their own exercise programs. As your child masters SHAPEDOWN, he or she will be more independent. You may feel upset by this and want your child to need you in the "old way."

3. SHAPEDOWN addresses the obstacles to good diet and exercise patterns. Most of us know what to eat and how much to exercise. So what really helps us is doing away with the obstacles, the things that keep us from making changes consistently. SHAPEDOWN helps with a wide range of these obstacles. Kids pick up techniques to improve their self-esteem and their mood. Parents sharpen their skills in listening to and setting limits with their children. Families change their food and activity patterns, and the focus of time together moves away from food.

4. SHAPEDOWN accommodates individual needs. We use self-directed change so that you concoct your own program. We talk about lots of topics important to kids and weight. Then you and your child pick the topics and strategies that sound right for you.

Also, as questions or problems arise, we encourage you to draw upon the physician, registered dietitian, mental health professional or exercise specialist affiliated with your program.

5. SHAPEDOWN sets attainable goals that promote long-term change. You want results, of course. But the goals we suggest stop short of promoting quick weight loss at the expense of health and well-being in the long-term.

1

The goals you set will be realistic. For a child who has rapidly gained weight in the last year, stopping the weight gain is a reasonable goal. For a family at odds or even hostile over weight, a realistic goal is to develop more harmony and a new commitment to healthy living. On the other hand, for some children a ten-pound weight loss may be quite attainable.

6. SHAPEDOWN gives you long term support. Weight problems don't appear or resolve overnight. This SHAPEDOWN program only lasts 10 weeks. For the majority of families, is only just a start. Most families will continue this progress with ADVANCED SHAPEDOWN. This advanced program gives families more support, more training and more motivation to face the changing needs of the child and family to lose weight and to keep it off. Ask your instructor about ADVANCED SHAPEDOWN.

We hope that SHAPEDOWN is an important experience for your family, one that boosts your health and happiness. If you have comments or questions about SHAPEDOWN, we want to answer them. Just ask your SHAPEDOWN instructor or write to us at Balboa Publishing.

SELF-ASSESSMENT

1. GETTING STARTED

Each parent should complete each self-assessment. One parent should circle the response chosen, the other parent should put an "X" on his or her responses. Discuss your responses with one another prior to the group session.

1. Which of the following are you willing to do?

1) Attend all sessions.	YES	UNSURE	NO
2) Agree that all family members will not attend a particular session if any family member did not bring his or her book with assignments completed.	YES	UNSURE	NO
3) Read the parent's guide and complete the self-assessments, quizzes and records.	YES	UNSURE	NO
4) If needed, help my child with his or her readings, practices, quizzes and records.	YES	UNSURE	NO
5) Take 10 minutes each day for FAMILY TIME to review our records and praise one another for our progress.	YES	UNSURE	NO
6) Address any barriers to success before joining.	YES	UNSURE	NO
2. I have read the SHAPEDOWN goals and philosophy and feel they are appropriate for my child and family.	YES	UNSURE	NO

1

The nutrition and activity advice in SHAPEDOWN is appropriate for most people but may not be adequate to treat your weight problem. Conversely, other weight programs may not be compatible with SHAPEDOWN. Here is our advice:

CONSIDER YOUR NEEDS

Treat yourself to the same care you have lavished on your child. Before beginning any treatment for weight, assess the effect of your weight on your health and happiness. Consider what caused your weight gain and what has contributed to its persistence.

To check the medical risk of your weight, consult your physician. To check the psychosocial disadvantage of your weight, consider its influence on your psychological well-being and relationships. When identifying the causes of your weight problem, evaluate your food and activity patterns, but move beyond them to the factors which increase your susceptibility to overeating or inactivity. Are you an emotional overeater or do you have poor lifestyle habits or both? Is the main cause of the weight inactivity? What social, emotional, cultural, and genetic factors keep those patterns in place?

Tailor support to match the nature of the contributors to your problem. If you are depressed, an appropriate prelude to weight therapy might be counseling. If you are an emotional overeater, physical activity, active hobbies or a behavior intervention might be reasonable choices. Perhaps you are isolated and idle (the-go-to-work-come-home-and-flop syndrome). Then becoming socially and physically active and developing new interests might be the best route to weight loss. If you simply love the fat in food, advice from a registered dietitian might be in order. What if it's just genetics that makes you gently rounded, and your habits are great and you have no trace of emotional overeating? Then no treatment may be in order.

PROGRAMS COMPATIBLE WITH SHAPEDOWN

Are all programs compatible with SHAPEDOWN? No. Although we support you in finding a program that best suits your needs, if a program promotes rapid weight loss without addressing emotional overeating, moderate dietary intake and physical activity, then your child is likely to be confused. If you are already engaged in a fast, it may be less conflictual to your child if you wait until the maintenance phase to begin SHAPEDOWN. In addition, avoid using any other diet products (such as over-the-counter liquid diet programs and diet pills) or weight loss gimmicks. We also recommend that you do not engage in a program with a set, restrictive diet pattern. They just teach dieting, and a goal of SHAPEDOWN is to avoid getting your child stuck in the topsy-turvy dieting psychology.

Your child is biting the bullet, knuckling down and learning how to manage his or her emotions and behavior. A loving gift to your child is to begin to work toward doing the same with the additional programs, counselors and support you find helpful.

2. UNDERSTANDING YOUR CHILD'S WEIGHT

It's difficult to understand your own child's weight problem. First, we're so close to it that we can't see the forest for the trees. Second, weight problems have many facets—your child's biology, behavior, and feelings can all contribute to weight gain. And third, your child is part of many systems, particularly the family system, but also peers, school, day care and church. These systems—the interactions, roles and environments they involve—can have profound influences on our child's weight.

While it is true that for your child's activity level and body chemistry he or she has eaten too much, that is where simple explanations stop.

Suzi came into the world hungry, or rather, starved. Formula never satisfied her. She went right into solid foods. Getting enough food is a constant struggle for her. It's like her body wants so much more than it needs.

Rebecca has always been a sensitive child. Until three years ago weight had never been a problem. But the last few years have been rough ones. My mother got terribly ill and Rebecca's dad and I were having trouble. Then last March he got laid off. Rebecca never seemed upset. But a lot of food just disappeared.

My daughter, Jennie, actually eats less than Aynsley, her older sister. Aynsley has everything

going for her. She's thin, pretty and smart. Jennie, unfortunately, is just the opposite. To me, it's a matter of genes. Jennie is so much like her grandmother. She has her large build, walks the same, even carries her purse the same way. It's so unfair.

Justin's weight was normal or even low until he was 7 and diagnosed as diabetic. We had a hard time regulating the insulin at first and he gained a lot of weight. Lately the diabetes has gotten out of whack again. Justin has gained another 10 pounds this year.

WHY IS MY CHILD TOO FAT?

You need to know what factors have contributed to your child's weight problem. Only then can you construct a plan for treating the weight.

With a clear understanding of your child's weight problem, you can begin to construct a plan for action.

If the primary cause of your child's excess weight is the cookies and ice cream that stuff the kitchen — and your child — then a nutrition overhaul is in order. If it's sadness, taking care of the weight means taking care of the depression, typically with counseling. If it's family chaos that's getting in the way of healthy diet and exercise habits, then finding ways to add structure and order at home is key. Typically a host of factors is involved.

The idea is to first find out what's going on with your child. You'll be able to change some of the factors affecting your child's weight. You won't be able to change others. But with a clear understanding of your child's weight problem, you can begin to construct a plan for action.

Biological contributors — Is your child destined to be round because Grandma Mary was portly? Does obesity in the family guarantee a rounded body for life? Not necessarily. Studies reveal that fatness does travel in families. If one parent is obese, a child has a 40% chance of becoming obese. If both parents are obese, that percentage jumps to 70.

But how many of the family fatness similarities are caused by genetics? How many by environment? In a recent study, weights of adopted adults were more like their biological parents than their adoptive parents. That's an indication that genes may be quite important in determining weight.

But wait a moment. Other studies show that weight, even among the fattest and thinnest, is very changeable — that when we change diet and exercise habits, our weight goes up or down. Other studies show that the prevalence of obesity varies dramatically among various regions of the country. (It's highest in the northeast and midwest!) And by season. (You guessed it, there's more obesity in the cold months when the easy chair and banana bread, dripping with butter warm us.) So if weight is highly variable, environment and habits are important in determining weight.

Your child may or may not have an inherited tendency toward roundness. If you child does have a biological susceptibility to gain fat, he or she will probably never look pencil thin. And your child will probably have to eat a little less and exercise a bit more than his friend who sports spaghetti-arms. In addition, your child will need your help in accepting a healthy, higher weight.

However, the child with a genetic tendency to gain fat is not destined to be severely obese. Given some pretty healthy habits, he or she can probably attain a healthy, moderate weight.

Marie's Story

Marie was cute — more than cute — adorable. Plump, pink cheeks, sparkling eyes and an absolutely charming manner. She glowed. And she ate. Marie loved cookies, cakes, pies, ice cream — anything that would make her dentist cringe. She could describe a cookie in infinite detail, her face lighting up, relishing every word.

Marie was not alone in her love of sweets. Mom relied on them to untwist the knot of tension from the day of unrelenting telephone calls and endless paperwork. And they filled the void that having a mate work late nights had caused. In the evenings she cozied up on the couch, cradling a handful of cookies or a rounded bowl of smooth, sweet ice cream.

Marie's family was generally a happy one. Mom and Dad's relationship was stable and loving even though Dad had been preoccupied with work — starting a software company — during the past two years. Marie was an adored, and perhaps indulged, child. However, when the baby was born three years ago, Marie — who had always been a little chunky — got noticeably bigger. It was then that the lure of the cookie jar heightened.

It was also then that Mom began finding Marie to be enormously needy. She seemed to whine more and to always want more from her. Mom adored Marie, but found her very draining to parent. Marie was very effective at getting what she wanted. She knew just how to badger Mom when she got in the door at night to get the food she wanted. Mom would say "no" the first four times Marie asked, and, finally, the fifth time, "yes," throwing up her arms in exhausted frustration.

They decided that Mom's reliance on sweets to relieve anxiety and loneliness, her difficulty with setting consistent limits with Marie, the decreased attention to Marie precipitated by the baby's birth, Dad's being too removed and Marie's voracious appetite for sweets all contributed to Marie's weight problem.

Mom and Dad agreed that setting limits was a problem for them. Dad had a hard time setting limits with his work and coming home consistently by 7:00 p.m. Mom had difficulties setting limits with Dad — telling him what she needed and expected — and with Marie — saying "no" and sticking with it.

Mom began to re-examine her own use of sweets and to look for ways to relieve anxiety other than by eating. She chose early morning walks and started playing the piano after a three-year hiatus. She talked to Dad about spending more time with her. Mom retired the cookie jar to the attic and stopped baking so often.

Dad and Mom began looking at ways to meet Marie's needs. Mom and Marie began doing special things together without the baby along. They enrolled Marie in some new, enriching activities, starting her on piano lessons and gymnastics classes.

Both Dad and Mom began setting limits more effectively with themselves and with Marie. Dad made a commitment to give more time to Marie and to Mom. Mom switched her evening routine so that she took half an hour to relax all by herself when she first got home at night while Marie watched television. At the end of her private time Mom took a few minutes to give undivided attention to Marie. They sat on the sofa and Mom listened attentively to her daughter.

In addition to genetic differences, there are other bodily causes. Take illnesses, for instance. Any condition that causes children to sit more — like asthma, broken bones, or heart problems — clearly contributes to weight. What's more, medications like cortisone or insulin can promote weight gain in your child. In a very small proportion of children, rare syndromes cause the obesity. Your pediatrician, family physician or pediatric endocrinologist is well aware of these syndromes, and can rule out the possibility that your child has one of them.

Think about when the weight problem started. What changes occurred then?

Life events — Often illnesses, deaths, job problems, economic hardships, marital difficulties, alcohol or other drug problems trigger weight gain in kids. This is particularly likely to happen with passive, depressed or sensitive children. Some distressed children show their feelings through getting into fights, blatantly disobeying, withdrawing, or doing poorly in school. Others express their feelings by overeating.

It was the divorce that set off Marcy's weight. Both Julie and I felt so awful about putting her through it that we unconsciously spoiled her — with food, toys, anything she wanted.

Jake was always a healthy child. No problems. It's his brother Mark who's a terror. The last few years there has been one crisis after another for us. Mark has taken all of our attention — first truancy, then drug problems. Jake was always stable and didn't seem to miss the attention, except that he's gained 20 pounds a year — and that's too much.

Richard lost his job 18 months ago. It crushed him. To him, his importance in the family was based on bringing home a paycheck. He got to drinking too much and really cut off from us. Brian felt it the most, as he had been close to his dad. It was a really serious emotional loss for Brian to see his dad like that and to not have any closeness between them. That was when he developed this enormous appetite. You just wouldn't believe how much he can eat.

Diet — Your child orders a super scoop cone. The ice cream scooper rolls his eyes and smugly chalks up your child's fatness to gluttony. It may not be true. Some kids with weight problems eat the same or even less than their skinny counterparts. Others eat a lot more.

A few children have enormous appetites, a bottomless hunger, that usually have their roots from early deprivation — not having their needs met early on. Others with tremendous appetites were well-nurtured in early childhood but currently have stressors or feelings of deprivation that fuel their appetites.

It's hard to know what our kids eat. Sometimes we're aware that they are overeating. The food disappears! Other times we aren't. Some kids only overeat when they are home alone, at school or at a friend's house.

Common patterns that lead to weight problems in children are skipping meals, snacking excessively in the afternoons and eating mainly high-fat or high-sugar foods.

Exercise — Chances are your child is inactive. Even if once soccer was his passion or life centered around her dance classes, when fat accumulates, kids slow down. Often they can't keep up with the others. It's harder for them to move around well and excel at sports. Their enthusiasm for sports wanes and the television beckons. But there are many exceptions. Some kids find a niche for themselves on the swim

1

team or as a goalie in soccer. Others are quite skilled at sports despite their weight.

Inactivity reduces the amount of food your child requires and thus is a contributor to weight gain. But we are even more concerned about inactivity when it's part of a downward spiral of overeating, social isolation, withdrawal into the home, television viewing and unhappiness.

Moods — Children with weight problems do not have more psychological problems than kids who are normal weight. However, moods can trigger a weight gain. If a child is anxious, depressed or has low self-esteem, eating is one way to block those feelings.

Jeffery really went into a funk last year. He hated his teacher, and as a result, school. He was always losing his homework or forgetting about it. When his report card came it said he was *performing below grade level. The grades themselves were almost all unsatisfactories. It wounded Jeffery and his self-esteem really took a nosedive. He didn't seem to have the energy or drive to exercise. He took to eating instead.*

Family diet, exercise and weight — Your home environment is the launching pad for your family's diet. Family members eat what comes through the door. If your eating environment is laden with fatty and sugary foods, that's what the kids will eat. If you cook with cheeses, fatty meats, oils, butters and the like, your kids will eat fatty meals. Your family meal and home food environment are excellent predictors of what your child consumes.

What's more, your own food habits, exercise patterns and weight greatly influence your child. Your child will do what you do, not what you say. The first step to getting in control of your child's eating and exercise is getting in control of your own. If you don't know how to put into practice a healthy diet and exercise plan for yourself, how can you be expected to do so for your child?

Family System — When the family is having difficulties functioning smoothly kids are more likely to gain weight. Families that are most likely to function well are typically not too removed nor too overinvolved, but somewhere in between. There are clear roles and responsibilities, but rules bend when there is an important individual need. Family members speak to each other freely and communication clearly. They speak intimately with each other and talk about the things that are difficult to talk about.

In these families the parents are skilled at nurturing and at setting limits. They know how to stimulate their children to cooperate without resorting to nagging, threats or abuse. And the kids listen to them and cooperate, because their parents set limits well, and because they get so much warmth and appreciation from their parents. The kids know that their parents love them no matter what. The parents sometimes don't like how a child acts, and clearly tell him or her so. But the child gets messages day in and day out that he or she is loved and respected, that he or she does many things that make the parents proud.

Our difficulties with warmly nurturing or consistently setting limits contribute to our kid's weight problems.

Other Systems - Beyond the family, other social systems clearly influence kids. School, peers, church, and day care strongly affect your child's weight and well-being. You create a nurturing life for your child at home only to learn that several bullies at school are teasing her mercilessly about weight. Snacks at home are reasonably healthy but he gets greasy crackers and butter-soaked popcorn from day care. When things are going pretty well at home, disaster may be brewing at school. All these systems influence weight and are worth your scrutiny in sorting out the handful of causes of your child's overweight.

Also consider isolation. Life is more isolating these days for most of us. It's especially true for obese children. It's not always clear why. Teasing by peers. Poor social skills - being the clown, withdrawn or inappropriate. Or not truly connecting with parents. For instance, a child may be overly close to one parent, substituting for an absent or unavailable spouse. This enmeshment puts the child in a false adult role and, because the role is false, the intimacy suffers. On the other hand, a child can be distant from a parent, due to anything from incompatability to job demands that shrink time together. Both ends of the spectrum - when children are too removed or overinvolved - with a parent, a sense of isolation can result.

Often, for obese kids who are isolated, food or television becomes their comfort and companions. The child blunts his or her distress with activities like eating, watching television, playing repetitive games, and compulsive reading. Getting bigger, gaining another layer of body fat, is another form of self-comforting.

Before starting the SHAPEDOWN Program, your child and family may have had an assessment to identify the underlying issues, causes and consequences of your child's weight. In this chapter you will reflect on the contributors to your child's weight as a prelude to setting goals for change.

1

SELF ASSESSMENT

2. UNDERSTANDING YOUR CHILD'S WEIGHT

To assess your family, please read each of the sentences below. Choose the one response for each question that best describes what you or your child did or felt **during the last week**. Afterwards you will score this questionnaire. At the end of the SHAPEDOWN program you will complete this questionnaire again to assess your progress.

FAMILY HABIT INVENTORY

Example:

	always	4
	often	3
My child snacked on fruit, vegetables or other low fat, low sugar foods.	sometimes	2
✓	rarely	1
	never	0

	always	4
	often	3
My child snacked on fruit, vegetables or other low fat, low sugar foods.	sometimes	2
	rarely	1
	never	0
	always	0
	often	1
My child had fried or fatty foods like fried chicken, bacon, eggs, fries, chips or ice cream.	sometimes	2
	rarely	3
	never	4
	always	4
	often	3
My child ate at least one cup of vegetables a day.	sometimes	2
	rarely	1
	never	0
1. The foods my child eats.	Total	_____

My child had second helpings of food.

	always	0
	often	1
	sometimes	2
	rarely	3
	never	4

My child ate a lot when he or she snacked.

	always	0
	often	1
	sometimes	2
	rarely	3
	never	4

My child ate small amounts at dinner.

	always	4
	often	3
	sometimes	2
	rarely	1
	never	0

2. How much my child eats.   Total _____

My child skipped breakfast.

	always	0
	often	1
	sometimes	2
	rarely	3
	never	4

My child ate at least four times a day.

	always	4
	often	3
	sometimes	2
	rarely	1
	never	0

My child ate regular meals.

	always	4
	often	3
	sometimes	2
	rarely	1
	never	0

3. How often my child eats.   Total _____

1

The meals at home consisted mainly of low fat and low sugar foods.

_____	always	4
_____	often	3
_____	sometimes	2
_____	rarely	1
_____	never	0

At home, there were cakes, pies, cookies, candy, ice cream or chips.

_____	always	0
_____	often	1
_____	sometimes	2
_____	rarely	3
_____	never	4

There was a bowl of cut-up, ready-to-eat vegetables in the refrigerator.

_____	always	4
_____	often	3
_____	sometimes	2
_____	rarely	1
_____	never	0

4. Light family food.   Total _____

We watched television while we ate dinner.

_____	always	0
_____	often	1
_____	sometimes	2
_____	rarely	3
_____	never	4

The family ate dinner together.

_____	always	4
_____	often	3
_____	sometimes	2
_____	rarely	1
_____	never	0

We enjoyed our food, eating slowly and savoring every bite.

_____	always	4
_____	often	3
_____	sometimes	2
_____	rarely	1
_____	never	0

5. Family eating style.   Total _____

My child exercised hard for an hour or more on school days.

_____	always	4
_____	often	3
_____	sometimes	2
_____	rarely	1
_____	never	0

My child had no time all day to exercise.

_____	always	0
_____	often	1
_____	sometimes	2
_____	rarely	3
_____	never	4

My child exercised for at least two hours on the weekend.

_____	always	4
_____	often	3
_____	sometimes	2
_____	rarely	1
_____	never	0

6. How much my child exercises.   Total _____

My child watched an hour or less of television per day.

_____	always	4
_____	often	3
_____	sometimes	2
_____	rarely	1
_____	never	0

My child seemed bored or idle.

_____	always	0
_____	often	1
_____	sometimes	2
_____	rarely	3
_____	never	4

My child had nothing, other than homework, to do after school.

_____	always	0
_____	often	1
_____	sometimes	2
_____	rarely	3
_____	never	4

7. My child's active lifestyle.   Total _____

1

My child was excited about learning new things.

_____	always	4
_____	often	3
_____	sometimes	2
_____	rarely	1
_____	never	0

My child did household chores.

_____	always	4
_____	often	3
_____	sometimes	2
_____	rarely	1
_____	never	0

My child had interests and activities that he or she really enjoyed.

_____	always	4
_____	often	3
_____	sometimes	2
_____	rarely	1
_____	never	0

8. My child's enriching lifestyle.   Total _____

On the weekends we took a walk, played sports or exercised together.

_____	always	4
_____	often	3
_____	sometimes	2
_____	rarely	1
_____	never	0

Our family time included exercising together.

_____	always	4
_____	often	3
_____	sometimes	2
_____	rarely	1
_____	never	0

All we did together as a family was talk, eat or watch television.

_____	always	0
_____	often	1
_____	sometimes	2
_____	rarely	3
_____	never	4

9. Active family time.   Total _____

I felt guilty, sad or fearful about my child's weight or eating.

_____	always	0
_____	often	1
_____	sometimes	2
_____	rarely	3
_____	never	4

I felt angry or resentful about my child's weight or eating.

_____	always	0
_____	often	1
_____	sometimes	2
_____	rarely	3
_____	never	4

I accepted completely the body build my child inherited.

_____	always	4
_____	often	3
_____	sometimes	2
_____	rarely	1
_____	never	0

10.   Feelings about my child's weight.   Total _____

I told myself that my child really isn't that heavy.

_____	always	0
_____	often	1
_____	sometimes	2
_____	rarely	3
_____	never	4

I thought that my child would grow into his weight.

_____	always	0
_____	often	1
_____	sometimes	2
_____	rarely	3
_____	never	4

I believed that the weight problem would take care of itself.

_____	always	0
_____	often	1
_____	sometimes	2
_____	rarely	3
_____	never	4

11.   Facing my child's weight problem.   Total _____

1

My child kept asking for food again and again until I gave in.

_____	always	0
_____	often	1
_____	sometimes	2
_____	rarely	3
_____	never	4

I felt that I could not make my child exercise.

_____	always	0
_____	often	1
_____	sometimes	2
_____	rarely	3
_____	never	4

I found it difficult to say "no" to my child and make it stick.

_____	always	0
_____	often	1
_____	sometimes	2
_____	rarely	3
_____	never	4

12. Setting limits and following through.   Total _____

When my child overate I lectured or scolded him or her.

_____	always	0
_____	often	1
_____	sometimes	2
_____	rarely	3
_____	never	4

When I wanted to reward or treat my child I gave him or her food.

_____	always	0
_____	often	1
_____	sometimes	2
_____	rarely	3
_____	never	4

I complimented my child on exercising or eating.

_____	always	4
_____	often	3
_____	sometimes	2
_____	rarely	1
_____	never	0

13. Rewarding my child positively.   Total _____

I asked my child about his or her feelings and needs.

_____	always	4
_____	often	3
_____	sometimes	2
_____	rarely	1
_____	never	0

I listened attentively to my child.

_____	always	4
_____	often	3
_____	sometimes	2
_____	rarely	1
_____	never	0

When I asked questions, I got honest answers from my child.

_____	always	4
_____	often	3
_____	sometimes	2
_____	rarely	1
_____	never	0

14. Communicating with my child.   Total_____

I reassured my child that despite discomfort he or she would be OK.

_____	always	4
_____	often	3
_____	sometimes	2
_____	rarely	1
_____	never	0

I praised my child.

_____	always	4
_____	often	3
_____	sometimes	2
_____	rarely	1
_____	never	0

I gave my child direct messages that I accept and value him or her.

_____	always	4
_____	often	3
_____	sometimes	2
_____	rarely	1
_____	never	0

15. Building my child's sense of well-being.   Total_____

1

We parent(s) exercised for at least 60 minutes three or more times.

_____	always	4
_____	often	3
_____	sometimes	2
_____	rarely	1
_____	never	0

We parent(s) were normal weight or slowly losing weight.

_____	always	4
_____	often	3
_____	sometimes	2
_____	rarely	1
_____	never	0

We parent(s) ate mainly low fat and low sugar foods.

_____	always	4
_____	often	3
_____	sometimes	2
_____	rarely	1
_____	never	0

16. Role model for exercise, food and weight.

Total _____

Now go back and score each group of three questions. Total each group of scores. Record the total scores on the Family Habit Inventory Summary on the next page.

—FAMILY HABIT INVENTORY SUMMARY—

BEHAVIOR OR FEELING	SCORE
Food	
1. The foods my child eats	_____
2. How much my child eats	_____
3. How often my child eats	_____
4. Light family food	_____
5. Family eating style	_____
Activity	
6. How much my child exercises	_____
7. My child's active lifestyle	_____
8. My child's enriching lifestyle	_____
9. Active family time	_____
Parenting	
10. Feelings about my child's weight	_____
11. Facing the weight problem	_____
12. Setting limits and following through	_____
13. Rewarding my child positively	_____
14. Communicating with my child	_____
15. Building my child's sense of well-being	_____
16. Role model for exercise, food and weight	_____
TOTAL SCORE	_____

Scores for each area range from 0 to 12. Total scores range from 0 to 192. Higher scores indicate behaviors and attitudes associated with successful weight management in children.

1

Identify three or more areas with the highest scores. These are your family's THIN HABITS. They are the ways your child and family act or feel that keep weight down.

1. _____
2. _____
3. _____
4. _____
5. _____

Next identify three or more areas with the lowest scores. These are your family's FAT HABITS. They are the ways your child or family feel or act that put on weight. Focus on these areas during SHAPEDOWN.

1. _____
2. _____
3. _____
4. _____
5. _____

Look back at your FAMILY HABIT INVENTORY SUMMARY and at pages 10 to 14 to review the wide range of possible contributors to your child's weight. What factors do you believe contributed to your child's weight?

_____

_____

_____

_____

_____

_____

_____

You probably have some strong feelings attached to your child's weight. These feelings are likely to have their roots in the current attitude of Western culture toward excess body fat. We are taught from the cradle that fat is ugly and lethal and that overweight people are out of control, lazy, over-indulgent, stupid, dishonest, amoral and sinful. All of these attitudes, of course, are without basis. But they do represent our current cultural bias. Therefore these attitudes influence our feelings about our child and about ourselves as parents.

Our feelings about our child's weight — guilt, fear, sadness, anger, frustration and blame — only worsen when we begin to "help" our child lose weight. Efforts to prompt our child to eat less usually just make him or her feel deprived and punished. That makes us feel guilty, ineffective and angry. These feelings chip away at our family's sense of closeness and harmony. The guilt creeps around our dinner table and the exasperation pops out at just the wrong times.

My frustration comes from how awful he is about his diet. He knows what he's supposed to eat, but after school he just goes right for the sugary cereal or the cheese. I can't believe my eyes. We talk diet and then he eats whatever he darn well pleases. I end up yelling at him. That's right, yelling at him.

1

Become aware of your feelings about your child's weight. Only then can you consistently give support.

When Suzi gets that sad look on her face when I say "no" to an ice cream bar in the afternoon, I melt. It just strikes a cord in me that is so deep. I feel so sad about depriving her. I just hate hurting her. I tell myself, "Just one cookie won't matter."

My husband blames me for our daughter's weight problem. He has his nerve. His work consumes him these days and he ends up acting like the classic absent father with little time for the kids. He sabotages and criticizes but won't help one bit. He's the one who treats her to ice cream and doughnuts in place of really talking to her. And that's after I've made her healthy lunches all week.

Feelings of guilt—The most common feeling is guilt, a feeling that we have done something wrong. Perhaps we have done something wrong. After all, our food habits or exercise patterns are not perfect. Family stresses that worsened the weight problem could have been prevented in the best of all worlds. We don't devote all of our intellectual and emotional energy to parenting. And some of us passed along fat genes to our kids.

In reality we parented our kids the best we could. Life was the way it was. We gave them the best genes we could. And now, did you contribute to your child's weight problem? Perhaps. If you did, and if you feel guilty about it, you can do some things to feel less guilty. You can give your full support to turning the weight problem around.

Lisa is such a needy child. No matter how much I give her she wants more. At 11 she's had more lessons, special trips and extras than her two older brothers combined. I guess anger is my main feeling, yet guilt is in there, too. Even though I give her more, I feel worse about how well I'm mothering her.

Amy's weight has bothered me for a long time. She's not huge, just rather big—like her mother. My wife tells me that it's all in my mind, which, of course, is convenient on her part. She says that I am overly concerned about weight and am creating Amy's weight problem. To some extent that's true. What I find is that the extent to which her weight bothers me depends on me. When I'm worried about my own weight, I get down about hers.

If you really confront me with it I'll tell you that what I do—or did—isn't rational. Why do I keep ice cream in the house when I know Megan devours it? Lots of reasons. I like ice cream. Her dad likes it. That's my normal answer. But now I recognize that it's also because I'm angry at Megan. I expect her to have the willpower not to eat it.

Joshua's mother and I have been divorced for three-and-a-half years. Now our chief communication is about Josh's diet. My new wife is doing her best to help Josh but all his mother does is feed him. I feel powerless, I can't forbid him to see his mother and yet I know that from the moment he arrives until the time he drives home, she's stuffing him with all the food he loves.

Feelings of sadness—When your child hurts, you hurt. You feel sad that your child is experiencing the negative consequences of being overfat. When the clothes don't fit and friends don't call, you feel wounded. Often parents of obese

You have a right to feel sad about your child's weight.

kids are overly involved, overprotective and excessively close to their kids. If this is the case in your family, the intensity of the sadness is only magnified.

Also, you may feel your own separate sense of sadness. Perhaps you have missed out on the joy of watching your son make goals in soccer or your daughter excel in dance. Or, if you were overweight as a child, their weight may bring up old sadnesses for you.

You have a right to feel sad. Being overweight is a disadvantage. However, there are many problems far worse than too much body fat. And weight can be treated. What's more, taking care of the weight has its rewards. Mobilizing to help a child's weight often triggers a family to operate and communicate better, and to develop a healthier lifestyle.

Feelings of fear — Your child's weight and eating seem out of control. It is frightening. What if your child keeps on gaining? What is he doing to his body? Will his health be compromised for good? Will the stretch marks ever go away? What lies in store if you and your child don't get hold of this problem before adolescence strikes? What then?

Of course you are fearful. There is a possibility that your child could weigh 200 or 300 pounds. Some kids do. But not many. Perhaps there will be stretch marks and emotional scars because of weight. But few of us arrive at adulthood without some leftover mind or body hurts. Like most kids, regardless of weight, your child will cope, adapt and develop. In addition, you have started early instead of letting the weight go

up and up. So there is less reason for you to be fearful. These feelings of sadness and fear can lead to control struggles with our kids. How? Sadness and fear make us feel out of control. When we're feeling out of control our kids can sense it. That leads to battles for control that only widen the gap between our kids and us.

Feelings of anger, frustration, and blame — If you've tried to do anything about your child's weight, you probably recognize these feelings.

I bought Jake a soccer ball and it sits in the closet - I think he only used it once! I do my part to support him and it seems like he doesn't even try!

I cook skinless chicken and rest of the family good-naturedly downs it. Then I find candy wrappers in Emily's desk drawer. She's ruining it, not us.

Why doesn't your child just take care of it, stop eating, get out of the chair and move? Why can't he accept some responsibility and use some willpower? You are struggling with other problems — work, relationships and getting older — why do you have to deal with this, too?

The frustration, anger and blame don't stop at the child. The other individuals who influence your child's weight are probably not totally cooperative. If you are doing your part and they are not doing theirs, there are bound to be negative feelings.

Ron came home last night with two half gallons of ice cream. Last Saturday he took the girls for hamburgers, fries and shakes. He uses it as an excuse to eat too much himself. I work hard and he ruins it all.

Situations and the people involved with them that have been critical to your child's weight are usually the brunt of such feelings, too.

1

The divorce, that's when Amy's weight started to go up. It was a reasonably good marriage until her dad started seeing another woman at work. I don't have the least doubt that the affair caused the breakup—which fueled the weight problem.

Jack had make a career move from Seattle to San Francisco. It was a lateral move within his company. Jack's performance had suffered in recent years. His drinking had something to do with that. So we didn't have much choice. We went. Sarah left all her friends. Next thing I knew she had this voracious appetite. The insult of the move was what caused the problem. I'm sure of it.

You are frustrated and angry because things aren't going the way you want them to go. You wish things were different. You may feel angry on a very basic level because you care about your

child and yet he or she hurts or ignores you. It's important to talk about these feelings. As you explore them you may find that they help you and your child. If they do, they are probably worth keeping. If they do not, if the anger makes you genuinely upset, if it really blocks you from getting on with making changes, then it's worth looking into, and you should consider other ways of responding.

A child's weight loss requires a family to function with symphonic precision. Some frustration—when the orchestra falters—is inevitable.

Don't allow your feelings about your child's weight to be discounted. If people tell you that you are wrong to feel a certain way, they are not

IDEAS TO COOL ANGER

Your child probably is not willfully trying to gain weight. Extra body fat comes from diet and exercise behavior. One can't change genetics. Behavior is learned. Your child eats and exercises this way because he has learned that it is okay. Learning to exercise and eat differently takes time.

Your child is a concrete thinker. This limits his motivation. Your child is still thinking concretely. He or she cannot think abstractly and clearly about cause and effect and the future. Therefore he or she won't be motivated to eat celery instead of cookies today in order to weigh less in the future. It is unrealistic to expect your child to have built-in willpower.

Your child's eating is shaped by other influences. Your child's eating and exercise are influenced by his family, school and peers. Typically kids are influenced by the systems they live within. If the family and other systems are supporting his or her weight loss, the child usually loses weight.

The rewards necessary to motivate change have not been set up for your child. Your child is exercising and eating the way he is because there are more benefits to doing so than to changing. Just the way you need the motivation of a paycheck to get you up when the alarm rings, your child needs rewards and consequences to motivate him. He or she does not have them now.

---

helping you. Your feelings are real and need to be listened to. Besides friends, relatives and the group, there are other resources for clarifying and ventilating these feelings. Your SHAPE-DOWN instructor is on hand to talk about these issues, as are counselors who are affiliated with your program.

All of these feelings are normal. They are uncomfortable feelings, but they are common reactions to dealing with children's weight problems. It is maddening to see your kid eat a bag of doughnuts when you've told him not to. It is frightening to see the buttons pop on his new, larger clothes. These uncomfortable feelings are normal.

Managing these common feelings will make it easier for you to help your child. That's because these feelings make it difficult for you to make consistent changes. For instance, feelings of guilt, fear, sadness and anger can cause you to really

struggle, yet only give sporatic support to your child. Or worse yet, they may prompt you to discourage your child's progress—without realizing it—actually sabotaging his or her efforts.

Some of these feelings will subside during SHAPEDOWN. Some feelings, such as fear and sadness, may lessen as you talk with other parents in the group and learn more about kids' weight problems. Feelings of guilt may decrease as you invest energy in making changes.

You can manage your feelings by separating them from your actions. Sometimes the feelings of guilt, fear, anger or sadness do not subside. How do you prevent them from blocking your effectiveness in helping your child lose weight? By separating your feelings from your actions. For instance, you can still feel guilty but not act as if you are wrong. You can feel fearful but act calm and reassuring.

1

I look at Casey and I feel sick. I've done it to him, I know I have. I was so busy with school and my work when he was young. He was in a family day care home that pushed food on him. If I had been more tuned in to his needs earlier maybe this wouldn't have happened. Now his appetite is so big that I really don't know how to respond without always nagging or forever saying "no." I feel at my wit's end about the whole thing.

I guess you'd say that I don't feel much about Roxanne's weight. I'm really here because her doctor insisted. The whole family's always had a weight problem, so to me, Roxanne looks like a normal 7-year-old. She seems happy and healthy. I know this child is more than 50 pounds overweight, but I just am not in the habit of worrying about it.

Matt was such a cute, happy little boy, always laughing, really loving life. This is the first year—he is 10 now—that he couldn't make the soccer team. *We pretended that he just decided not to play this year, but in reality, he couldn't have made it, even as goalie. Lately he has looked sullen. His face has been set in kind of a blank, dejected look. It makes me feel so sad.*

Sometimes feelings that persist benefit from counseling. Clarifying your feelings and gaining insight into their origins can be enormously helpful. One or more sessions with a counselor connected with your SHAPEDOWN program can be the ticket to managing these feelings effectively.

Rather than brushing off these feelings, focus on them. They can be powerfully influential. Getting them managed or out of the way puts you in a position to consistently support your child's weight loss. By identifying and resolving these emotional barriers, you can make changes with relatively little effort that are otherwise terribly difficult to make.

SELF-ASSESSMENT
3. CHECKING IN WITH FEELINGS

1. How often do you have these feelings about your child's weight problem?

	never		sometimes		always
GUILT	1	2	3	4	5
SADNESS	1	2	3	4	5
ANGER	1	2	3	4	5
RESENTMENT	1	2	3	4	5
BLAME	1	2	3	4	5
FEAR	1	2	3	4	5
FRUSTRATION	1	2	3	4	5
OTHER: _____	1	2	3	4	5

	not at all				a lot
2. How much do these feelings affect you?	1	2	3	4	5
3. How much do you think these feelings affect your child?	1	2	3	4	5

4. What are your plans for managing these feelings?

_____ Talk about them with other parents in the group.

_____ Talk about them with friends or relatives.

_____ Try to be more aware of my feelings as weight issues come up with my child.

_____ Start focusing on making changes that help my child lose weight.

_____ Consider talking about these feelings with the SHAPEDOWN instructor or counselor.

_____ Other _____

1

Directions: After you have read Section 1, answer this practice quiz. Check your answers below. Then complete the final quiz. At your next session, you will check the answers to the final quiz.

TRUE OR FALSE

PRACTICE

___ 1. The parents but not the child brought their book to the session so the family cannot attend.

___ 2. A goal of the SHAPEDOWN program is to decrease the child's weight quickly.

___ 3. To get weekly rewards in SHAPEDOWN, only the child must meet all of his or her goals.

___ 4. Parents are entitled to whatever feelings they have about their child's weight.

FINAL

___ 1. The reward system in SHAPEDOWN is based on only the child making changes.

___ 2. Children and parents in SHAPEDOWN go on a diet.

___ 3. Only parents who are overweight need to record their food and track their activity.

___ 4. Fear or sadness about a child's weight can keep a parent from helping the child lose weight.

Practice Quiz Answers: 1.T 2.F 3.F 4.T

2

THE ACTIONS

Each of us agrees to the following this week:

1. Complete the readings, practices and quizzes for Section 2.

2. Record on my SUPPORT record each day.

3. Meet at least 4 of my 5 SUPPORT goals.

4. If overweight, lose weight: □ ¼ + pound **OR** □ 1 + pounds.

THE REWARDS

If **we all** do all of these actions, then **we all** receive our rewards:

_____'s reward:_____
    child's name   provided by when?_____

_____'s reward:_____
    parent's name   provided by when?_____

_____'s reward:_____
    parent's name   provided by when?_____

When the family receives the rewards, _____ will be responsible for
                                            parent's name
rewarding the child. The child will be sure the parents have given themselves their reward.

_____   _____
    parent's signature   child's signature

_____   _____
    parent's signature   date

PARENT SUPPORT #2

	MON.	TUES.	WED.	THURS.	FRI.	SAT.	SUN.	TOTAL	MET MY GOAL?
We took FAMILY TIME each day to review these records and to praise each other.								___ days	YES NO
I watched no more than 0 2 4 6 8 hours of TV								___ hours	YES NO
I EXERCISED for 50 100 200 300 400 minutes or more.								___ minutes	YES NO
I filled out correctly MY FOOD! each day.								___ days	YES NO
GOAL OF THE WEEK: I did something fun with my child on ___ or more days.								___ days	YES NO

TOTAL NUMBER OF GOALS MET ⇒

HOW TO USE: MY FOOD!

You are filling out food records, yes. But you are not on a diet. You are just eating in a reasonably healthy way. Right now, you will categorize your foods as FREE, LIGHT, HEAVY or JUNK to decrease the fat and sugar in your diet. In addition, you will track whether or not you ate regular meals, that is, breakfast, lunch and dinner. Eating regular meals has been associated with improved nutrition and weight loss. Later you will assess your diet for its protein, vitamin and mineral content and check that you eat when you are hungry and stop eating before you are full.

Here's how to use MY FOOD!: Every time you eat or drink, write down the time, the food or beverage, and the amount. At the end of the day, use your FOOD SUMMARY and check the group that best fits each food: F = FREE, L = LIGHT, H = HEAVY and J = JUNK.

For your diet to be about 30% or less fat and consistent with current health guidelines for healthy Americans older than two years of age, choose a variety of foods from the FREE FOODS and LIGHT FOODS. Most people find that they need to keep their HEAVY FOODS and JUNK FOODS to no more than a few per day in order to stay within the guidelines for fat.

If you or your child are emotional overeaters or have a history of dieting, be sure that you get enough of the HEAVY and JUNK FOODS. Allowing you or your child to feel deprived will only stimulate overeating later on.

If you desire a more precise calculation of your diet, check with the registered dietitian affiliated with your SHAPEDOWN program. However, we suggest that you avoid any overfocus on the diet. The game-playing and false security that comes with counting grams and calculating calories makes food more important, whereas our goal with SHAPEDOWN is to make food less important while making life more active and fulfilling.

Total each of the four categories of foods. Because serving sizes vary, adding up the number of times you ate each kind of food will not give you an accurate picture of your diet, but it will give you a rough idea of whether or not you are eating mainly FREE FOODS and LIGHT FOODS. In addition, determine whether or not you had breakfast, lunch and dinner, that is, regular meals.

If your goal is to lose weight and you don't, consider decreasing the amount of food you eat, eating fewer HEAVY FOODS and JUNK FOODS and/or exercising more. If your goal is to maintain weight, use these same guidelines, but eat enough so that your weight remains stable.

On the following pages are seven MY FOOD! records. If two parents are participating, use the food records in the back of this guide to make additional copies. There are three different food records that you will use in SHAPEDOWN. Check to be certain that you are copying the same food record that is used in each particular week's lesson.

2

Day _Tuesday_

2

		Food Type			
Time	Food or Drink	Amount	Free	Light	Heavy	Junk
6:30 a.m.	wheat flakes	1 cup		✓		
	non-fat milk	1 cup		✓		
	coffee	2 cups	✓			
11:00 a.m.	bagel, wheat	1		✓		
	butter	1 t				✓
1:30 p.m.	apple	1		✓		
2:30 p.m.	diet soda	1 can	✓			
3:30 p.m.	cookies	2				✓
5:15 p.m.	beer	12 oz.				✓
	cottage cheese non-fat	1½ cups		✓		
	strawberries	1 cup		✓		

Totals

Ate mainly FREE & LIGHT Foods? (yes) no   Ate breakfast, lunch & dinner? (yes) no

===================== MY FOOD! =====================

Day _____

		Food Type			
Time	Food or Drink	Amount	Free	Light	Heavy	Junk

Totals

Ate mainly FREE & LIGHT Foods? yes no   Ate breakfast, lunch & dinner? yes no

Day _____

Time	Food or Drink	Amount	Food Type			
			Free	Light	Heavy	Junk

Totals

Ate mainly FREE & LIGHT Foods?   yes   no   Ate breakfast, lunch & dinner?   yes   no

═══════════════ **MY FOOD!** ═══════════════

Day _____

Time	Food or Drink	Amount	Food Type			
			Free	Light	Heavy	Junk

Totals

Ate mainly FREE & LIGHT Foods?   yes   no   Ate breakfast, lunch & dinner?   yes   no

Day _____

| | | | | Food Type | | |
Time	Food or Drink	Amount	Free	Light	Heavy	Junk

Totals

Ate mainly FREE & LIGHT Foods?   yes   no   Ate breakfast, lunch & dinner?   yes   no

Day _____

| | | | | Food Type | | |
Time	Food or Drink	Amount	Free	Light	Heavy	Junk

Totals

Ate mainly FREE & LIGHT Foods?   yes   no   Ate breakfast, lunch & dinner?   yes   no

MY FOOD!

Day _____

Time	Food or Drink	Amount	Food Type			
			Free	Light	Heavy	Junk

Ate mainly FREE & LIGHT Foods?   yes   no   Ate breakfast, lunch & dinner?   yes   no

MY FOOD!

Day _____

Time	Food or Drink	Amount	Food Type			
			Free	Light	Heavy	Junk

Ate mainly FREE & LIGHT Foods?   yes   no   Ate breakfast, lunch & dinner?   yes   no

45

4. MOVING INTO ACTION

2

You have a clearer understanding of your child's weight and your family's patterns. Now it is time to be specific about what you will change. Although in the self-assessment at the conclusion of this chapter, you will describe briefly your long term goals for your child and family, the major emphasis will be on specific changes you will target in this SHAPEDOWN program. You will target additional changes in ADVANCED SHAPEDOWN, all in support of your overall goals for your child and family.

The goals you set will be for specific changes you have the authority to change. For instance, you cannot eat or exercise for your child, however, you can prepare healthful meals and give the nurturing and limit setting that curbs an emotional appetite.

So, implicit in the goals you will set is the understanding that you and your child will share the responsibility for his or her weight. You will try to do your part. You expect your child to his or her part to begin to normalize weight within his or her genetic potential.

We recommend that you talk directly with your child about this division of responsibility. Here is a three-step plan to doing so, that research has shown to be effective with children:

1. Express confidence in your child. "I know it's difficult to lose weight, but I truly feel you can handle it. You have done other difficult things well. I believe you can do this, too."

2. Give appropriate responsibility to your child. "I cannot eat or exercise for you. I'll do my part to eat and exercise in a healthy way, to make our family life healthy and to give you the love and discipline you need. Other than that, it is up to you. If you eat and exercise in a healthy way, your weight will go down. If you don't, it won't."

3. Express willingness to help. "I am available to help you. Whatever you need, come and talk with me about it. I'll be there to help you."

This process lets the child know that you will strive to do your part and that you expect the same of him or her. You are not treating him or her as an adult, nor accepting that he or she is as irresponsible as a younger child. Moreover, it makes it clear that you are not rescuing him or her from the weight problem. Nor is the program. This discussion is a vote of confidence that sets the stage for your child to mobilize for change.

**Kids do what we do.
Changing them begins
with changing ourselves.**

THE NUTS AND BOLTS
OF CHANGING HABITS

Changing habits is very different from going on a diet. Instead of going on a crash diet, you make small changes each week. After a while those changes add up and make a big difference in your weight. When you go on a diet you know that sooner or later you'll go off it. When you change habits you do it for the long run. The changes are gentle ones. You get used to eating and exercising differently. Before long the new healthier ways feel normal and good and you stick with them.

Focus on habits in addition to weight. Weight change is slow. It takes playing in a lot of soccer games and missing many second helpings to lose a pound of fat. Since healthier habits cause weight loss, concentrate on behavior. Make changes in your behavior goals in and of themselves. Focus on habits and the fat will slowly disappear.

Measure weight once a week — no more. Weight day-to-day is not a reliable indicator of body fat. But over a period of weeks, it is. Weight week-to-week gives you feedback on whether the daily grind of habit changes is working. If your child is not losing ½ to 1 pound a week, the message is clear: too much food, too little exercise or both.

**She crunches her way
through a bag of chips,
then weighs. Down a pound.
What does that mean?**

Pick habits you are ready to change. If your child loves mashed potatoes with a puddle of butter, don't cut them out. Instead say farewell to pie and ice cream. Work on minimizing the painfulness of losing weight.

Experiment. Concoct your own approach by experimenting with different strategies. In SHAPEDOWN you sample lots of different strategies. From them you devise your own special blend! Try a strategy. If it works, consider using it again. If it doesn't, learn from it and move on.

Give your child a limited range of choices. Your child needs guidance and leeway. Propose a handful of changes. Let your child choose one or two of them. Without your guidance your child is apt to choose changes that are too big or

47

2

too small. Provide a safe framework and allow him or her to make choices within it.

Plan small wins. Children tend to plan unrealistic goals. They fail. So plan small wins — switching to two cookies rather than to two celery stalks. Savor small changes. Give your child the motivation to stick with it.

Teach your child about trade-offs. When your child raises a demand, respond to it. Teach him or her about trade-offs. "You want a cookie after dinner? Tell me how you'd change your diet or exercise to make up for it!"

What we're doing is difficult. Little baby steps of progress are courageous.

Avoid the perfectionist trap. The pizza delivery business thrives on all those dieters tearing themselves down for that one ice cream cone and consoling themselves with a large combination pizza. If you change a habit four days out of seven that's success! Help your child develop reasonable expectations.

Expect backsliding. Backsliding is when your child returns to an old habit. Keep in mind that backsliding is normal — even desirable. Why? Because it is inevitable. Diet and exercise are influenced by internal and external factors that are constantly in flux. Stops and reversals are to be expected.

Learn how to get back on track. Each time you backslide you have a chance to learn how to get back on track. How many adults do you know who have stuck to a strict diet to lose 50 pounds? The first time they waivered led them to non-stop cookies and candy and regaining those 50 pounds. Getting back on track early is a skill worth building.

Expect a crunch time. After a few weeks, when the newness of SHAPEDOWN wears off, you may experience a crunch time. That's the time when the real work involved in making changes becomes clear to you. At the crunch time you either decide to give up on the idea of helping your child lose weight, or you renew your commitment. If you decide now is not the time for you and your child, fine. Consider SHAPE-DOWN again when the time is right.

Losing weight isn't a barrel of laughs. It does build a child's self-respect.

Keep losing weight in perspective. Weight is only one of your child's characteristics. We all know that losing weight is not a cure-all. Your child may feel, act and look better when he loses weight, but other problems and worries are not likely to disappear. In fact, as weight recedes as a problem, other priorities and concerns surface. For instance, losing weight may stop the taunts from other kids, but your child still may have some catch-up work to do on developing social skills or on sharpening up soccer techniques.

PROMPTING OTHERS TO COOPERATE

It takes an incredible amount of cooperation from everyone for a child to lose weight. There are so many people who influence him or her. One grandmother who insists on clean plates or one parent who delights in giving your child food "treats", can stall or reverse his or her progress. What's more, this kind of sabotage can lead to strained relations, if not outright hostility.

Richard just doesn't get it. He knows Donnice is not supposed to be filling up on junk, but where does he take her for a treat on the way home from school? For an ice cream . . . or some chips and soda. He just smiles. "A little doesn't

48

hurt." It doesn't matter one bit what I say, he just keeps on feeding the child.

I wasn't aware of it until just this week, but Rhonda has gotten in the habit of taunting her brother about food, eating chips in front of him and calling him "fat." This has been going on for some time, but my son is not a complainer. He just kept it to himself.

Allisa has the classic grandmother who thinks the only way to show love is to feed. If it's not cookies, then its coffee cakes, doughnuts and pies. I cannot control my mother, that's for sure. What she does in her home she says is her own business. There isn't anything going to stop her from overfeeding my daughter.

It is your role to gain the support of these individuals. Your child cannot be expected to orchestrate their cooperation. That is part of your role.

You cannot expect your child to tell Daddy not to bring home ice cream or Mommy not to make a goopy casserole. Kids are not adequately prepared to ask Grandma to put a hold on baking cookies or to ask the after school program to give up chips and cupcakes for snacks. You must do these things. If you don't take rather assertive action these individuals will threaten your child's success.

If you can't keep Grandma from stuffing her with goodies, is success really possible?

Find out who these individuals are. Ask your child who influences him. Think about it yourself. Then list their names. What would you like them to do differently? Tell them precisely what you want them to do. Ask them to discuss what makes it so difficult. Get a commitment. Follow up at least weekly, asking how the changes are going and praising them for their support.

2

STEPS IN GAINING COOPERATION

1. Tell these individuals precisely what changes you would like them to make.

2. Discuss with them the difficulties or barriers they think they will encounter.

3. Get a commitment from them that they will make changes.

4. Follow up and praise them for their cooperation.

Easier said than done? Here's how one 34-year-old high school teacher gained her former husband's support:

I want you to give Donnice only fruit snacks. It would go such a long way to helping her lose weight.

OK, OK, I know.

But its hard for you to do. What makes it so difficult for you to feed her fruit?

I resent that she's so deprived. Why can't she have what other kids her age eat? It's like she's in prison.

You really enjoy feeding her.

Yeah, I do. That's part of it. The other part is that I try to tell myself that Donnice is not that fat. That it really isn't a problem.

What do you really believe about her weight? How serious of a problem do you think it is?

It is a problem. It clearly is.

Is there something else you could do with Donnice that you'd enjoy as much as feeding her ice cream?

No. Nothing. But I am worried about the weight. I think I'm going to have to just tough it.

I know it's difficult. Will you try it for one week?. Just fruit for a week and then we can talk about it again?

I can last a week. If Donnice is going to try to do this, then I'm going to try to help her however I can.

Sometimes it's difficult to assess an individual's influence. For instance, if Grandma offers your child crackers and butter for a snack twice a week, how negative is that? Creating a fuss over it may cause more of a sense of deprivation in your child and may not be worth it. Yes, there are a lot of gray areas that are difficult to assess. However there are a few patterns that are clear, that require your concerted attention to alter:

- **a sibling who teases the child about weight or eating**

- **another adult who cares for your child regularly — after school or evenings — who is not supporting healthy eating and exercise habits.**

- **another adult who blatantly sabotages your efforts, such as bringing home junk foods.**

Call on the support of your SHAPEDOWN staff or group if you find it difficult to enlist the support of the people who influence your child's weight. You are putting time, effort, money and more into this program and deserve some cooperation.

Given all of the priorities in your child's life and family time during the next few months, what are realistic goals to accomplish during SHAPEDOWN? What changes will you orchestrate in the people who influence your child's weight?

2

SELF-ASSESSMENT
MOVING INTO ACTION

MY GOALS FOR MY CHILD
Please describe your goals for your child's weight (e.g., weight, food, activity, attitudes).

_____

_____

_____

MY OWN GOALS
Please describe your goals for yourself. Include a broad range of goals that support your child's weight loss.

My food:

_____

_____

My activity:

_____

_____

My health and weight:

_____

_____

My parenting practices:

_____

_____

Our family's lifestyle and communications:

_____

_____

GIVING APPROPRIATE RESPONSIBILITY TO YOUR CHILD

I discussed with my child our division of responsibility for his or her weight loss:

YES   NO   UNSURE

2

I used the three-step method:

1. express confidence in your child

2. give appropriate responsibility to your child

3. express willingness to help

YES   NO   UNSURE

PROMPTING OTHERS TO COOPERATE

A person who influences my child's weight:

_____

_____

What I want this person to do differently:

_____

_____

I discussed it with this person:	YES	NO	NOT SURE
Will he or she change?	YES	NO	NOT SURE

Another person who influences my child's weight:

_____

_____

What I want this person to do differently:

_____

_____

I discussed it with this person:	YES	NO	NOT SURE
Will he or she change?	YES	NO	NOT SURE

The way of eating that is best for overfat kids is also best for the rest of the family. It not only helps overfat people lose weight, but also lowers the whole family's risk of diseases—heart disease, diabetes, high blood pressure, stroke and some types of cancer—and is rich in the nutrients we all need. When a family eats this way the parents and kids all reduce their risk of nutritional deficiencies and disease. In addition, the children—fat, medium and skinny—learn healthy eating patterns to continue into adulthood.

This is good news for the cook. There is no slaving over one meal for the people in the family who are losing weight and another for those who aren't.

It is even better for the overfat child. He or she need not eat foods that are different from everybody else. Thin family members simply cannot justify that salami sandwich or bag of chips because of their weight. A diet of heavy, greasy, fatty, sugar-drenched, salt-soaked foods is not good for the body—thin or fat.

The entire family eats the same foods.

It is inexpensive. There are no magic formulas or liquid potions to buy. No special foods dipped in sure-fire fat remover to seek out from special get-thin-quick companies that devastate your

53

2

wallet. No, it's plain, wholesome, fresh, crispy, crunchy, natural food—that's all.

It is not even a diet. It doesn't taste like a diet. You don't have to measure and calculate. And best of all, you never have to go off of it. Because it isn't that different from how you eat now. Your favorite foods aren't forbidden, and you don't have to stick with it to the letter or feel that you've blown it. It would be more fun if it was a diet. You could count. And cheat. And boast about the six pounds lost you lost in six days only to regain them.

This way of eating has just about everybody's stamp of approval on it. It has been recommended by many, many health organizations to help prevent or to treat diseases that you either don't want to get or already have. The federal government recommends this way of eating for all healthy Americans to provide essential nutrients and decrease risk of degenerative diseases. In addition to maintaining desirable weight, these U.S. Dietary Guidelines are:

U.S. DIETARY GUIDELINES*

Eat a variety of foods.
Avoid too much fat, saturated fat and cholesterol.
Eat foods with adequate complex carbohydrates and fiber.
Avoid too much sugar.
Avoid too much sodium (salt).
If you drink alcohol, do so in moderation.

---

*excluding weight guideline

Sounds easy? It isn't. If you make minor changes, you'll get insignificant results. Changes need to be substantial and consistent. In particular, if you don't de-fat your family's food, the changes you're aiming for just won't happen.

How do these general guidelines translate into what to fix for dinner or what to put into your shopping cart? One way is to use the SHAPEDOWN Food Summary in this chapter. It will help you increase the complex carbohydrates and fiber in your family's diet and decrease your intake of fat, saturated fat, cholesterol, sugar and alcohol.

In the FOOD SUMMARY there are four groups: FREE FOODS, LIGHT FOODS, HEAVY FOODS and JUNK FOODS. Foods are classified based on their nutritional value and their caloric density—that is, calories per unit of volume.

FREE FOODS and LIGHT FOODS are low in fat, sugar and alcohol. Less than 30% of their calories are fat, and less than 10% of their calories are sugar. Most of these foods are rich in nutrients essential to growth and development and to keeping people looking and feeling in top shape.

In addition, FREE FOODS are very low in calories, with only 35 or fewer calories per serving. They are primarily vegetables, flavorings and beverages that have a very low caloric density—that is, few calories per unit of volume.

LIGHT FOODS are low in calories, too. Some of these foods are naturally low in fat and sugar. They give you essential vitamins and minerals. You'll probably notice that many LIGHT FOODS are high in starch. Starch, or complex carbohydrates, are good foods that have about half the number of calories found in fried and fatty foods.

HEAVY FOODS and JUNK FOODS are high in fat, sugar or alcohol. They contain more than 30% fat or more than 10% sugar. Some of these

FOOD SUMMARY

FREE FOODS	artichokes asparagus bamboo shoots broccoli broth brussels sprouts cabbage carrots cauliflower celery cinnamon coffee cucumbers	dill pickles eggplant flavorings garlic green beans green onions greens herbs horseradish jicama lemons lettuce limes	mineral water mushrooms mustard onion powder onions peppers popcorn, plain radishes salad dressing, no oil sauerkraut soda, diet soda water sour pickles	soy sauce spices sprouts summer squash tabasco sauce tea tomatoes tomato juice vegetable juice vinegar water water chestnuts zucchini

LIGHT FOODS	apples
	applesauce, canned
	  without sugar
	apricots
	bananas
	bagel (plain)
	blackberries
	black-eyed peas
	beans, dried
	beans, refried
	biscuits
	bran
	bread
	bread sticks
	bulgar
	buttermilk
	cantaloupe
		cereal, unsweetened
		cheese, reduced fat
		cherries
		chicken, light
		  meat, no skin
		clear soups
		cottage cheese
		  low-fat
		crackers, low-fat
		english muffins
		fish
		fruit, canned
		  in water
		fruit, canned
		  in juice
		grapefruit
		grapes
			hamburger buns
			hominy grits
			lentils
			meat, lean red,
			  all fat removes
			milk, non-fat
			milk, low fat (1%)
			nectarines
			oranges
			papaya
			peaches
			peas
			pineapple
			plums
			potatoes
			prunes
			raisins
				rice
				rice cakes
				spaghetti, plain
				split peas
				strawberries
				sweet potatoes
				tangerines
				tortillas
				tuna, canned
				  in water
				turkey, light
				  meat, no skin
				vegetable soups
				watermelons
				winter squash
				yogurt, plain
				  low-fat

HEAVY FOODS	almonds
	applesauce,
	  sweetened
	avocado
	cereal, sweetened
	cheese
	chicken, fried
	chicken or turkey
	  dark meat
	chicken or turkey
	  with skin
	chili
	coconut
	corn bread
		cottage cheese,
		  creamed
		crackers, high-fat
		cream soups
		eggs
		fish, fried
		fish sticks
		french toast
		fries
		fruit, canned
		  in syrup
		fruit rolls
		granola
		hash browns
			macaroni &
			  cheese
			macaroni salad
			meat, red
			milk, chocolate
			milk, ice
			milk, low-fat (2%)
			milk, whole
			muffins
			pancakes
			peanut butter
			peanuts
			pizza
			popcorn, buttered
				potato salad
				pudding
				stuffing
				sunflower seeds
				taco shells
				tofu
				tuna, pack in
				  oil
				turkey hot dogs
				vegetables in sauce
				waffles
				yogurt, flavored
				yogurt, low-fat
				  frozen

JUNK FOODS	bacon beer butter candy candy cereal cakes chips chocolate chocolate topping cookies cream cheese cream sauce croissants	doughnuts fruit drinks granola candy bars gravy gum half and half honey hot dogs ice cream jam jello jelly	kool-aid lard liquor margarine marmalade mayonnaise oil olives pastries pies popsicles salad dressing salami	salt salt pork sausage shakes sherbet sodas, regular sour cream sugar sweet pickles syrup tartar sauce whipped cream wine

2

foods are naturally higher in fat or sugar. Others are foods that have been processed with added sugar or fat. HEAVY FOODS have a higher caloric density than LIGHT FOODS.

JUNK FOODS have the highest caloric density. They are mainly fat or sugar and have many, many calories per bite. JUNK FOODS have little or no nutritional value other than calories. Some JUNK FOODS are ready to eat—like potato chips. Some you add to other foods—like jam on toast.

We have categorized foods, but suggest that you be careful not to make judgments about these foods. All foods are OK. FREE FOODS are not good and JUNK FOODS bad. You are not good when you eat FREE FOODS and bad when you eat JUNK FOODS. If we shift toward eating more lighter foods, we become leaner and healthier, that's all. Being judgmental about a food just unnecessarily empowers it.

To make changes in the kinds of foods your family eats, choose more often FREE FOODS and LIGHT FOODS and less often HEAVY FOODS and JUNK FOODS. Initially, follow these steps:

1. Accept your family's eating preferences just the way they are. The way you eat now must have some benefits, or you wouldn't be eating that way. You like the foods you eat. Don't discard all of them.

2. Buy and serve more FREE FOODS and LIGHT FOODS. Choose some FREE FOODS and LIGHT FOODS that your family members like or at least are willing to try. These foods will begin to crowd out heavier foods.

Her brother is skinny and growing like crazy. I need to keep the cookies in the house because he needs the energy.

Brother can grow and have plenty of energy without bags of cookies. In addition, he is learning healthy habits to decrease his risk of heart disease, diabetes and other diseases.

My husband really enjoys ice cream after dinner. He's worked hard all day and deserves to enjoy his food.

Dad's health would benefit from lowering fat in his diet, too. If he really needs some ice cream, there are plenty of times and places to get it other than after dinner at home.

My son won't eat vegetables.

His preferences for high fat, high sugar foods have been indulged. He needs to learn to enjoy—or at least tolerate—other foods.

Vegetables will taste better to him when he is hungry and when other, tastier foods aren't available.

My child will feel different from the other children if he doesn't have chips and cookies in his lunch.

Your child's peer relationships are affected far more by his fatness than by his lunch. Many other parents are concerned about nutrition, regardless of their child's weight. If you child protests with this one, view it as a "good try," not a reality.

The food doesn't taste good unless there's a certain amount of fat in it.

Children raised on non-fat milk think that low-fat milk tastes greasy. Families that cut the fat in their food notice it for a few weeks. Then their tastes change. The lighter foods begin to taste good to them.

3. Buy and serve fewer foods that are HEAVY FOODS and JUNK FOODS. Agree on some HEAVY FOODS and JUNK FOODS that you want to remove from the grocery list for a while. Make room in your family's diet for lighter alternatives.

Make gradual changes so nobody feels deprived. Start with small changes that lighten your family's meals. Wait a while until these lighter foods seem okay. Then make more changes. Over time, keep on lightening the diet to make it lower in fat, sugar, sodium and alcohol.

Don't completely forbid certain foods. That only adds to their appeal. Keep a few touches of heavier foods in your meals. Let this bit of heavier food scare away the binge monster.

Create a light but not depriving food environment.

Equally important, don't delude yourself. Adding a dab of peas on the plate twice a week is close to useless. Cutting down from chips and granola bars in the lunch every day to only chips won't do much to trim your little one's tummy.

If you don't make some important changes in the family's food, your child probably won't lose weight. Why? Because the food environment—the food on hand—is a major factor in determining what your child eats. If you change from no vegetables on the plate at dinner to a small serving of cooked frozen broccoli with sauce, it is a nice attempt, but you probably won't see any smashing results.

As long as you are doing it, you might as well really make some changes. Cover half of the plate with fresh broccoli with a squeeze of lemon. Your child and family will adjust.

SELF-ASSESSMENT

5. SHIFTING TOWARD LIGHTER FOODS

List at least 5 FREE FOODS from the SHAPEDOWN Food Summary that you will buy this week.

1. _____   4. _____

2. _____   5. _____

3. _____   6. _____

List at least 5 LIGHT FOODS you will buy this week.

1. _____   4. _____

2. _____   5. _____

3. _____   6. _____

List at least 5 HEAVY FOODS you will not buy this week.

1. _____   4. _____

2. _____   5. _____

3. _____   6. _____

List at least 5 JUNK FOODS you will not buy this week.

1. _____   4. _____

2. _____   5. _____

3. _____   6. _____

PRACTICE

Directions: Answer this practice quiz, check you answers below and then complete the final quiz. Check the answers to the final quiz at your next session.

1. Whose responsibility is it to approach others to cooperate in helping the child lose weight?
   a. the child's
   b. the parent's
   c. nobody's

2. Describe how habit change works:
   a. like an switch, turning on and staying on for good.
   b. like an elevator, first going up then going down.
   c. like a bus, going forward with stops or reverses now and then.

Which types of foods are these? (FREE, LIGHT, HEAVY, JUNK).

3. eggs   _____
4. cheese   _____
5. bread   _____
6. 1% milk   _____
7. pizza   _____
8. banana   _____

=================== **FINAL** ===================

1. Which of these techniques helps a person change habits:
   a. trying to have a perfect diet
   b. expecting to backslide now and then.
   c. being down on yourself when you get off track.

2. Which situation may **not** require a parent to gain another person's cooperation.
   a. a sister ridicules the child about being overweight.
   b. another parent brings home doughnuts every Sunday morning.
   c. a grandmother fixes beef hot dogs for the child monthly.

Which types of foods are these? (FREE, LIGHT, HEAVY, JUNK)
   3. lettuce   _____
   4. oil-packed tuna _____
   5. beef hot dog   _____
   6. spaghetti   _____
   7. carrots   _____
   8. potatoes   _____

THE ACTIONS

Each of us agrees to the following this week:

1. Complete the readings, practices and quizzes for Section 3.

2. Record on my SUPPORT record each day.

3. Meet at least 4 of my 5 SUPPORT goals.

4. If overweight, lose weight: ☐ ½ + pound **OR** ☐ 1 + pounds.

THE REWARDS

If **we all** do all of these actions, then **we all** receive our rewards:

_____'s reward:_____
    child's name   provided by when?_____

_____'s reward:_____
    parent's name   provided by when?_____

_____'s reward:_____
    parent's name   provided by when?_____

When the family receives the rewards, _____ will be responsible for
                                         parent's name
rewarding the child. The child will be sure the parents have given themselves their reward.

_____   _____
      parent's signature   child's signature

_____   _____
      parent's signature   date

PARENT SUPPORT #3

	MON.	TUES.	WED.	THURS.	FRI.	SAT.	SUN.	TOTAL	MET MY GOAL?
We took FAMILY TIME each day to review these records and to praise each other.								____ days	YES NO
I watched no more than 0 2 4 6 or 8 hours of TV								____ hours	YES NO
I EXERCISED for 50 100 200 300 400 minutes or more.								____ minutes	YES NO
I correctly filled out MY FOOD! each day.								____ days	YES NO
GOAL OF THE WEEK: On ____ or more days, I praised my child for something he or she did.								____ days	YES NO

TOTAL NUMBER OF GOALS MET ⇒

61

3

Day _Tuesday_ EXAMPLE

Time	Food or Drink	Amount	Food Type			
			Free	Light	Heavy	Junk
6:30 a.m.	wheat flakes	1 cup		✓		
	non-fat milk	1 cup		✓		
	coffee	2 cups	✓			
11:00 a.m.	bagel, wheat	1		✓		
	butter	1 t				✓
1:30 p.m.	apple	1		✓		
2:30 p.m.	diet soda	1 can	✓			
3:30 p.m.	cookies	2				✓
5:15 p.m.	beer	12 oz.				✓
	cottage cheese non-fat	1½ cups		✓		
	strawberries	1 cup		✓		

Totals

Ate mainly FREE & LIGHT Foods? (yes) no   Ate breakfast, lunch & dinner? (yes) no

---

Day _____

Time	Food or Drink	Amount	Food Type			
			Free	Light	Heavy	Junk

Ate mainly FREE & LIGHT Foods? yes no   Ate breakfast, lunch & dinner? yes no

Day _____

Time	Food or Drink	Amount	Food Type			
			Free	Light	Heavy	Junk

Ate mainly FREE & LIGHT Foods?   yes   no   Ate breakfast, lunch & dinner?   yes   no

3

MY FOOD!

Day _____

Time	Food or Drink	Amount	Food Type			
			Free	Light	Heavy	Junk

Ate mainly FREE & LIGHT Foods?   yes   no   Ate breakfast, lunch & dinner?   yes   no

Day _____

Time	Food or Drink	Amount	Food Type			
			Free	Light	Heavy	Junk

Ate mainly FREE & LIGHT Foods?   yes   no   Ate breakfast, lunch & dinner?   yes   no

3

Day _____

Time	Food or Drink	Amount	Food Type			
			Free	Light	Heavy	Junk

Ate mainly FREE & LIGHT Foods?   yes   no   Ate breakfast, lunch & dinner?   yes   no

Day _____

Time	Food or Drink	Amount	Food Type			
			Free	Light	Heavy	Junk

Ate mainly **FREE & LIGHT** Foods?   yes   no   Ate breakfast, lunch & dinner?   yes   no

3

Day _____

Time	Food or Drink	Amount	Food Type			
			Free	Light	Heavy	Junk

Ate mainly **FREE & LIGHT** Foods?   yes   no   Ate breakfast, lunch & dinner?   yes   no

3

Keeping a kid on a diet can be one of the most demanding jobs imaginable. It is constant. It takes extra food planning, preparing and presenting. It shakes our basic desire to nurture, slapping our wrists for doing what is so very basic to the parent-child relationship: satisfying our child's desire for food.

I've resorted to controlling everything he eats. As soon as I come in the door after work I demand, "OK, what did you eat?" just knowing he's either been into the ice cream, graham crackers or corn chips. The more I step up my checking on him, the more he stashes food. I just know he gets food from his friends or buys it at the store down the street. But you'll never get him to admit it.

Stacy starts on me as soon as she gets home from school, "Can't I just have one cookie, just one?" Some days I say no. Other days she wears me down. I get so angry and tired of the whole thing, I just give in. The constant struggle is so negative. It spoils our afternoons together.

Overcontrolling your child doesn't work. The "police" role of overcontrolling your child's eating—dictating each and every bite and responding to at least a dozen "Can I have . . ?" questions hourly—is tiresome, ineffective and just plain negative.

3

SIGNS OF OVERCONTROL

- Your child overeats when home alone.

- Your child "pigs out" with friends.

- Your child won't eat in front of you.

- Your child has to ask you about every thing he or she eats.

- You focus most of your conversation with your child on food.

Undercontrolling your child doesn't work either. Being too removed from guiding your child's food patterns can result in weight gain. If you back off and put diet and exercise out of your mind, the weight almost always keeps going up and up.

SIGNS OF UNDERCONTROL

- You give in after your child repeatedly requests JUNK FOODS.

- It hurts you deeply to say "no" to your child.

- Your child still has sweets or chips in his or her school lunch.

- Your child pouts, sulks or cries when he or she doesn't get his way about food.

So what can a parent do that is positive and effective? How can we stimulate change without going into "overcontrol," draining ourselves emotionally or thoroughly boring ourselves and our kids?

"You met your goal! You snacked on vegetables four out of five school day afternoons. That is really tremendous! Now for your reward. Which friend do you want to invite to the movie?"

"Sarah, I do not want you to mention food all afternoon. We have better things to talk about. When you are ready for your snack, go to the SNACK LIST on the refrigerator and choose something. I am proud that you are big enough to pick out and fix your own snack."

Jack's response to his son's second, third and fourth request for a piece of cake: . . . Silence . . .

I know you don't like baked chicken, Andrew but that's what we're having for dinner. I realize you prefer it fried. But I know you will be okay. It's not the worse thing in the world to eat something that isn't your favorite.

"You ran across the field so much faster today."

"You've been going through six or eight glasses of milk a day. I expect you to limit it to three. When would you like to have each of those three glasses?"

STIMULATING CHANGES POSITIVELY

1. Negatives are costly to you and ineffective with your child. We all resort to them. More often on blue days or when energy wanes. But negatives just don't do our kids or us any good. Quizzing our children about food, playing the role of policeman, nagging him or her to eat less, saying "You can't have that", and accusing our child of "cheating" are ineffective. We have all

3

I expect you to go to the party and eat reasonably, Amy. What does that mean to you?

Have a hot dog but no chips. One glass of soda, not two and one piece of cake.

That sounds fine. How will you make sure that you don't eat chips, Amy?

I'll tell Becca's mom that I don't want any.

How about the second glass of soda?

I'll get water if I'm still thirsty.

You've really planned well, Amy. Let's talk about it after the party to see what you did.

————————

Did you have fun at the party, Amy?

Yeah. They had a magician and I got to help him pull a bunny out of the hat.

What fun! What did you do well about food at the party?

I didn't have the chips and I only had one glass of soda.

Terrific. You acted on your own. You were

really responsible with the chips and soda. That's just great, Amy. What didn't go well?

I had cake and ice cream. And the cake was a big piece. A very huge piece.

Why was that a mistake, Amy?

Because there are probably two bags of chips worth of fat in that cake and ice cream.

That's right. What could you have done differently so that you would have had less cake and no ice cream?

I don't know.

Yes, you do. I bet you can think of something to say so that won't happen.

When Becca's mother gave me the plate of cake and ice cream I could have said I wanted a smaller piece and no ice cream.

Exactly. It is so important to me that you were responsible about the chips and sodas, Amy.

Next time I'll know what to say when they give me the cake.

Good. See, you are becoming more and more responsible.

been there, and the only direction to move is toward the more positive.

2. You cannot control everything your child does. You can not eat or exercise for your child. If you are now in "overcontrol," relax. Being overly intrusive just backfires. A certain number

of decisions can only be handled by your child. If you are in overcontrol your child will sense your anxiety or react to your intrusiveness. Typically that means he will create a struggle for control, openly by eating candy in plain sight of you or secretly, by eating non-stop at a friend's. So just sigh and let go. Over controlling is futile.

3. Unless you exert moderate, consistent control, your child will not change. Even if your child is acutely distressed about weight, he or she is unlikely to independently lose weight. Children's "now" orientation, difficulty delaying gratification and lack of knowledge about what to change and how to change it mean that they need your involvement and support. Backing off totally usually means continuing the weight gain.

4. Your child should assume some responsibility for his or her diet, exercise and weight. You have to support your child's changes, but he must assume some responsibility, too. Use your FAMILY TIME to promote a sense of responsibility in your child.

- Tell your child precisely what you expect of him or her.

- Praise and reward your child for responsible behavior.

- Give your child feedback on irresponsible behavior: why was it a mistake? what were his or her alternatives?

- Remain patient as your child gains the experience and information to act responsibly.

5. Draw upon your special relationship with your child to motivate him or her. Your child wants your approval and relishes your rewards. Apart from rewards of movies, sleepovers and the like, you can reward him or her with your approval. This is more motivating to most kids than any toy you can buy them. Because of your relationship with your child you have a special advantage as a motivator. Use it.

6. Accept the fact that your child will find improving his or her diet and exercise uncomfortable. Your child will not like eating carrots instead of chips at snack time. Nor will your child like turning off the television and heading for the basketball court. Anticipate negative reactions. Expect hunger strikes, pouting and angry outbursts. Reassure your child that being a little uncomfortable is part of life. Learning to do things that aren't fun or easy is the ticket to building self-respect and to achieving meaningful goals. The idea is to give your child the message that protesting slight discomfort or displeasure just doesn't make it.

3

Become comfortable with making your child uncomfortable.

7. Reassure yourself that you are being a good parent even while making your child uncomfortable. Perhaps more important than reassuring your child is reassuring yourself. Unless you are comfortable setting limits, observing your child's discomfort and still sticking with those limits, you will not consistently encourage your child to lose weight. In other words, unless you become comfortable with making your child uncomfortable, SHAPEDOWN won't work.

You are acting lovingly to your child when you encourage changes that make him uncomfortable now but set him up for a healthier and happier future. Since children do not have much of a future orientation it is difficult for them to pass up an ice cream today for weighing less next week. They won't like passing up the ice cream, but your praise, acceptance and respect for them—and a trip to the movies—will assuage some of that discomfort. Some discomfort is inevitable. You need to reassure your child and yourself that this discomfort is okay.

3

8. Tell your child what eating and exercise behavior you expect, then give him or her choices. How much exercise do you expect your child to engage in each day? Decide . . . and then tell your child. Next offer your child a few choices of activities.

Children desire structure. Being clear about what you expect is essential to giving them that structure. However, take the next step that encourages your child to assume responsibility without undue resentment. Develop a list of choices you think are reasonable and can be monitored. Allow your child to make choices within that list.

9. Reward your child for changes in behavior and weight. Use the daily FAMILY TIME to reward your child. Praise what went well that day and problem solve about what didn't. Each day that your child performs his or her target behavior, use the reward of your approval and appreciation. If your child met his or her goal for the week, give a reward of something special such as a privilege, object or activity.

FAMILY TIME is a time for closeness and intimacy. You talk through the ups and downs and give your child praise and rewards. You are developing your child's self-concept as a competent and successful individual. This positive self-concept will help him or her continue to exercise and eat well during the times when enthusiasm wanes.

NEGATIVES THAT DON'T WORK

GIVING ADVICE: *You shouldn't have eaten that cookie.*

WHY IT DOESN'T WORK: You are treating your child like a peer. It is ineffective in promoting change, and only makes your child anxious. Your child is not a peer. By treating him like one you give him more authority than he can handle.

NAGGING: *Don't eat that. That's too much. You've had enough.*

**About to criticize?
Take a deep breath. Praise
your child for something—
anything!—first.**

WHY IT DOESN'T WORK: Intrinsic in nagging is that you know it doesn't work. If it worked you wouldn't have to say it over and over. Once would be enough.

THREATENING: *If you keep eating like that you'll be as big as a house.*

WHY IT DOESN'T WORK: You don't believe yourself and neither does your child. You look foolish in your child's eyes and in your own. What you are threatening won't happen and has scant chance of motivating your child to eat less.

POSITIVES THAT DON'T WORK

FOOD REWARDS: *If you lose a pound you can have an ice cream sundae.*

WHY IT DOESN'T WORK: By rewarding with food, you are further reinforcing the idea that eating is the primary source of pleasure, relaxation and nurturance. That doesn't help your child value ways other than eating to take care of his or her needs.

MONEY REWARDS: *If you lose a pound I'll give you a dollar.*

WHY IT DOESN'T WORK: A nice idea that works on occasion, but "money for flesh" is somewhat degrading. Besides there are so many other possible rewards that ennoble the child or stimulate healthy development. They are better choices.

LONG RANGE REWARDS: *If you lose weight we'll get you a new wardrobe.*

WHY IT DOESN'T WORK: Kids can draw on the motivation of an immediate reward—for instance, your praise during FAMILY TIME for having one cookie rather than a fistful. A far-off reward does little to stimulate kids to say "no" and give up that immediate pleasure.

POSITIVES THAT WORK

TAKE FAMILY TIME DAILY: *I know you have to do your homework, but it's our time to talk about SHAPEDOWN.*

WHY IT WORKS: FAMILY TIME gives your child the accountability for making diet and exercise changes. It's also a time for problem-solving. How can he get that exercise? What could she do next time someone offers her chips? But mainly FAMILY TIME is intimate parent-child time and this direct hit on isolation makes the appetite take a nosedive.

CAREFULLY MONITOR BEHAVIOR: *Your goal is to exercise one hour or more per day, five out of seven days. Today you exercised 1-¼ hours. You met your goal. Let's write that down on your STROKES record.*

WHY IT WORKS: Children want structure and limits. It is one way that we as parents show them we care. They want to be held accountable for what they do, and they want the positive attention that comes with feedback. Looking carefully at what they have done shows them

3

that we really care. It also gives them objective feedback that motivates.

PRAISE POSITIVE CHANGES: *Did you really say "no" to Cynthia when she handed you some chips? That's fantastic!*

WHY IT WORKS: Changes are difficult to make. Kids focus on their failures and want to throw in the towel. You help them smell the roses and see themselves as successful. Positives motivate. Negatives don't. Use the positive approach, congratulating them even on modest changes to motivate them to continue making more and more changes. Whenever you are about to criticize, preface it with praise.

PROBLEM SOLVE: *How could you have changed your afternoon so that you exercised? Let's work together to list some changes you could make.*

WHY IT WORKS: Often the reason kids don't eat well or exercise is because they don't know how to make it happen. Think about the complex set of cognitive and social skills it takes to decide what to do and then to do it. Kids need your guidance and instruction.

REWARD POSITIVE BEHAVIOR: *Let's look at your STICKER STROKES. You exercised for one hour or more five of the last seven days. You met your goal. You did it. I admire you for it. Which friend would you like to have spend the night tonight?*

WHY IT WORKS: Positive reinforcement is motivating. It stimulates children to snack on carrots rather than candy. Anticipating a reward stimulates them to go for that jog even when the television beckons.

10. Limit your discussion of food, weight or diet. That's right. Do praise you child every time you see positive changes — the flush on his cheeks after a bike ride, the carrot for a snack rather than a chocolate chip cookie. Take FAMILY TIME daily. Otherwise, let your conversation drift to other topics. It's quite easy to focus all of our attention on that child and on his or her diet. That gives the child the message that he **is** his weight. Nothing else matters. For that child it makes no sense to lose weight, and with it, all that attention.

Give it a try. Experiment this week with various positive techniques for stimulating healthier eating and more exercise in your child.

SELF ASSESSMENT

6. STIMULATING CHANGES WITH POSITIVES

1. To what extent do you:

	not at all				a lot
Believe that negatives are costly to you and ineffective with your child?	1	2	3	4	5
Recognize that you cannot control everything your child does?	1	2	3	4	5

	not at all				a lot
Believe that unless you exert moderate, consistent control your child will not change?	1	2	3	4	5
Recognize that your child should assume some responsibility for his or her diet, exercise and weight?	1	2	3	4	5
Draw upon your special relationship with your child to motivate him or her?	1	2	3	4	5
Accept the fact that your child will find improving his or her diet and exercise uncomfortable?	1	2	3	4	5
Reassure yourself that you are being a good parent even while making your child uncomfortable?	1	2	3	4	5
Tell your child what eating and exercise behavior you expect, then give him or her choices?	1	2	3	4	5
Reward your child for changes in behavior and weight?	1	2	3	4	5
Limit your discussion of food, weight or diet?	1	2	3	4	5

2. In the last week did you:

	not at all				a lot
Take FAMILY TIME daily?	1	2	3	4	5
Use the SUPPORT Form?	1	2	3	4	5
Praise positive changes?	1	2	3	4	5
Problem solve about difficulties?	1	2	3	4	5
Carefully monitor behavior?	1	2	3	4	5
Reward Positive behavior?	1	2	3	4	5

3

7. PROMPTING YOUR CHILD TO EXERCISE

Most kids underexercise. In our automated society we have stopped walking, put an end to active chores and cut sports to a minimum. This sedentary lifestyle isn't good for any of our children, but it's particularly detrimental to obese kids. The inactivity just furthers their weight gain, detracts from their ability to keep up with peers in sports and activities and retards their sense of competence and pleasure in moving their bodies.

Sandra is a little queen. She sits in front of the television and when it's time to turn the channel, she badgers her brother into getting up. If I suggest that she walk to school instead of being paraded in by the "domestic chauffeur," she turns on her best theatrics: whining, moaning and grimacing until her mom gives in and takes her to school.

Jeremy loves sports and has always been on the soccer team. Last year he could only play goalie, and this year he didn't even make the team. He told us he had lost interest in soccer. But we knew differently. It's so hard to see him being left out more and more on account of his weight.

I take time late in the day to walk around the neighborhood. Between 5:00 and 6:00 is my time to unwind. I've brought Stacy with me on my walks, but she's so slow it ruins the walk for me.

You may turn on the TV after your hour of exercise.

You are well aware of what a miracle worker exercise can be for an overweight child:

Burns up calories—Moving uses up energy. Each minute your child moves rather than sitting, he or she expends more calories. On the average, sitting uses up 1.5 calories per minute whereas brisk walking uses up 6 calories per minute. If your child moves more and eats the same, he or she will slowly let go of body fat.

Speeds up metabolism—Physical activity increases your child's metabolic rate during exercise. If your child has a biologic make-up that encourages fat accumulation, exercise can cause his or her metabolism to become more like a thin person's. What's more, as your child's body becomes leaner and fitter, exercise revs up his body for hours after exercise, too.

**The message is clear.
Get the kid off the couch and
out the door. Get that child moving.**

Helps get rid of fat—Bodies that have exercised are a lot more fit than bodies that haven't. Fit bodies tend to burn up more body fat than unfit bodies. Bodies that exercise are less likely to turn food into fat. And they have more calorie-burning muscle, too.

Makes your child's body feel firm—Exercise tones muscles so they are firm instead of flabby. Firm muscles make your child's body look better. They smooth out body contours and give a leaner looking appearance.

Diminishes your child's appetite—Slow, steady exercise makes your child's hunger vanish. A slow jog around the block can take your hunger away as much as eating an ice cream cone. A child preoccupied with hunger at the beginning

of a tennis game will have little interest in food by its conclusion.

Helps your child gain a more positive body image—Children say that their bodies feel better—thinner, healthier and more attractive—after they exercise. Kids say that they actually feel lighter and leaner.

Puts kids in a super mood—Being on the move can destroy blue moods. Exercising promotes a strong sense of well-being. Children learn that feelings of lethargy, boredom, anger and sadness abate with exercise. They learn how to create for themselves a healthy sense of well-being.

Sets your child up for lifelong fitness—Teach your child to play tennis. Give him or her encouragement, even when the ball sails over the fence and into the berry bushes. The result? Your child develops the skills and positive attitudes toward exercise. You set up your child to continue to be active and fit in his or her adult years.

3

**GUIDELINES FOR
CHILDREN'S PHYSICAL ACTIVITY**

daily

one hour

low intensity

continuous

safe

Did you say daily? That's right. Your child sleeps daily. Your child should exercise daily. Regardless of weight, a healthy body makes a healthier mind. It's good for the spirit and the flesh. Weave the exercise into your child's daily routine. Besides, there will always be exceptions. Children become sick, the coach is on vacation, the tennis class is cancelled. Whatever the reason, even when exercise is planned daily for an hour or more it sometimes doesn't happen. So structure your child's day—each day—to include an hour or more of exercise, and keep your fingers crossed that most of the time it happens.

3 **School and television are physically depriving. Our kids' bodies yearn to shake off that restlessness, move those limbs and play.**

Why for an hour? It takes long duration exercise to boost your child's mood. Most children resist exercise at first. They feel uncomfortable and awkward. During the last half hour of the bike ride, children begin to relax and enjoy the activity. Life feels good. Plus, only long duration exercise affects weight significantly. It takes your child a full 10 minutes of jogging to burn off the calories from an apple. For exercise to cause weight loss—and to take some emphasis off of restricting food intake—it must be done regularly and for long periods of time.

Keep the intensity lower—Studies of obese children show that the weight that kids carry affects their cardiorespiratory system significantly. That means that higher intensity physical activity can cause exhaustion, injuries and poor functioning. Keep the intensity lower and the duration longer. You'll want your child to plan several episodes of exercise each day at first, to avoid exhaustion and yet maximize the benefits.

Make it continuous—Stop and start exercise isn't as effective in building up your child's cardiorespiratory fitness. Sure, jumping rope during recess for a few 30-second bursts of energy expenditure can't hurt, but compared with an extended romp around the playground or a brisk walk around the block, it doesn't make it.

Keep safety in mind—Check with your child's doctor to discuss any special needs or restrictions your child has for exercise. If your child bikes, skate boards, roller skates or does any other sport, be certain that he or she knows the safety rules and precautions and has appropriate safety gear. In addition, start slowly. If your child hasn't been exercising much, start with low intensity exercise, such as walking, bouncing on a mini-trampoline or bike riding. As your child becomes more fit, begin including sports, dance and other activities that involve more complex and vigorous movements.

THE ABC'S OF FITNESS

There are three kinds of fitness that keep your child and family in top shape: flexibility, strength and endurance. All three work together to maximize fitness!

Flexibility—If you are flexible, your body is loose and your joints have a wide range of motion. The muscle-bound football player who can barely turn his head is not flexible. The yoga master who makes her body into a pretzel is very flexible. To boost flexibility you and your child can try stretching exercises like dancing, sports, calisthenics and warm-up/cool-down stretches.

Strength—The ability of muscles to be forceful is called strength. Strength is usually measured by how much weight you can lift. For instance, the child who can lift a twenty-pound barbell is twice as strong as the child who can lift only ten pounds. Strength is also measured by how many times the muscles can lift—such as how many sit-ups you can do in one minute.

Both strength and flexibility exercises help you and your child move better, but strength and flexibility exercises alone burn little fat. Spot reducing—for example, doing sit-ups to get rid of stomach fat—doesn't work. Sit-ups do tighten your stomach muscles. But they don't remove the fat on your stomach.

Endurance—What kind of exercise helps burn fat? Exercise that improves endurance, that is, aerobic exercise. Aerobic exercise requires the steady use of the large muscles in the body, like legs and arms. Using these muscles causes the body to need more oxygen and, therefore, to breathe harder. Breathing harder causes the heart to beat faster, the metabolic rate to increase and energy to be expended.

How can you be sure that you and your child are doing aerobic exercise and causing these good changes? Just check heart rates after exercise:

Find your heart rate—Stop the activity, find the pulse on the side of the neck or on the wrist right behind the thumb and count the number of beats in six seconds.

If the number of beats is greater than the top of your range you are exercising too vigorously for your current fitness level. Slow up.

If the number of beats is less than the bottom of your range you are not exercising vigorously enough for your current fitness level. Speed up.

FAMILY EXERCISE TESTING[1,2]

To assess the effectiveness and safety of each family member's favorite exercises, test them! Just count how many times your heart beats during the **six seconds** right after you exercise. Assess it using one of the methods below. For simplicity, use the FAMILY METHOD. If you prefer, estimate each individual family member's appropriate heart rate range by referring to the INDIVIDUALIZED METHOD.

HEART BEATS PER 6 SECONDS

FAMILY METHOD FOR EVERYONE:
Use a Heart Rate of 12 to 15 Beats

INDIVIDUALIZED METHOD:
Find Your Heart Rate Range
on the Table below:

	healthy obese low fit 60 to 75% max heart rate	healthy normal weight fit 70 to 90% max heart rate
children	12 to 15	14 to 19
adolescents	12 to 15	14 to 19
adults		
20 years	12 to 15	14 to 19
25 years	12 to 15	14 to 19
30 years	11 to 14	13 to 17
35 years	11 to 14	13 to 17
40 years	11 to 14	13 to 16
45 years	10 to 13	12 to 15
50 years	10 to 13	12 to 15
55 years	10 to 13	11 to 14
60 years	9 to 12	11 to 14
65 years	9 to 12	11 to 14

[1]Katch, FI, McArdle, WD, Nutrition, Weight Control, and Exercise. 3rd edition, Lea & Febiger, Philadelphia, 1988.
[2]Binkhorst, RA, Kemper, HCG, Saris, WHM, Children and Exercise XI. International Series on Sports Sciences. Volume 15, Human Kinetics Publishers, Inc., Champaign, Illinois, 1985.

The ranges used in the FAMILY METHOD and the lower intensity INDIVIDUALIZED METHOD are based on approximately 60 to 75% of maximal heart rate. Maximal heart rate is the number of beats per minute immediately following 3 or 4 minutes of all-out running or swimming. We use this 60 to 75% level because it has been associated with better exercise compliance and fewer injuries, it accommodates even the less fit, decreasing the chance we'll reach our

anaerobic threshold, build up blood lactate and feel tired. It also allows us to exercise longer so that we expend more calories.

For family members who are healthy, normal weight, fit people, use the higher intensity INDIVIDUALIZED METHOD. It is based on 70 to 90% of maximal heart rate. Of course, check with your physician for exercise recommendations and approval before beginning any exercise program.

STRATEGIES TO TRY

Exercise with your child. A national study has shown that kids are more fit when a parent exercises with them. Your little one probably won't get up, turn off the television and go for a walk unless you do it with him. It's a good excuse for us to get off the sofa, too, and to get involved with our child. Hiking, skiing, walking, skating,

shooting baskets and kicking a soccer all require our physical and mental presence. They are great ways to make that shift from thinking about ourselves to thinking about our kids.

Be a good role model. Engage in daily exercise. That means taking extra time for you. Weaving some time for exercise into your day is a strong step toward your child's success in losing fat. Children do what we do, not what we say. Consider getting up a little earlier to go for a morning walk, or asking your children to cook dinner so you can go for a jog after work.

**Exercise is a family affair.
Anybody strong enough to eat is
strong enough to exercise beforehand.**

Start with low intensity, non-competitive forms of activity. Walking, biking, bouncing and

GETTING STARTED IN EXERCISE

Walking   Walk the dog, walk to the store, walk around the mall, stroll around the neighborhood, walk after breakfast, walk before dinner, walk after dinner, walk to school, walk home from school, walk to a friend's house, park four blocks from the store and walk, just walk. It's safe, cheap, low intensity, long duration and continuous. Kids like it when they are walking some place they want to go, with someone they enjoy getting attention from. They love it when the dog comes along.

Bouncer   The mini-trampoline or "bouncer" is worth its cost, no question about it. Kids love it, which is good for the child and good for us — there's less complaining. They can do it in any weather. It is non-competitive and can be done privately, a big plus for children who at first feel self-conscious about exercising. Children can bounce while they watch television.

IMPORTANT WARNING: The bouncer is potentially unsafe. Children should bounce in the middle with their feet barely leaving the platform to increase safety. Use with adult supervision.

Swimming   Give them lessons. Early and often. Swimming is ranked number one nationally in children's exercise outside of school. Sure, lolling in the pool, playing in the water doesn't offer the cardiovascular benefits of a jog around the park, but it teaches them to experience their bodies in motion, to enjoy a wide range of body movements, and it improves flexibility. In addition, it gives them a skill that can benefit their fitness throughout their adult years.

Biking   The stationary bike offers the benefits of the bouncer. Some kids enjoy it, others don't. It's more expensive and harder to store than the bouncer, so the bouncer is a lower risk investment. If your child doesn't know how to ride a bike — lots of obese kids don't — he or she should learn. Biking is a great family sport. Long bike rides are terrific for endurance. Keep in mind, however, that for some kids biking means straddling a bike while standing and talking with their friends. Although meandering around the school yard on a bike sure beats parking in front of the cookie jar, it stops short of providing a good workout.

Soccer   Soccer is big these days. Peewee soccer begins at age three and by age 7 or 8 many children are playing on intramural teams. More boys than girls play competitively, but outside of team playing, it's ideal for the entire family. We can all dribble, kick and drill. With a few family members we can form teams. If your child has not yet become involved with soccer, consider signing him or her up. When your child first starts, he or she will be less skilled than their peers, so give him or her extra praise and extra practice.

3

GETTING STARTED IN EXERCISE (Continued)

Dancing

Dancing is fun, lyrical, creative and expressive. If there was a minimum daily requirement of dance, we'd all have more smiles and fewer crow's feet. Dance picks up on children's love of music, motion and aesthetics. It can also give a great workout. Dance classes offer the added benefit of having others teach and stimulate your child. It is programmed exercise that others orchestrate. Also, consider gymnastics and tumbling.

Baseball

Next to soccer, baseball is the most popular team sport for kids. How does it stack up? Again, better than munching chips in front of the television. It's a physical skill, can be continued in adulthood, and has social dividends. Unfortunately, it also involves higher intensity, stop-and-start, short duration movement, and so is less than ideal. A competency in all sports is good for children, so by all means consider signing your child up for the team. But if stand-around baseball games followed by soda and candy as team snacks crowd out substantial aerobic exercise, a change is in order.

Jump rope

A popular recess activity, and one that fills up an important corner of most women's childhood memories. If your child enjoys jumping or skipping rope, encourage it. Kids are likely to do it for a few minutes at a time, which can't hurt. But don't rely on jumping rope for the meat and potatoes of your child's exercise program. It is high impact—particularly problematic for obese kids—and high intensity, which means it is usually of be short duration or stop-and-start.

Playground

In the early school years, kids go to the playground a lot, often more for parental mental health than for their own physical exercise. Giving kids time to play, climb on the play structures, swing on the bars and on the swings and run through the grass is good for their bodies and their attitudes. They learn to use and enjoy their bodies. Some kids are very busy at the playground, romping non-stop from one structure to another. Other kids take a slower pace and get little exercise. In either case, bracketing playground time with walks that get our kids huffing and puffing a bit, guarantees that the playground experience benefits the heart and lungs.

Skating

A giant *yes* to roller skating! Some children will skate for hours and wake up the next morning with sore muscles. Skating improves flexibility and endurance and strengthens muscles in lower extremities. The intensity and duration vary according to the child's fitness level—they'll stop when their feet hurt or their legs tire. The risks, especially for obese children, involve injury—the more one weighs, the harder one falls. But skating is great fun and most kids when reminded to roller skate do it enthusiastically.

the like. These activities bridge the fitness gap until your child becomes more physically fit. Once he's mustered more fitness he can more readily engage in complex movement without injury and keep up with his peers.

Start with short intervals of 10 to 20 minutes. At first your child will tire easily. Keep the walks, soccer matches and bike rides brief. For instance, take a 10-minute morning walk to school and a 15-minute stint on the bouncer in the afternoon. If you are consistent with the short interval activity, within a few weeks, your child will work up to being fit enough to exercise 30 or 40 minutes straight.

Monitor your child's and your own heart rate often. Use the post exercise heart rate test and count heart beats right after exercise. Since we know it should be in the range of 12 to 15 beats per 6 seconds, we can learn a lot from this simple test. Go for a walk then test your heart rate. Was it less than 12? Speed up the walking. Bounce on the bouncer slowly. Test your heart rate. Then bounce hard and fast. Take your heart rate again. This is a wonderful mechanism for keeping us all in touch with our bodies and our current levels of fitness. And it's great fun!

3

7. PROMPTING YOUR CHILD TO EXERCISE

EXERCISE PLAN FOR YOUR CHILD:

We recommend that your child exercise daily for one hour.

On weekdays when will your child exercise?

before school   after school   before dinner   after dinner

On weekends when will your child exercise?

morning   afternoon   evening

List the kinds of exercise he or she will engage in this week:

1. _____

2. _____

3. _____

3

PARENT EXERCISE PLAN:

For how many minutes will you exercise in one day?

30 minutes   60 minutes   90 minutes   other_____

How many times per week will you exercise?

4   5   6   7

On weekdays when will you exercise?

morning   afternoon   early evening   evening

On weekends when will you exercise?

morning   afternoon   early evening   evening

List the kinds of exercise you will engage in this week:

1. _____

2. _____

3. _____

PRACTICE

Directions: Answer this practice quiz, check you answers below and then complete the final quiz. Check the answers to the final quiz at your next session.

1. Marsha's daughter, Christy, age 11 won't eat in front of her. Marsha is in:

   a. overcontrol
   b. undercontrol

2. Paul sees his 10-year-old step-son, Mark, playing a computer game. Which response is most effective?

   a. "You shouldn't be playing that thing. Turn it off."
   b. "I keep reminding you not to play that computer game. When are you going to stop?"
   c. "I know you love your computer game. You can watch it as soon as you've finished your homework and exercised for an hour."

3. Jennie came home from work and found Katie eating chips and watching television. The most effective response would be:

   a. "I expect you not to watch television after school and not to eat chips as a snack. You will have to do the dishes after dinner as a consequence. Now, tell me what went well today."
   b. "Get up off the couch and put those chips away. I can't believe you!"
   c. "You really shouldn't be eating chips now. It's better to wait until dinner to eat."

4. What are the benefits of exercise?

   a. can decrease body fat
   b. increases lean body mass
   c. improves one's mood

5. How much exercise per day is recommended for an overweight child?

   a. 30 to 60 minutes minutes
   b. 45 minutes
   c. 60 or more minutes

FINAL

1. Sean comes home from school. His mother, Barbara, has a business at home and is on the telephone with a client. She calls to him periodically, "turn off the television" but he doesn't listen. Barbara is in:

   a. undercontrol
   b. overcontrol

3

2. Jake goes to pick up Meredith from softball practice and sees her finishing a candy bar. The response likely to be most effective is:

   a. "I thought you knew you weren't supposed to have candy."
   b. "When you want candy, what are you supposed to do? That's right, talk to me about it. How can you plan your food for the rest of the day to be sure your diet is still healthy?
   c. "That candy just makes you fat. Don't you care about how you look?"

3. After a birthday party, Brian told Connie that he had two pieces of cake. How could Connie respond effectively?

   a. "I'm so happy that you felt comfortable telling me. It was a difficult situation and you could have eaten four pieces of cake. What do you plan to do about it now?"
   b. "That's OK. I know what we can do about it. Let's just skip dinner tonight."
   c. "That's it. No more parties. You obviously can't act responsibly at them, so no parties until you get this weight off."

4. Which of these forms of exercise is the most appropriate for overweight children who are not yet physically fit?
   a. walking
   b. baseball
   c. soccer

5. An activity is the correct intensity for you if your heart rate afterwards is:
   a. 10 to 15 in 6 seconds
   b. 15 to 20 in 10 seconds
   c. 12 to 15 in 6 seconds

Practice Quiz Answers: 1.A 2.C 3.A 4.A, B, C 5.C

84

THE ACTIONS

Each of us agrees to the following this week:

1. Complete the readings, practices and quizzes for Section 4.

2. Record on my SUPPORT record each day.

3. Meet at least 4 of my 5 SUPPORT goals.

4. If overweight, lose weight: □ ½ + pound **OR** □ 1 + pounds.

THE REWARDS

If **we all** do all of these actions, then **we all** receive our rewards:

_____'s reward:_____
     child's name   provided by when?_____

_____'s reward:_____
     parent's name   provided by when?_____

_____'s reward:_____
     parent's name   provided by when?_____

When the family receives the rewards, _____ will be responsible for
                                          parent's name
rewarding the child. The child will be sure the parents have given themselves their reward.

_____   _____
     parent's signature   child's signature

_____   _____
     parent's signature   date

PARENT SUPPORT #4

	MON.	TUES.	WED.	THURS.	FRI.	SAT.	SUN.	TOTAL	MET MY GOAL?
We took FAMILY TIME each day to review these records and to praise each other.								___ days	YES NO
I watched no more than 0 2 4 6 or 8 hours of TV								___ hours	YES NO
I EXERCISED for 100 200 300 400 minutes or more.								___ minutes	YES NO
I correctly filled out MY FOOD! on 4 or more days.								___ days	YES NO
GOAL OF THE WEEK: We went for a family walk on ___ or more days.								___ days	YES NO

TOTAL NUMBER OF GOALS MET ⇒

USING THE "FOOD PYRAMID" WITH "MY FOOD!"

Use the **Food Guide Pyramid,** also known as "My Pyramid" to help you eat better every day. It will help you make sure you eat different kinds of foods and get enough vitamins, minerals and protein. Each of the food groups in the Pyramid provides some, but not all, of the nutrients you need. No one group is more important than another -- for good health you need to eat some foods from each of the groups. Go easy on fats, oils and sweets.

On the pages that follow, you will see that the Pyramid is made up of five food groups: grains, vegetables, fruits, milk and meat & beans. The chart below the Pyramid suggests the amounts of each food group that should be eaten each day for a 2,000 calorie per day diet. You may visit www.mypyramid.gov to find the amount of each group that is right for you. The chart also recommends the amount of physical activity that is best for you to lose, maintain or sustain weight loss.

Remember, the Pyramid is not a diet, but a tool to remind you of the variety of foods that you should eat to stay healthy. It is also intended to stress the importance of regular exercise. Are there groups in which you don't consume any foods? Get a feel for whether or not you eating is healthy. Try to do well but don't worry about being perfect.

Notice that the "MY FOOD!" form now includes the five Pyramid Food Groups. In the columns below each group, make a check in the appropriate column for the food group you have eaten.

4

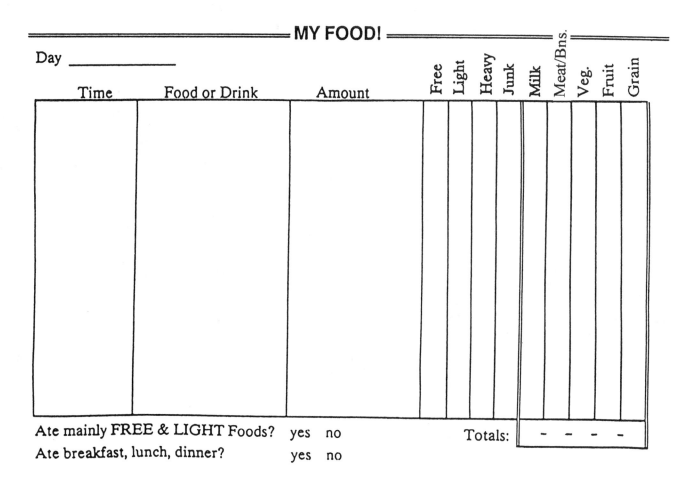

MyPyramid

STEPS TO A HEALTHIER

MyPyramid.gov

GRAINS | VEGETABLES | FRUITS | MILK | MEAT & BEANS

FAT-FREE MILK

1% MILK

PEACHES

RAISINS

TUNA

GRAINS
Make half your grains whole

Eat at least 3 oz. of whole-grain cereals, breads, crackers, rice, or pasta every day

1 oz. is about 1 slice of bread, about 1 cup of breakfast cereal, or ½ cup of cooked rice, cereal, or pasta

VEGETABLES
Vary your veggies

Eat more dark-green veggies like broccoli, spinach, and other dark leafy greens

Eat more orange vegetables like carrots and sweetpotatoes

Eat more dry beans and peas like pinto beans, kidney beans, and lentils

FRUITS
Focus on fruits

Eat a variety of fruit

Choose fresh, frozen, canned, or dried fruit

Go easy on fruit juices

MILK
Get your calcium-rich foods

Go low-fat or fat-free when you choose milk, yogurt, and other milk products

If you don't or can't consume milk, choose lactose-free products or other calcium sources such as fortified foods and beverages

MEAT & BEANS
Go lean with protein

Choose low-fat or lean meats and poultry

Bake it, broil it, or grill it

Vary your protein routine – choose more fish, beans, peas, nuts, and seeds

For a 2,000-calorie diet, you need the amounts below from each food group. To find the amounts that are right for you, go to MyPyramid.gov.

| Eat 6 oz. every day | Eat 2½ cups every day | Eat 2 cups every day | Get 3 cups every day; for kids aged 2 to 8, it's 2 | Eat 5½ oz. every day |

Find your balance between food and physical activity

Be sure to stay within your daily calorie needs.

Be physically active for at least 30 minutes most days of the week.

About 60 minutes a day of physical activity may be needed to prevent weight gain.

For sustaining weight loss, at least 60 to 90 minutes a day of physical activity may be required.

Children and teenagers should be physically active for 60 minutes every day, or most days.

Know the limits on fats, sugars, and salt (sodium)

Make most of your fat sources from fish, nuts, and vegetable oils.

Limit solid fats like butter, stick margarine, shortening, and lard, as well as foods that contain these.

Check the Nutrition Facts label to keep saturated fats, *trans* fats, and sodium low.

Choose food and beverages low in added sugars. Added sugars contribute calories with few, if any, nutrients.

U.S. Department of Agriculture
Center for Nutrition Policy and Promotion

4

MyPyramid.gov
STEPS TO A HEALTHIER YOU

Limit-setting is a close cousin to old-fashioned discipline. It is telling your child what you expect him to do. It also means following through to be sure that your child experiences positive consequences for acceptable behavior and negative consequences for unacceptable behavior. Limit-setting is how parents create order out of chaos and efficiently teach their children to adopt good habits.

Kids benefit when their parents devote their time and energy to limit-setting. Children want structure. They need to know how far they can go before their behavior is unacceptable to their parents. When parents draw the line and set limits for them, children feel less anxious. They know that they are not expected to be adults. The important separation of the generations is acknowledged. They can be children, do their part, yet be protected by the limits their parents set. Limit-setting can improve their sense of security in a world of constant change.

Nobody listens to me around here! I ask you over and over again to keep your stuff out of the living room and to keep your rooms picked up! Does it happen? No! Who do you think I am, your maid? What do I have to do to get your attention? I've had it!

Limit-setting is also good for parents. We need to exert some controls in order to make our

90

home lives run smoothly. Limit-setting is a way to effect our children's behavior so that we avoid the rising tension that comes from telling them to pick up their clothes over and over and over again. As we teach our kids acceptable behavior, our homes become more orderly and relaxing. With effective limit-setting, recurrent problems arise less frequently. Most of the time the wet towels are picked up off the bathroom floor, the dog gets fed and the trash is taken out.

Children want structure. When we set limits we give them that structure.

Difficulties with limit-setting are common among parents of overfat kids. Problems with limit-setting — and the resulting family chaos — can contribute to weight problems in kids. Without a certain amount of organization and structure, it's hard to have much control over the family's lifestyle, including diet and exercise. If we're drained by the long day's stresses, and then sit in bumper-to-bumper traffic on the way home, when the refrigerator is bare except for mustard, what will we do? Order out for pepperoni pizza, of course. If we live in a family in which there is little pre-planning and follow-through, we miss the deadline on joining the soccer team. Somehow broccoli and turkey breast don't always find their way into the fridge.

Kelly has dimples and plump pink cheeks and even strangers remark that she is totally captivating. She sure has captivated me. She loves ice cream and cookies, and charms me right into giving in.

Also, many overfat kids are so extraordinarily cute and charming that even parents who are great limit-setters succumb. These kids know just how to tilt their heads and speak in their sweetest voices when asking for another cookie. The result? We melt and give in. They know our weaknesses and hit every one of them.

In addition, many parents set limits well with school work, friends and clean up . . . but when it comes to food and exercise they strike out. Limit-setting about food and exercise are often blocked by our own attitudes toward them. These barriers are usually based on our early experiences with eating or exercising. If we've been deprived of food — because of scarcity or dieting — we don't want our kids to be deprived. In avoiding deprivation, we are likely to overindulge them. If sports meant failure, humiliation, excessively intense competition, boredom or dreary work to us as kids, we'll find it next to impossible to prompt our children to join the team or to walk a couple of miles to school.

When we set limits we are giving them the message that it's safe for them to be kids. We set limits to protect and guide them.

On many occasions limit-setting is unnecessary. Kids often make good choices all by themselves. We encourage them to act responsibly by praising them when they make good choices independently. We sprinkle our dialogue with "it's your choice," "you decide what you feel is best" or "if you wish." We also encourage positive behavior by heaping on the praise. We praise them as soon as we notice the positive behavior, describing what they did and indicating our approval. *I see you're eating fruit for a snack. That's a terrific change.*

So my daughter takes out the garbage strewing coffee grounds and half-eaten sandwiches along her path. On her way back she picks up the mess. I pause. I say, "Good clean-up job Marcie." I must be a saint.

4

Sometimes children make decisions to act in ways that are intolerable to us. They may behave in ways that are unhealthy, dangerous or destructive. Setting limits becomes desirable in these situations.

How does limit-setting differ from old-fashioned discipline? After all, many kids react to authority with hostility and resentment, resorting to lying, cheating, hiding feelings and striking back. Old-fashioned discipline, that is, resorting to the traditional "power approach" of threats and demands is rarely effective overall. Parents end up causing needless resentment and hostility. Setting limits is an alternative approach to authoritarian discipline that usually produces the desired behavior change without causing so many negative feelings.

If our child's discomfort wounds us deeply, we won't set limits. We must learn to tolerate making our child uncomfortable.

THE HOW-TO'S OF SETTING LIMITS

Here are the steps to setting limits with your child. Some of these steps you probably already do. Others you may want to brush up on.

STEP 1. Tell your child what you expect of him or her.

STEP 2. Attach a reward or a negative consequence to your expectation.

STEP 3. When your child acts acceptably, follow through consistently with praise and rewards.

STEP 4. When your child acts unacceptably, follow through consistently with negative consequences.

Now let's go through each step and talk about how to make each one work for you and your child.

STEP 1. Tell your child what you expect of him or her. You have expectations of your child. Don't keep them to yourself. Tell your child directly and specifically what behavior you expect.

Expect acceptable, not perfect, behavior. Don't confuse acceptable behavior with perfect or ideal behavior. Acceptable behavior is the behavior that you can tolerate and accept. For instance, *I expect you to join a sport. Right now that means soccer, football, karate or gymnastics* . . . rather than . . . *I expect you to play on the soccer team.*

Sandwich your expectation between praises. Say a "positive" to your child. Then tell your child your expectation. Then finish it off with another positive. *I know you are trying to exercise more, but I expect you to exercise for at least an hour a day. You've improved in your exercise to the point that you can do more of it. I'm proud of you* . . . rather than . . . *I expect you to exercise for at least an hour a day.* Few children resent you and fight complying with your expectations when you wrap it in acceptance, praise and love.

Begin sentences with, "I expect you to . . ."

Put out small fires. Your child may do quite a number of things that irritate you right down to your toes. He or she may disappoint you right and left. Don't save up these feelings until you explode in anger. Instead, keep a running dialog going with your child. Tell him or her 20 times a day if need be, what you expect. *I don't like it when you interrupt me. I expect you to wait until I am finished before speaking.* . . . rather than . . . *Stop interrupting me! You've been pestering me all night and I can't stand it any more!*

Use "I" messages. Verbally attacking a child doesn't make either of you feel good. Besides, your child is no match for you. Bullying or lecturing kids leads nowhere. It also strikes out as a motivator for behavior change. So, liberally sweeten your remarks with "I feel," "I expect," "It is important to me that you" and the like. Using "I" messages keeps your emotions in check and opens the door to your child really listening to you. *When you keep asking me about food, I feel angry. I expect you to remember that you can have as much salad as you want* . . . rather than . . . *Stop asking me for food! Can't you remember that you can have as much salad as you want?*

Keep your tone positive. Of course there are times when you are red hot mad and setting limits at the same time. But, as much as possible, keep the emotional tone positive. You do not need to be angry when you set limits. In fact, getting you angry just reinforces the undesired behavior. A child who can get Mom or Dad really angry has an awful lot of power. So, try to state your expectations calmly and directly. When you provide consequences, you are letting your child know you're serious and that you are not angry with him, just with his actions.

Make room for choices. Boost your child's sense of self-esteem. Decrease his or her resentment and hostility. How? By giving your child choices. *I expect you to exercise for one hour a day. One half hour of it should be taking a walk. What would you like to do the other half hour?* . . . rather than . . . *I expect you to take a walk for an hour each day.* Giving unlimited choices doesn't work. Kids may decide to do sit-ups for an hour or walk at a snail's pace for 20 minutes. Giving them choices within an acceptable range is motivating and positive.

STEP 2. Attach a reward or a negative consequence to your expectation. Often you tell your child what you expect and he or she does it. Sometimes it isn't so easy. If simply telling your child what you expect hasn't worked, add a consequence to it to get better results. The purpose of adding a consequence is to motivate the child, just as our paycheck motivates us to arise with the alarm each morning.

When possible, use positive consequences. Positives are more reinforcing than negatives. Your child feels rewarded rather than punished. We all respond better to positive statements. So use positive consequences first.

POSITIVE REWARDS

I will give you a sticker each day that you snack only on fruit or veggies after school.

I will let you bring the dog on our walk tomorrow, if you keep up and don't complain during our walk today.

I will let you stay up an hour later if you weed the vegetable garden.

If you bike to the store and back, I'll let you invite a friend over for dinner.

Use negative consequences when positives don't work. Negative consequences (punishments?) are very appropriate at times. Some negative consequences are motivating. They are appropriate for certain expectations and are saviors when you're "all out" of positives!

Avoid consequences that involve food. We are guiding your child to being less food-focused and using other activities, objects and relationships to feel pleasured and gratified. Rewarding your child with a hot fudge sundae may make you feel better, but is not good for your child.

She is our baby but let's stop babying her.

have an important opportunity to prompt the continuation of that behavior. Simply praise and reward it liberally, until to you it almost feels excessive. Probably only then will the child understand that you think what he has done is good. Follow through consistently. Praise your child — show how his actions make you feel, the reward he will get and how much you enjoy and respect him for his actions.

Far-off rewards of new wardrobes and shiny new bikes don't blunt the allure of today's cookie jar.

Use immediate consequences. A reward of new clothes when 20 pounds disappear is not a powerful motivator. Getting a new blouse if this week's weight goal is met, is. An even more compelling reward is something received today for today's action. Keep things here and now.

NEGATIVE CONSEQUENCES

If you ask me for another cookie again, I will have you sit on the punishment chair for 10 minutes.

If you don't go to soccer practice, you will have to get your exercise around here. You can wash, fold and put away the laundry.

If you choose to go slowly or complain on our hike, you will have to do five miles on the stationery bike when we get home.

STEP 3. When your child acts acceptably, follow through consistently with praise and rewards. Once your child acts acceptably, you

Look what you did! You rode your bike to White Hill and back. That means you're getting stronger! I feel so proud of what you have done.

I feel so happy about the way you said "no" when Martha offered you those cookies. You are making such good decisions all by yourself!

You walked the entire way without complaining or lagging behind. I really enjoyed walking with you. It makes me happy to think that we can go on fun walks together. Tomorrow you can bring the dog!

STEP 4. When your child acts unacceptably, follow through consistently with negative consequences. Consistently and immediately tell your child what you expected. Compare what he did to what you expected him to do. Tell him how you feel using "I" messages. Remind him what the consequences of his actions will be. Follow through in letting him experience the negative consequences.

How you handle giving negative consequences is extremely important. Handled incorrectly, negative consequences can actually stimulate more unacceptable behavior. The idea is to avoid giving him extra attention for doing something "bad." So remain calm. Administer the consequence in a matter-of-fact way, without emotion or concern. He chose to act in a certain way, this is the consequence. Period.

I told you that I expected you to bounce on the trampoline during the first half hour that you watched TV. Here you sit watching TV without having bounced on it. I feel very angry. I don't like what you have done. I would like you to get up now, turn off the television and do the dinner dishes and then bounce on the trampoline for a half an hour without the TV.

I told you that I expected you to stop asking me for cookies. I feel very irritated when you keep on asking for them. I get tired of telling you this over and over again. Go sit on the punishment chair for 15 minutes.

You chose not to go to soccer practice today. You must wash, fold and put away the laundry before you go to bed.

COMMON LIMIT-SETTING BREAKDOWNS

Alexa talked about food—what she could and couldn't have—constantly. Her parents set limits and followed through consistently with their food goals, but got worn down by Alexa's incessant food talk. Their limit-setting had failed in that Alexa got all sorts of attention that was unpleasant to the parents. They had set limits with what Alexa should eat, but not with another behavior they found intolerable: focusing the entire family's attention on Alexa and her weight. Once they recognized the pattern, Alexa's parents told her that they were responsible for when she ate and the foods served. She was responsible for whether she ate and how much. There was a list of afternoon snacks she could choose from taped to the refrigerator. They expected her not to talk about food except during their FAMILY TIME each night.

Jennifer had two girls with weight problems. As a single parent she was stretched to the limit. When she got home at night the girls would inundate her with dozens of questions and demands. Jennifer felt beaten down before the evening began. She barely had the energy to tell the girls what she expected of them, let alone to follow through. They didn't even pay attention to what she said because they knew she wouldn't make it stick. Jennifer

COMMON LIMIT-SETTING BREAKDOWNS (Continued)

got to the point that she wanted to move out—or get the girls to move out. The situation was intolerable. She recognized that setting limits and following through were very demanding activities. They required structure, focus and her emotional well-being. Once Jennifer was convinced that she had to take care of herself in order to parent the girls well, she had little trouble turning things around. The first step was to change the evening routine. When Jennifer got home at night she asked the girls to watch 30 minutes of television while she unwound. After 30 minutes she gave each girl one-on-one time to talk about the day and see how they were doing. Then the evening began. Jennifer had regained the composure and focus she needed to begin following through on some of her limit-setting.

Marjorie and Tom instigated a policy that Bobby had to do his hour of exercise prior to watching television each day. Their limit-setting about how much he exercised was effective. However, Bobby began expressing a lot of anger at them by scowling and giving them hateful stares. For a while they tolerated it. Finally they asked him about his feelings and he lashed out at them, "How could you do this to me? How could you make me sweat like this?" Then the scowling and stares continued. Bobby had won. He had found a response that got their attention. The parent's unreasonable guilt about making their child exercise made them willing to put up with his manipulative behavior. When they recognized the pattern for what it was—a behavior they had taught him that worked to get their attention—they quickly treated it as such. Tom began saying, "I know you don't like to exercise but it's important to your health, regardless of your weight. I know you are angry. I

know this doesn't make you happy. But I expect you to exercise one hour per day. I do not like the way you are acting when you scowl and look hateful. Please go to your room until you can behave well."

Cindy began to think about setting limits with Kelly. She watched her daughter help herself to another plate of lasagne at dinner. That same evening she looked on as her husband had his nightly three double scotches, and then felt too fuzzy to make love or talk intimately. Later she finished off the rest of the half gallon of rocky road ice cream. Cindy began to see her own pattern. She had difficulties setting limits with herself and with others. No wonder she felt so helpless, hopeless and out of control. She wasn't shaping herself, her relationships or her life the way she wanted to. Cindy requested a referral from the SHAPEDOWN instructor who recommended several possible counselors to support Cindy in making some changes.

Marna felt guilty about what Tommy had gone through when she and his dad had split up. His dad had been verbally abusive and physically violent to her toward the end. Tommy had observed too much of it. Now she wanted to protect him from any further hurt. Marna took Tommy to a therapist weekly. It seemed to help, but not with the family interaction. Marna kept indulging Tommy, giving in whenever he expressed discomfort. Tommy quickly learned to cry, throw his body on the floor, saying, "You hate me! You're ruining my life" whenever Marna demanded that he do something. The change came when Marna developed a close relationship with, and then married, Jack. With Jack's emotional support Marna set a limit with Tommy: no more

---

COMMON LIMIT-SETTING BREAKDOWNS (Continued)

granola bars and chips in his bag lunch. Tommy reacted predictably: "The kids at school will laugh at me. I'll have no friends. You hate me," and rolled on the floor and shed huge tears. Marna told herself that the limit she had set was reasonable and that she was being a good mother to take action to improve Tommy's health. Jack reminded her that Tommy's behavior was learned. Marna had taught him over and over again that it worked to throw tantrums. He could shed tears and get his way. Marna cried, but stuck with it. Tommy's protestations diminished. The next time Marna set a limit, it was easier to deal with Tommy's behavior. By the end of four weeks he had stopped his tantrums altogether.

He had learned that they didn't work.

Chet advised Randy, "You shouldn't have so many sweets" and "I don't know why you don't exercise." He would become disgruntled when Randy didn't do what he had advised. Chet's limit-setting wasn't working because he was treating Randy like a peer not like a child. this made Randy more anxious, knowing that he had more authority than his dad did. No one was protecting him from adult responsibilities and demands. Rather than advising Randy, Chet began telling him what behavior he expected. "I expect you to have fruit rather than sweets for dessert" and "I expect you to exercise one hour each day."

4

WHY IT'S SO HARD TO SET LIMITS

Sometimes our beliefs, experiences or feelings call a halt to our limit-setting. They make what seems rather simple, unbearably difficult. See if you have experienced any of the most common barriers to consistent limit-setting:

You don't want to deprive your child. Denying your child food seems mean. It goes against the grain of being a nurturing parent. You are not depriving your child when you feed him healthy foods. You are switching from nurturing with food he doesn't need to nurturing with your time, attention, and affection, all of which he does need.

You don't want your child to feel punished about his or her weight. The other kids eat chips, why can't your child? What anger and resentment must seethe within your child when others get goodies and he doesn't? Your child will pick up your attitude. If you don't feel that eating healthfully or exercising is punishment, your

child won't. Besides, your child is not alone. Plenty of parents enforce healthy habits regardless of their children's weights.

Now and then all kids skip meals or eat foods they don't like. They survive it just fine.

You fear that your child will not get enough to eat. Your child has overfed himself, habitually consuming more calories that his body requires. His body needs less food than you've been used to feeding him. Cutting back moderately will not starve your child. A missed meal now and then is not terribly detrimental to his health. Relax and avoid letting your fear of his not eating keep you from setting effective limits.

You feel sad when your child looks sad. You want your child to be happy and satisfied. That's not how he or she looks when you set limits and stick with them. You can learn to feel comfort-

4

able with a certain amount of negative feeling or expression of anger. His discomfort and yours will be short term. It helps to keep in mind that you are setting the stage for a healthier and happier life for your child.

You feel you or your child have failed if you need to set limits. You think that your child should eat lightly and exercise without having limits set. He should just do it. He has disappointed you. You have disappointed yourself. Kids need encouragement to develop healthy habits. It doesn't usually happen without parents taking a guiding role.

You fear that setting limits with your child will cause him or her to stop liking you. You work long hours. You're not home much. You wish you had more patience and time with your child. With all that guilt, one thing you can't tolerate is feeling that your child doesn't like you. You

cannot afford to alienate your child because that must mean that you are a bad parent. So you indulge him or her. Actually, the opposite is true. The overall impact of consistent limit-setting is not only positive for your child, but also for your relationship. He knows you are concerned and involved. Besides, indulgence clearly doesn't make up for time spent communicating intimately. It doesn't make your child feel more secure or cared for.

You find it hard to set limits, because your child is very close to you and it hurts you as much as it hurts him or her. You are terribly close to your child. Perhaps it's because he or she is a sensitive, giving child. Or because the marriage isn't working and you rely on your child for emotional support. Just the way parents who are very removed, very detached, have difficulty meeting their child's needs, so do parents who are over-involved and enmeshed. A certain amount of distance will allow you and your child to function more positively.

**In the long run,
if you don't set limits,
you'll express more anger,
not less.**

You feel that to set limits you need to feel angry, which you dislike. You were brought up with anger and yelling and you detest it. You don't like the feelings of getting angry or having your child experience your anger. It is normal to experience a wide range of emotions toward your child, including envy, resentment and anger. Actually, setting limits is a very calm act. You clearly lay out what you expect your child to do and the rewards and consequences if he or she chooses not to do it. Acting hostile is not necessary.

In summary, since each child, parent and situation differ, there are no hard and fast rules for how much "muscle" to use in shaping your child's behavior. In general, start with a little and escalate only if necessary. Begin with "Power 1" and use more muscle only if this doesn't work. Then use "Power 2" and, if that is not effective, use "Power 3."

Power 1. State your expectations.

I expect you to go on our walk without complaining.

Power 2. State your expectations. Attach a positive consequence.

I expect you to go on our walk without complaining. If you do, you can watch TV for 30 minutes when we get home.

Power 3. State your expectations. Attach a negative consequence.

I expect you to go on our walk without complaining. If you do not, you cannot watch any TV tonight and you will do the dinner dishes by yourself.

The difficulty inherent in setting limits is also what makes it so potent in deflating your child's sense of isolation that fuels the appetite. Limit setting requires that you reach into yourself and decide exactly what you are willing to take, where you draw the line. You bring to the limit-setting task exactly who you are and open up the risk of your child confronting you, ridiculing you or ignoring you. Your response requires the child to do the same. As a result, in the rush of the day, parent and child's souls have encountered one another.

As you launch into brushing up on limit-setting, be reassured. It is roughest in the beginning. Your child will test you thoroughly. He or she will want to see if you really mean it. Will you care enough to remember to follow through with a consequence? Will you buckle when it comes to negative consequences? When your child pulls such manipulations as crying, pouting, shouting and the like, congratulate yourself. You have a creative kid. Then go on to be consistent; stick with the limits you have set. And finally, begin to enjoy your child more—even to like your child more—as his or her behavior improves.

SELF-ASSESSMENT

8. SETTING LIMITS

1. How often do you:

	never	sometimes			always
Tell your child what you expect of him or her?	1	2	3	4	5
Attach a reward or a negative consequence to your expectation?	1	2	3	4	5
When your child act acceptably, follow through consistently with praise and rewards?	1	2	3	4	5
When your child acts unacceptably, follow through with consequences?	1	2	3	4	5

2. Which of these barriers to effective limit–setting do you experience?

You don't want to deprive your child.	YES	NO	NOT SURE
You don't want your child to feel punished about his or her weight.	YES	NO	NOT SURE
You fear that your child will not get enough to eat.	YES	NO	NOT SURE
You feel sad when your child looks sad.	YES	NO	NOT SURE
You feel you or your child have failed if you need to set limits.	YES	NO	NOT SURE
You fear that setting limits with your child will cause him or her to stop liking you.	YES	NO	NOT SURE
You find it hard to set limits, because your child is very close to you and it hurts you as much as it hurts him or her.	YES	NO	NOT SURE
You feel that to set limits you need to feel angry, which you dislike.	YES	NO	NOT SURE

100

Your child's losing weight, but is he or she okay nutritionally? Is your child getting enough to eat? Is he or she setting out for school each day with the necessary vitamins and minerals? Probably. When we cut down on fat and sugar in the diet, our kids eat more nutritious foods. Often the real risk is not making the diet too nutritious. Our goal is to lighten their diet yet avoid that deprived feeling that makes honest kids into cookie bandits.

Margaret doesn't like milk so we've relied on cheese for her calcium. Now cheese is on the outs so I'm not sure what's going to keep her leg bones from bending!

I've been giving Charlie two apples and a banana for lunch. Is that enough?

To determine how much your child should eat check his or her weight change. Aim for a pattern of food intake that produces a one-half to one pound weight loss per week. Most kids do fine planning their diets without calculating calories. Besides, energy requirements during childhood are very individual. Even if you calculated calories, you'd probably be off by quite a bit. And kids—and parents—have better things to do than count calories.

Serve fewer high calorie foods and more low calorie foods. The number of calories in one cup

4

of food ranges from 10 for lettuce to 1600 for butter. So, the amount of food to eat depends on the kind of food you are eating.

FREE FOODS—Because these foods are mainly water and fiber, the quantity your child can consume is unlimited. Even if you filled up a telephone booth with lettuce, it would still be a thin amount! Your child can enjoy all of the FREE FOODS he wants.

LIGHT FOODS—A thin amount of these foods is ½ to 1 cup. A thin amount of LIGHT FOODS is a large apple, ½ cup of rice, 1 cup of low-fat milk, 2 slices of bread, 1 chicken breast, 1 cup of beans.

HEAVY FOODS—These foods contain more calories than LIGHT FOODS, so a thin amount of HEAVY FOODS is smaller. A thin amount of HEAVY FOODS is ¼ to ½ cup. One piece of pizza, 1 cup of chili, ½ container of flavored yogurt and 1 ounce of cheese are thin amounts.

JUNK FOODS—Because JUNK FOODS are mainly fat or sugar, thin amounts of them are tiny, between 1 teaspoon and ¼ cup. Half a doughnut, 5 potato chips, 1 teaspoon of butter, a sliver of cake, and 1 cookie are all thin amounts of JUNK FOODS.

4

MyPyramid

MyPyramid.gov

GRAINS VEGETABLES FRUITS MILK MEAT & BEANS

In SHAPEDOWN, you will use a variety of ways to determine whether or not you are getting what you need from your diet. First, you used eating regular meals and the kinds of food (FREE, LIGHT, HEAVY, JUNK) to determine the nutrient and caloric density of foods. Second, you have been using the **Five Food Groups** from the **Food Pyramid** to estimate whether or not you are getting enough vitamins, minerals and protein. This system doesn't tell you how much food to eat. It just tells you the minimum.

Now your child is beginning to take into account how hungry he or she is. Later in SHAPEDOWN, you and your child will keep track of how hungry you are when you start eating and how full you are when you stop eating. By starting eating when you are hungry and stopping when you are just satisfied, not full, you are less likely to overeat.

ARE YOU HUNGRY?

Why all the fuss about amounts? Won't kids just eat what they need? Sure, some kids will, but some won't. Hunger is not as simple as a growling stomach after a missed meal. It's biological, but it can be psychological, too. The perception of hunger easily gets mixed up with feelings of anger, boredom, depression and loneliness. We can teach ourselves to be hungry at 4:00 p.m. or even 1:00 a.m. We can "feel hungry" just by seeing the chocolate coating being poured over the nougat candy bar on television. Encourage your child to check in with his or her internal cues of hunger and satiety before initiating eating and to stop eating when barely satisfied, not stuffed.

In addition, keep these general guidelines for healthy nutrition in mind:

1. Serve regular meals — breakfast, lunch and dinner.

2. Limit snacking — usually one snack is acceptable — in the afternoon.

3. Serve mainly FREE FOODS and LIGHT FOODS.

4. Serve mainly unprocessed foods -an orange rather than orange juice, whole wheat bread rather than white bread.

5. Serve large portions of vegetables and smaller portions of other foods. Try half a plate of veggies and half a plate of other foods.

6. Include foods from at least three of the four food groups at each meal.

7. Include a small amount of a HEAVY FOOD or JUNK FOOD each day to chase away the cookie bandit.

8. Ask each family member to pick a favorite food and include it in the family's light meals that week.

Dinner is easy.
Serve half a plate of veggies,
and half a plate of other foods.

CUTTING THE FAT

The most important part of eating healthfully is to eat very little fat. That's because fat has lots of calories — 9 per gram whereas protein and carbohydrates only contain 4. What's more, fat is more likely to become fat on your body. Excess calories have to be converted to be stored as fat, but fat doesn't have to be converted. It can be stored as is, so becomes body fat more readily than other foods do. If you only make one change, "cut the fat."

4

Buy low fat foods and add little or no fat to the foods you prepare. Frying, sauteing or smothering food in heavy sauces adds extra fat and calories. If you bake, broil, steam or boil your food instead, you won't be adding extra fat and calories. When you do fry or saute, use PAM, or not more than a tablespoon of fat. Better yet, cook with broth or water and herbs.

THE CALORIE COSTS OF ADDED FAT

	calories
toast with ½ teaspoon butter	91
toast with 1 tablespoon butter	177
1 potato with ½ teaspoon butter	161
1 potato fried in oil	456
1 cup broccoli with lemon and pepper	47
1 cup broccoli with ¼ cup Hollandaise	232
2 cups salad (lettuce) with 1 tablespoon dressing	100
2 cups salad (lettuce) with ¼ cup dressing	340
4 oz. of tuna canned in water	144
4 oz. of tuna canned in oil	327

If you only do one thing, de-fat your family's food.

LIGHT SHOPPING

Be particular about the food you buy. Be a critical purchaser and look for the foods that are low in fat, sugar and sodium. Pick out lean ground beef rather than regular ground beef. Find sandwich meats that are naturally low in fat and scan the shelf for canned fruit packed in water or juice rather than fruit canned in syrup. What you bring into the house, the family will eat.

Special "dietetic" foods are unnecessary. Many foods sold as "diet foods" have just as many calories as regular foods. In addition, they are often more expensive. Any food claiming to be a diet food has to provide nutrition information. Before you buy, be sure to check and compare the labels for numbers of calories and quantities of fat, sugar and sodium. If you find a few "diet" foods that your family likes, fine. But avoid using too many. They just perpetuate the myth that you must eat special foods and be on a "diet" to lose weight.

Before putting it into your cart ask, "Should we really be eating this?"

Use the information on food labels. Find where it says "Ingredients" on a label. The ingredients are listed in order of predominance. The food has the most of the first ingredient listed, less of the second ingredient, and so on. If one of the first three ingredients listed is some kind of fat or sugar, that food is probably a HEAVY FOOD.

For instance, the only ingredient in Shredded Wheat cereal is 100% natural whole wheat. Shredded Wheat is a LIGHT FOOD. The first three ingredients in Wheaties are whole wheat, sugar and salt. Wheaties is a HEAVY FOOD. Start checking out what's on labels. You may find some surprises!

Determine which foods derive less than 30 percent of their calories from fat. It's easy to figure out. Remember that there are nine calories in each gram of fat. Multiply nine times the number of grams of fat in a serving and divide by the

---IS IT A LIGHT FOOD?---

Spaghetti sauce

Nutrition Information

calories per serving	80
protein (grams)	2
carbohydrate (grams)	14
fat (grams)	2

Ingredients: water, tomato paste, tomatoes in tomato juice, sugar, soybean oil, dried onions, salt, garlic powder, Romano cheese, parsley, black pepper, basil, oregano

You already know that plain spaghetti is a LIGHT FOOD, right? But what about spaghetti sauce? Let's put it to the test. The first three ingredients are water, tomato paste and tomatoes in tomato juice, so it should be a LIGHT FOOD. Let's double check by looking at the fat it contains. Multiply 2 grams by 9 calories. That's 18. Divide 18 by the number of calories per serving: 80. The result? About 23% of the calories are from fat. That's 30% or less, so spaghetti sauce is a LIGHT FOOD!

Again, here's the formula: % calories from fat = $\dfrac{\text{grams of fat x 9}}{\text{calories per serving}}$

4

number of calories. That's all there is to it. If it is 30% or less it is a LIGHTER FOOD, if it is more than 30%, it is a HEAVIER FOOD.

Consider including your child in grocery shopping. Does your child ask for everything he or she sees in the cereal and cookie sections? Some parents deal with it by shopping alone, especially at first. Others turn the tide around and tell the child what they expect: "You can go with me to the store if you don't ask for any HEAVY FOODS or JUNK FOODS. When we are at the store you can pick out one vegetable, one fruit and one bread of your choice."

The idea is to know your limitations. Shopping at 6:30 p.m. after a hectic day and terrible traffic and constant food requests from kids can only trigger a buying spree of chocolate fudge ice cream, little butter cookies, and cinnamon rolls. Good prevention for those days is to leave little ones at home.

Yes, you can shop with me. You can pick out one fruit, one vegetable and one bread!

Empty your basket. That's right. Just before it's time to check out, STOP. Empty the child's seat of all foods. Then go through the entire basket, putting all of the HEAVY FOODS and JUNK FOODS in the child's seat. Do you really want your child to eat these foods? If so, keep them. If not, give your child some exercise putting them back.

YOUR EATING ENVIRONMENT

What adults see, they consider eating. What children see, they devour. If chocolate chip cookies are there, they'll eat them. Pizza in the fridge? Its lifespan is a matter of seconds.

The cure for the see-it-eat-it syndrome? Clean up the food environment. Lots of families find that it helps. Some find that it is the entire solution. Can the eating environment be too "clean?" Yes! If it makes your child feel deprived, he or she will find a way to compensate. Need some examples? Downing an entire box of raisin bran. Hitting the candy bar stash that lives between the mattresses. Conning friends out of their lunches. Create a depriving food environment at home and stand back and watch how creative your child becomes at getting in those calories!

Out of the house, out of the mouth.

So adopt a moderate approach. The kitchen becomes a place where there are healthy, good-tasting foods that people can fix and eat when they are hungry. It does not feel barren. Nor does it feel packed with goodies and junk that are all-too ready to eat.

Put food in the kitchen only — Keep food in the kitchen and nowhere else. Put away the peanuts that were next to the television and the potato chips that were on the coffee table.

Keep all food out of sight — A loaf of bread or a jar of cookies on the counter can signal your child to eat. Be sure that all food is in the cupboard or refrigerator. Out of sight, out of mind, out of mouth.

Move most JUNK FOODS out of the house — If ice cream, chips, cakes and cookies are always around, they will probably be eaten. Foods that are tasty and can be prepared with little effort are particularly troublesome. Frozen pizza bread, frozen cakes, heat-and-eat burritos and the like are strong cues to eat. Although no foods are forbidden in SHAPEDOWN, discuss with your child the foods that are best kept out of the house.

Keep a VEGGIE BOWL in the refrigerator— Discuss with your child the kinds of vegetables he or she wants on hand, already washed, sliced and ready for munching! Look back at the FOOD SUMMARY together for ideas. Vegetables sleeping in the vegetable bin are not a viable alternative to a handful of crackers. But washed, cut and ready—stored in ice water—they are.

Have a VEGGIE BOWL at the center of your table - A large bowl of salad, cut-up veggies or cooked vegetables, all with little or no fatty dressing or sauces, quiets cries for "seconds". Plates are served up and then those still hungry can help themselves to more from the VEGGIE BOWL.

Always have fresh fruit on hand—Almost everybody likes some kind of fresh fruit. Because fruit is a LIGHT FOOD and is always ready to eat, it makes a good snack. Look at the FOOD SUMMARY with your child and pick out fruits he or she likes. Make plans so that these fruits are available at home on a regular basis, particularly those your child tells you he or she is willing to eat.

Veggies cut, cleaned and crisp,
smile at you from the fridge.
They get eaten. Their cousins
in the crisper wilt, weep and die.

Leave food, except for a fresh VEGGIE BOWL, off the table during your mealtime - Putting bowls of food on the table is an invitation to have seconds. Instead, after the

4

107

plates are served, leave the extra food off the table and out of view. Keep butter and high-fat or high-sugar sauces, toppings and salt off the table.

After you eat, put all food away — Wrap up the leftovers and put them out of sight. That way your child will be less apt to have second helpings or to nibble after the meal is over.

With these ideas in mind, experiment with lightening your family's food. If you don't get a reasonable amount of resistance you're probably not lightening up enough. The fuss is fun for the kids. Don't take it too seriously. They will not starve. Somehow they will survive. And your entire family will be healthier for it.

SELF-ASSESSMENT

9. MORE ON HEALTHY EATING

1. How often do you:	rarely		sometimes		always
Put food in the kitchen only?	1	2	3	4	5
Keep all food out of sight?	1	2	3	4	5
Move most JUNK FOODS out of the house?	1	2	3	4	5
Keep a VEGGIE BOWL in the refrigerator?	1	2	3	4	5
Have fresh fruit on hand?	1	2	3	4	5
Leave food, except a VEGGIE BOWL, off the table during mealtime?	1	2	3	4	5
Have a VEGGIE BOWL at the center of your table?	1	2	3	4	5
Put all food away after you eat?	1	2	3	4	5

PRACTICE

1. Dan wanted his 12-year-old, Jake, to take responsibility for watering their plot in the community garden. Jake was not particularly interested in plants and in the past Dan had given up nagging him and just done the watering himself. With which type of limit should Dan begin?

   a. Power 1. State his expectations.
   b. Power 2. State his expectations. Attached a positive consequence.
   c. Power 3. State his expectations. Attach a negative consequence.

2. Which is an example of a Power 2 limit for prompting a child to exercise?

   a. "I expect you to finish your hour of exercise by 6:00 p.m."
   b. "I expect you to exercise for an hour. Then you may watch a half hour of television."
   c. "I expect you to do the dishes; if they are not done by 8:00 p.m., you can do them tomorrow night, too."

3. Which is an example of a Power 3 limit for stimulating a child to eat breakfast?

   a. "You have to start eating breakfast whether you want to or not."
   b. "Breakfast is really important. You really should start eating it."
   c. "You may not go to school until you have prepared and eaten at least one milk, one fruit and one grain food. If you are late for school, you will go to bed that night at 7:00 p.m."

4. It is healthy to stop eating when you are:

   a. hungry
   b. just satisfied
   c. full

5. Which two of these are NOT part of a healthy food environment?

   a. put a bowl of spaghetti on the table at dinner
   b. leave the pan of macaroni on the stove after dinner
   c. keep a plastic container full of cut up carrots in the refrigerator.

4

1. Janice wanted 7-year-old Jimmy to start taking out the trash. Jimmy liked taking out the trash, but might have difficulty remembering to do it. With which type of limit should Janice begin?

a. Power 1. State your expectations.
b. Power 2. State your expectations. Attached a positive consequence.
c. Power 3. State your expectations. Attach a negative consequence.

2. Which are examples of effective Power 2 limit for prompting a "latchkey" child to exercise?

a. "I expect you to vacuum the apartment and sweep the patio after school and get your home work done. If you do, then tonight we will do an exercise video together and then you can watch an hour of any TV program you like."
b. "I expect you to go to soccer practice after school and to be able to tell me that you played really hard. If you don't, then I'll store your computer game for the remainder of the week."
c. "I expect you to ride 10 miles on the stationary bike. It's odometer is at 254 miles now so it should be at 264 when I get home from work. If it is, we can visit Marguerite and Susan tonight."

3. Which of these Power 2 limits are likely to be successful in prompting a child to do the dishes?

a. "I expect you to help out with dinner. You can either prepare the dinner and set the table or you can clear the table and do the dishes. When we're all done, I will play a game with you."
b. "You are now old enough to do the dishes. It's a huge help to me. I want you to start doing them tonight. When you are done, call me so I can look at and appreciate what you have done."
c. "I really want you to start doing the dishes. You could get a start on them tonight. The first week I'll help you so you'll get the idea down. Then next week you can do it on your own. When you finish tonight, I'll read you any book you wish for 20 minutes."

4. It is healthy to <u>start</u> eating when you are:

a. very hungry
b. hungry
c. just satisfied

5. Which of these are NOT part of a healthy food environment?

a. put a VEGGIE BOWL at the center of the table at dinner
b. place a platter of fruit on the table for dessert
c. put a bowl of potato salad on the table at dinner

Practice Quiz Answers: 1.B 2.B 3.C 4.B 5.A, B

THE ACTIONS

Each of us agrees to the following this week:

1. Complete the readings, practices and quizzes for Section 5.

2. Record on my SUPPORT record each day.

3. Meet at least 4 of my 5 SUPPORT goals.

4. If overweight, lose weight: □ ½ + pound **OR** □ 1 + pounds.

THE REWARDS

If **we all** do all of these actions, then **we all** receive our rewards:

_____'s reward:_____

child's name   provided by when?_____

_____'s reward:_____

parent's name   provided by when?_____

_____'s reward:_____

parent's name   provided by when?_____

When the family receives the rewards, _____ will be responsible for

parent's name

rewarding the child. The child will be sure the parents have given themselves their reward.

_____   _____
parent's signature   child's signature

_____   _____
parent's signature   date

5

111

PARENT SUPPORT #5

	MON.	TUES.	WED.	THURS.	FRI.	SAT.	SUN.	TOTAL	MET MY GOAL?
We took FAMILY TIME each day to review these records and to praise each other.								____ days	YES NO
I watched no more than 0 2 4 6 or 8 hours of TV								____ hours	YES NO
I EXERCISED for 100 200 300 400 minutes or more.								____ minutes	YES NO
I correctly filled out MY FOOD! on 4 or more days.								____ days	YES NO
GOAL OF THE WEEK: I played a sport with my child on ____ or more days.								____ days	YES NO

TOTAL NUMBER OF GOALS MET ⇒

5

112

MY FOOD!

Day _____

Time	Food or Drink	Amount	Free	Light	Heavy	Junk	Milk	Meat/Bns.	Veg.	Fruit	Grain

Ate mainly FREE & LIGHT Foods?   yes   no   Totals: -   -   -   -

Ate breakfast, lunch, dinner?   yes   no

5

MY FOOD!

Day _____

Time	Food or Drink	Amount	Free	Light	Heavy	Junk	Milk	Meat/Bns.	Veg.	Fruit	Grain

Ate mainly FREE & LIGHT Foods?   yes   no   Totals: -   -   -   -

Ate breakfast, lunch, dinner?   yes   no

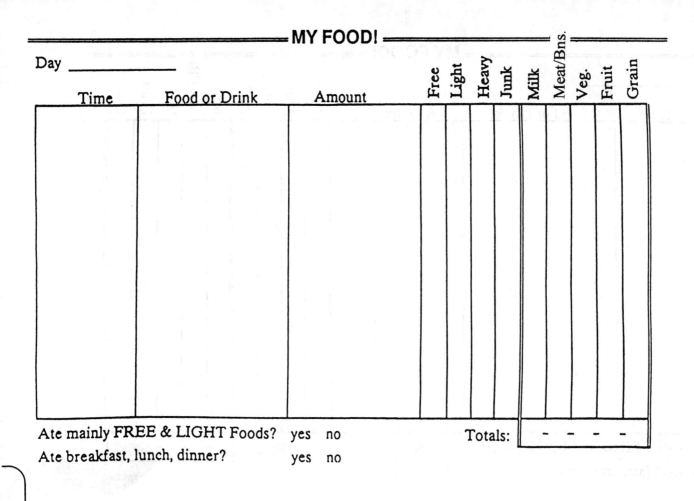

MY FOOD!

Day _____

Time	Food or Drink	Amount	Free	Light	Heavy	Junk	Milk	Meat/Bns.	Veg.	Fruit	Grain

Ate mainly **FREE & LIGHT** Foods? yes   no

Ate breakfast, lunch, dinner? yes   no

Totals: – – – –

5

MY FOOD!

Day _____

Time	Food or Drink	Amount	Free	Light	Heavy	Junk	Milk	Meat/Bns.	Veg.	Fruit	Grain

Ate mainly **FREE & LIGHT** Foods? yes   no

Ate breakfast, lunch, dinner? yes   no

Totals: – – – –

10. STOCKING UP ON FOOD IDEAS

You haven't seen many recipes so far in SHAPEDOWN. That's because you really don't need them. Eating more vegetables and fruits, a greater share of complex carbohydrates and less fat, are pretty straight forward changes. But when you've had it with steamed broccoli and when diet frozen dinners leave you cold, some fresh ideas on food are usually welcome.

So come on into the SHAPEDOWN kitchen and stock up on a few tricks for making appealing and satisfying meals and snacks. We serve great food with minimal amounts of fat.

RISE AND SHINE BREAKFASTS

For most of us, designer breakfasts are out of the question. There is simply not time. In addition, breakfast is an opportunity to start the day with a mind toward health. Somehow greeting the morning with a gooey plate of syrup-laden french toast or greasy, fatty bacon and eggs is a shame. In the morning most people don't crave variety. It's perfectly okay if it's wholesome yet somewhat routine. In fact, most don't care about breakfast being absolutely delicious and are content if breakfast stops short of being memorable.

STANDARD WHOLESOME BREAKFASTS

a bowl of unsweetened cereal, non-fat milk, ½ glass of orange juice, water, or

a slice of whole grain toast with a touch of butter and some low-sugar jam, ½ of an orange, a glass of non-fat milk, water

Bored to tears with toast and cereal? If breakfast has become a tad too monotonous, try these fun breakfasts for a change:

FRUITY CEREAL—Top dry cereal with two kinds of fruit: use strawberries, bananas, pineapple, apples, raisins, apricots, or peaches. When fresh fruits are not in season, try fruit canned in water or juice.

APPLE OATMEAL—Make your favorite unsweetened oatmeal, with half the salt, one cut-up apple and a shake of cinnamon. Serve with non-fat milk and a sprinkle of wheat germ.

CLOWN CREAM OF WHEAT—make your favorite farina/cream of wheat cereal with half the salt and an added ¼ cup of bran per serving. Serve with non-fat milk. With raisins make a clown face and watch your child smile!

LIGHT FRENCH TOAST—make french toast with whole grain bread and a batter of eggs—with every second yolk tossed out—milk and a drop of vanilla. Cook in a non-stick pan and serve with a sprinkling of powdered sugar, a dollop of flavored yogurt or a tablespoon of syrup.

DOLLAR-SIZED PANCAKES—use your favorite pancake mix, cutting the oil in half and being sure to use Pam or a non-stick pan. Shape the pancakes into dollars or even your child's initials. Serve topped with flavored, non-fat yogurt.

BLUEBERRY MUFFINS—add ¾ cup of bran to a 13-ounce package of blueberry muffin mix. Use two egg whites for each egg the mix requires. Serve with non-fat milk and sliced bananas.

LUNCH

Lunch for most families means weekday brown bags. Most kids bring to school sack lunches from home. Packing a lunch from home gives you a chance to make up a healthy lunch for your child.

Does you child buy lunch at school? If so, perhaps you should go back to brown bags. Often food sold in schools or available through school lunch programs are high in fat, sugar, sodium and calories. Your own homemade fare is typically a far better choice.

It's atrocious what they feed them in school lunches—salami sandwiches, chocolate pudding, sugar cookies and syrupy canned fruit. The sticky, sugary stuff they can buy at school is even worse. If I were a dentist, I'd shoot those vending machines!

What about milk at school? Most children can purchase milk at school on a quarterly or annual basis. Milk is good food, particularly if it is non fat. It's a real joy not to have to face the soured milk thermos at the end of the day, so if your child can get non fat milk, or even low fat milk at school, it's probably worth signing up for. On the other hand, if the milk is regular, whole milk, you're better off going back to the thermos.

Below are standard lunches for kids. These lunches are not depriving. They are just healthful. Health-aware parents of skinny kids and in-between kids also keep fat and sugar to a minimum in bag lunches.

How full should the bag be? Some kids haul around grocery bags full of lunch. How much should you pack? The amount of food in that sack depends upon such things as your child's size, activity levels and weight goals. A child who is smaller needs less food than a larger child or an adult. The lunch that fuels a child to run up and down a soccer field all afternoon is bigger than the lunch of a child who turns on the TV or lolls around the soccer field. The child who is losing weight needs less than the child who is maintaining weight. If your child is not losing at least a half pound a week — on the average — he or she is still eating too much for his energy expenditure. Part of that excess may be in the brown bag.

I finally realized that Sarah really didn't need the entire sandwich, two pieces of fruit, a box of raisins and the peanut butter filled celery stalk. She quickly got used to half that much. I was astounded.

STANDARD BROWN BAGS

a half or a whole sandwich made with whole grain bread and low-fat filling

one or two pieces of fruit

a baggie full of veggies

non-fat milk

Come up with some healthy treats for your brown bagger. So you have come to terms with the granola bars, chocolate chip cookies and potato chips. They have not seen the inside of your child's brown bag for weeks. Terrific! But you want to inject a little fun into the meal. Check out the ideas below for healthy treats.

TREATS FOR BROWN BAGGERS

ADD-A-THERMOS — For a change include anything you can thermos: broth, lentil soup, chicken noodle soup, a brown cow (non-fat milk with a touch of diet root beer), or hot chocolate (made with sugar-free cocoa mix)

SURPRISE BAGGIE — mix together and place in a baggie a couple of your child's favorite low sugar cereals, raisins, dry-roasted peanuts, cut up dried fruits, broken up bread sticks and other healthy dry foods you happen to have on hand. The surprise can be that there are always different things in it.

The kids clamor for surprise cups. I give them Cheerios and they're pleased. I add corn flakes, broken up crackers and raisins and put it in a paper cup and they're ecstatic!

LEAPIN' LEFTOVERS — Dinner may be marginal, but when it's served in a bag lunch the next day it is fit for a prince — or princess. Wrap up that vegetable lasagne, that turkey hotdog or that broccoli and rice casserole. Better yet, put it between two pieces of whole wheat bread. If you've never indulged your child with lasagne on whole wheat, you are in for some great reviews.

MOIST, LOW-FAT SANDWICHES — Granted, turkey on bread — dry — balls up in your mouth. Food shouldn't be depriving, right? The solution? Take your pick: mustard, catsup, lettuce, tomato, 1 teaspoon of light mayonnaise or ½ teaspoon of regular mayonnaise. If you use tomatoes, put them within layers of the meat so that they won't make the bread soggy.

LIGHT SALAD SANDWICHES — Water-packed tuna is light, right? But add half a cup of mayonnaise to it and it ends up heavy. Make tuna sandwiches with water pack tuna and moisten it with a mixture of half light mayonnaise and half

5

non-fat plain yogurt or low-fat cottage cheese. As for egg salad, use the same ingredients to moisten it and toss out every second egg yolk. Season both with anything non-fat from mustard to a teaspoon of pickle relish.

Pack the lunch with a liberal supply of non-edible treats—The chocolate cookie at the bottom of the sack meant Mommy remembered you. Skip the cookie, granola bars, fruit roll-ups, chips and the like but go whole hog on treats. Write a riddle on your child's napkin. Add a flexible straw. Decorate their bag with their full name or a drawing of the cat or of something they're studying in school. Pick a flower and stick it in. So what if it's wilted by lunch time. The message of care is still there.

At 11, Kristen doesn't want my hearts and flowers all over her bag any more so I give those little "care" messages by putting in a sticker or writing a riddle on her napkin.

SNACKS

Eating regular meals precludes constant snacking or heavy snacks. Kids who are engaged and active don't have time to think much about snacking. Some children—particularly those who are very physically active or are younger benefit from a light, small morning or afternoon snack.

In general, the idea is to make the snack not terribly appealing. It is designed to tide over a big appetite until the meal rather than to stimulate the appetite. If children are hungry they'll thoroughly enjoy the standard snacks. When you want variety, particularly after your child is well on his or her way with weight loss, vary the snacks, if you wish.

STANDARD SNACKS

carrot, celery or other raw vegetables

one piece of plain, whole grain bread

one piece of fruit

LIGHT SNACKS THAT PLEASE

sliced apple sprinkled with cinnamon
plain popcorn
warmed tortilla dusted with Parmesan
dry unsweetened cereal
crisp lettuce wedge
surprise cup (paper cup with mixture
    of cereals, dried fruit, pretzels, etc.)
unsalted pretzels
matzo crackers
rice crackers
plain whole wheat bread
plain yogurt topped with cereal or fruit
veggie sticks and yogurt dip
two kinds of fresh fruit, cut up
dried apples, apricots, peaches
fruit shake (fruit juice and banana)
frozen unsweetened juice bars
frozen banana (rolled in wheat germ)
banana milkshake (banana, milk, ice)
fruit soda (½ juice, ½ soda water)
red soup (½ tomato juice, ½ broth)

PURPLE SHAKE—Blend until smooth: 1 cup unsweetened grape juice, 1 cup plain non-fat yogurt, a handful of ice cubes. Pour into glasses. Makes two servings.

PEANUT BUTTER DIP—Blend until smooth: ¼ cup peanut butter, ¼ cup orange juice, ½ cup plain non-fat yogurt. Serve with cut up fruit or raw vegetables. Great with celery.

FRUIT FIZZ—Mix in small cups chopped oranges, sliced bananas, and sliced strawberries (optional). Top with a few raisins and fill the cups with sugar-free strawberry soda.

BANANA BOATS—Peel each banana and cut it in half the long way. Spread scantily with 1 tablespoon peanut butter. Sprinkle with wheat germ. Makes 2 servings.

ANTS ON A LOG—Wash and trim a stalk of celery. Spread the stalk scantily with 1 tablespoon of low-fat cream cheese. Dot with raisins.

TORTILLA CHIPS—Cut corn tortilla into chip-shaped wedges. Place on a greased baking sheet and bake at 300 for 8 or more minutes. Serve with salsa.

DINNER

Dinner is a ritual. It is also a time when we are hungry and tired. The dinner ritual is being updated. In some families this means abandoning the meal altogether, which usually means more overeating, not less. Other families are placing more emphasis on the evening meal. We have so little time together, it's important to make the most of it. Dinner is a time to relax but also a time to sit together showing physical recognition of your family closeness.

STANDARD LIGHT SUPPERS

half a plate of light foods, with no more than a teaspoon of fat or a small amount of heavier foods

half a plate of vegetables with no more than one teaspoon of fat per serving.

a glass of non-fat milk

Some families relax by cooking together. Sharing mealtime chores gets everyone into the kitchen and broadens the meal's spirt of closeness. It also cuts down on kitchen drudgery. Other families prefer to quickly fix-it-and-eat-it and then go about their evening.

DINNER IN A MINUTE

This particular night you have better things to do than cook. Here are some ideas for healthy eating that are quick, easy and good!

BAKED POTATO — Microwaved big baked potatoes, potato removed, mixed with cottage cheese, restuffed and broiled, green salad, whole wheat crackers.

TACO SALAD — start with a big mixed green salad on each plate, add a dollop of heated refried beans and/or canned pinto beans, topped with a little low-fat sour cream and salsa.

TUNA AND RICE — canned tuna, added to a rice mix, half the seasoning tossed out and no fat added, a double serving of broccoli seasoned with lemon, non-fat milk.

BROILED FISH — broiled fish served with tartar sauce made from mayonnaise, non-fat yogurt and pickle relish, frozen veggies, rice mix with half of the seasoning mix tossed out.

SOUP AND SANDWICH — low salt chicken noodle soup, half of a melted cheese sandwich on whole wheat bread (1 ounce of cheese per serving) and sliced tomatoes.

SOUP AND MUFFINS — cream of tomato soup made with water, plain corn muffins, non-fat milk, cut up orange and banana.

HAMBURGERS — made with ground round — five patties to a pound — on buns or whole wheat bread topped with lettuce, tomato, catsup, mustard, but no fat (mayonnaise, butter, margarine, cheese).

INSTANT PIZZA — split and toasted whole wheat English muffins, each topped with bottled pizza sauce, 2 tablespoons of lowfat cottage cheese and a tablespoon of Parmesan cheese and broiled for 5 minutes until cheese turns golden.

MACARONI AND CHEESE — from a box, topped with wheat germ, big mixed fruit salad, non-fat milk.

SPAGHETTI — made with canned spaghetti sauce with added zucchini and sliced mushrooms, topped with a little Parmesan cheese, wedge of iceberg lettuce, non-fat milk.

DINNERS WITH LEFTOVERS

Meals you can cook on Sunday that last through supper on Tuesday or sandwiches on Wednesday make for a more relaxed start to the week.

TERIYAKI TURKEY AND VEGGIES — turkey breast, baked or barbecued, basted with bottled teriyaki sauce and served with a large bowl of crunchy, raw vegetables and dip.

BEEF AND MACARONI SALAD — lean roast beef or London broil sliced thin and served with macaroni salad made with minced celery, grated carrots, macaroni and low-fat ranch dressing.

RICE BOWL — Start with 6 cups of sliced vegetables — onions, carrots, celery, zucchini and water chestnuts are good. Add 3 cups rice, 6 cups water, 6 bullion cubes and cook until water is absorbed. Beat and stir in 6 eggs whites and 3 yolks. Cook until set. Serve in small bowls with soy sauce. Try using chop sticks.

LEAN BEEF STEW—beef stew made with lean beef and double portions of carrots, mushrooms, celery and potatoes.

ALL-SEASON BARBECUE CHICKEN—broiled, skinned chicken pieces brushed with barbecue sauce and served with fresh or frozen corn.

HEARTY CHICKEN SOUP—chicken soup from chicken broth, light chicken meat, a can of beans, carrots, celery, onion and alphabet noodles. See if your child can spell his or her favorite words!

TURKEY LOAF—a meatloaf made from ground turkey, seasoned bread crumbs, egg whites, finely chopped onion and celery and topped with catsup. Great for sandwiches during the week.

VEGETABLE TRICKS

Not all kids hate vegetables. Nudge your child into enjoying them. Try these ideas for making vegetables easy and delicious.

GO FOR VARIETY—Let your child choose a brand new vegetable at the store each week. Try baked banana squash dusted with cinnamon, match sticks of jicama, eggplant topped with bottled spaghetti sauce. Fuel your child's enthusiasm by letting them explore the produce section and pick the vegetable of the week.

SALAD-FOR-A-WEEK—Most kids like crunchy salads. Make it easy on yourself. As you unpack your groceries wash the leaves from two or more heads of lettuce (mix different kinds!) Stack leaves on two or three paper towels and bundle them all up in a plastic bag. At salad time just take out some of the leaves and make an instant salad.

DIP FOR RAW VEGGIES—Kids stop turning up their noses to carrots sticks and cauliflowerettes when you pass the dip. Try adding dill weed, garlic and onion powder to a base of ½ sour cream, ½ low-fat yogurt. Still turned up noses? Try another dip mix at your store with the sour cream/yogurt base.

MARINATED VEGGIES—Lightly steam or microwave Brussels sprouts, tiny new potatoes, broccoli, carrots or other vegetables. Spoon on a bit of low-oil dressing and chill. Great for snacks, salads and lunch boxes.

LIGHT CARROT AND RAISIN SALAD—Grate several carrots, add a few tablespoons of crushed pineapple, half a handful of raisins, a pinch of cinnamon and moisten with plain yogurt. Keeps for four or more days!

SMOOTH AND CREAMY VEGGIE SOUP—Start with canned chicken broth. Heat in a large sauce pan. Add several cups of a vegetable of your choice—broccoli, zucchini, pumpkin, spinach are favorites—and simmer until soft. Puree in a processor or blender. Return to the heat and add a can of non-fat evaporated milk.

DESSERTS

Ah yes, desserts. Somehow we've left them for last. Desserts are fun. They are one of the pleasures of life. It's a myth that dessert eaters can't lose weight. Serve less food at dinner so there's more room for dessert.

Of course, the problem is that kids can get very dessert-focused. The evening revolves around what's for dessert. Not a good thing, particularly for a child with a weight problem. There are many possible strategies, and what works for a given family is highly individual. Here's a sampling of strategies that have worked for other families.

5

RED PLAN—No desserts. That's right. None. On a regular basis we don't eat them. We eat food, not sweets—holidays and birthdays excepted.

YELLOW PLAN—Fruit for dessert during the week. Small portions of desserts on weekends and on special occasions.

GREEN PLAN—Small desserts every night. Sweets are part of life and we can eat less or lighter the rest of the day and exercise more to balance things out.

When weight loss isn't happening, it's probably best to stick with the RED PLAN—no desserts. If you're on the right track with eating and physical activity, if the scale is showing slow but steady results, the YELLOW or GREEN plans may work out well.

When you do serve non-fruit desserts, dish up small portions. If you choose low-fat, low-sugar desserts, serve moderate portions. The choice is between fat-sugar goo in very small amounts or reasonably light sweets in moderate amounts. As you read this list you might wince a time or two. Yes, they are less than perfectly nutritious foods. But that's okay. Kept as an occasional choice, kids survive even twinkies.

FRUIT COBBLER—Mix together ½ teaspoon cinnamon, 1 tablespoon cornstarch and 3 tablespoons sugar. Stir into 4 cups of thinly sliced fruit. Place in the bottom of an oiled 8″ baking dish. In a separate bowl stir 1 cup baking mix, such as Bisquick, ⅓ cup milk, and 1 tablespoon sugar. Pour over apples. Bake for 50 minutes at 325.

CHOCOLATE PUDDING SANDWICHES—Make pudding from a chocolate sugar-free pudding and pie filling mix. Chill well. To make each sandwich, drop 2 tablespoons of pudding onto a graham cracker. Top with another graham cracker. Wrap and freeze.

APPLE CRISP—Spread 4 cups of sliced baking apples in an 8″ baking pan. Combine ¾ cups rolled oats, ⅓ cup flour, 1½ teaspoons cinnamon and sprinkle over the apples. Next sprinkle on ¼ cup water and dot on 2 tablespoons butter or margarine. Bake at 350 for 30 minutes. Serve topped with vanilla, non-fat yogurt.

DESSERTS ON THE LIGHT SIDE

an unfrosted cupcake from a mix that does not require oil

a slice of angel food cake topped with strawberry non-fat yogurt

unsweetened applesauce topped with cinnamon

a handful of plain animal crackers

a small cone or dish of low-fat ice cream, ice milk, or non-fat frozen yogurt

a baked apple topped with cinnamon and a tablespoon of whipped cream

sugar free pudding made with non-fat or 1% milk

sugar free strawberry jello made with sliced fruit—try bananas in raspberry jello or peaches, fresh or canned in juice or water

a bowl of sliced bananas topped with orange juice

JELLO CUBES—In a bowl mix two envelopes unflavored gelatin, two envelopes sugar free jello and 2½ cups boiling water. Stir until dissolved.

Pour into 8″ square pan and chill until firm. Cut into 1″ cubes.

STRAWBERRY ROLL-UPS — Make 3″ pancakes with your favorite pancake mix, minimizing the recipe's fat content (non-fat milk, half the oil, etc.) Spoon on each pancake a tablespoon of strawberry non-fat yogurt. Roll up and secure with a fancy toothpick. If available, top with sliced fresh strawberries (optional).

YOUR OWN FAVORITES

You probably have 10 to 20 recipes you couldn't do without. You know, Aunt May's rice casserole and that special chicken dish. There's no need to do without them! Keep each and every one. If they are truly straight fat or sugar you may want to have them less often. In most cases, you can lighten them up without unduly compromising the taste. As you change these beloved recipes, keep these ideas in mind:

- use no fat to cook with

- double the FREE FOOD ingredients

- keep the LIGHT FOOD ingredients the same

- decrease the HEAVY FOOD ingredients

- cut out the JUNK FOOD ingredients

- add no fat at the table

With some fresh ideas in hand, enjoy some quick and healthy eating. Like the other changes you've made, you may encounter some ruffled feathers at first, but in time this healthier way of eating will seem second nature.

5

FAVORITE RECIPES — LIGHTER!

Cheddar Rice Chicken Casserole

Original Recipe	Lighter Recipe
1 whole chicken, cut up	4 chicken breasts, skinned, cut up
1 cup rice	1 cup rice
1 can chicken broth	1 can chicken broth
1 can water	1 can water
1 onion, chopped	1 onion, chopped
1 T. parsley	2 carrots, sliced
1 t. dill	1 cup celery, chopped
1 cup shredded cheddar cheese	1 T. parsley
	1 t. dill
	¼ cup shredded cheddar cheese

SELF-ASSESSMENT

10. STOCKING UP ON FOOD IDEAS

Choose one idea you will use for:

breakfast:

_____

_____

lunch:

_____

_____

dinner:

_____

_____

snacks:

_____

_____

5

Write down the ingredients in one of your favorite recipes:

_____

_____

_____

_____

_____

_____

How will you change the recipe to make it lighter?

_____

_____

_____

_____

_____

_____

What is your dessert policy?   RED   YELLOW   GREEN

Now that you have brushed up on your limit-setting skills, let's turn to the warmer half of parenting: nurturance. If nurturing is not up to snuff, the child will be feel bad. To block out the bad feelings, the child may over-eat or hook into television and gain more weight.

What is nurturing? It's what happens to the children when we set aside our own drives and just focus on them, on their feelings, their needs and their requests. It gives them the warmth of pure sunlight not dimmed by our own egos. Our mirroring of our child's thoughts and feelings solidifies a sense of self in them that scares away the emptiness which otherwise beckons to food. When we nurture well, we both delight in their separateness and steep in the sanctity of the parent-child bond.

It is very difficult to nurture a child. We may be loving and accepting toward friends and work mates who are more distant from us. But close relationships bare our own inner workings. If we don't love and accept ourselves, we can't truly accept our child. If we don't feel a sense of our own separateness, our "boundaries", we cannot respect the child's separateness. It becomes difficult to love her for just being her, to delight in her exploring her own uniqueness and expressing her real self rather than donning the mask that buys her social acceptance.

Problems with nurturing travel in families. It is catching. Our parents may not have had a secure inner core, a loving sense of self. Perhaps our parents couldn't balance being separate and being close, but had to see-saw back and forth or get stuck in one or the

Not *always* lovable...

other. They didn't talk about feelings, much less the demons inside, the hates, angers and fears. We never learned different. Our kids pick it up from us. Somewhere along the line, someone needs to change the cycle.

If you are in this cycle, you may want to use SHAPEDOWN as an opportunity to hop off, that is, to get some additional help to cut the flow of these common family patterns to the next generation. SHAPEDOWN is not designed to give you more than a nudge toward working on these generation-to-generation patterns, but your SHAPE-DOWN instructor has resources on hand to refer to you for support.

Central to all of these issues is feelings. In trying to raise kids, we need to be finely tuned in to our feelings. Why? Because close relationships are irritating. Our child does things that bother us. If we are aware of these small feelings of irritation and are committed to telling our child the absolute and complete truth, we usually resolve them. But, if we have never learned the skill of tuning into our feelings or of expressing them to others early, before they become explosive, they fester into resentment toward our child. Left untended, the resentment often turns into rejection, which our kids can feel no matter how clever we are in trying to hide it.

Suppressing or stuffing our feelings can affect our child in another way through the "piston effect". Family members are emotionally connected; they work like pistons in an engine. When one piston goes down, another comes up. When we suppress our sadness or "keep it to ourselves", another family member experiences it. What we suppress, they express. Often it's the obese child that feels these suppressed feelings, as the obese child is usually very sensitive to the emotions of other family members. The anger we push down, our child feels and it confuses him or her. The child doesn't know

where the anger is coming from or what to do with it and turns to food or television to block it out.

That's right, our repressed feelings can trigger the eating and fuel the fat of the child. If this is the case, helping a child get over a weight problem requires us to express our feelings. The source of those feelings, like marital tension or a hopelessly miserable job - may need some attention, too.

I used to hide out from my daughter, not tell her what was really on my mind. I felt a little afraid, that if I let her know the real me, she wouldn't like me. I noticed that, on some level, she could feel my fears, the fears I didn't talk with her about. So we both ended up feeling a little afraid and it distanced us. It was a relief to talk with her straight out about me, my feelings, to be absolutely and completely honest with her. She started doing the same. It opened up in me all these blocked feelings of love for her.

For a long time Jack and I pretended to be happily married in front of the kids, but inside we were furious with each other. We protected the kids by not mentioning it directly or sharing our sadness about it. They ended up feeling our fury and grief and making our lives pretty miserable. The younger one with tantrums; the older one with sneaking food. It was a hard to learn to tell kids the truth about what is going on.

I used to avoid eating dinner. I'd deny my own right to eat. My not eating just made Patricia's appetite bigger. So I started eating three decent meals instead of dieting. Patricia seemed to relax and eat less. She didn't have to eat for me and for herself any more.

Below is a recipe for nurturing kids well. All the ingredients may not be in our cupboards right now, but as we stock up on them, our nurturing gets better and better.

RECIPE FOR NURTURING KIDS

Parents who:

love and accept themselves.

have a strong sense of who they are.

are in touch with their feelings.

openly express their feelings.

ask for what they need.

speak directly to people rather than use go-betweens.

discriminate between their problems those of others.

tell the absolute and complete truth in their close relationships.

accept the ways their child is different from them.

feel a loving bond with their child.

encourage their child to express his or her feelings.

teach their child to ask for what he or she needs.

redirect their child when he or she uses go-betweens.

help their child discriminate between his or her problems and those of others.

accept their child, limitations and all.

give their child direct messages that he or she is accepted and valued.

Have you slammed down this book yet? Can you imagine being able to do all those things well all of the time? I can't. The recipe confirms that parenting is the most difficult thing most of us ever do. And all we can do is the best we can do.

Safety in Boundaries

Marsha picks up on Dad's work troubles. She frets about them. Dad approaches her and says, "I have work problems but they are mine. Only I can do something about them. They are not your fault and there is nothing you can do about them. This job is the best option for me now. Sometimes I may be grumpy, but that is life. I will handle it."

Tell your child what is and is not her problem. Does she have the authority to do anything about the problem? If not, she needs clear messages not to take responsibility - to let go of it.

Keeping it Direct

"If you have a problem with someone, talk to that someone." Good advice from Grandpa. Sounds like common sense, but it really gets its power when you witness what **not** following it can do: create triangles. Triangles are trouble.

Mary is mad at her dad for embarrassing her in front of a friend. Mary goes to Mom and complains. Mom could think, "Is this my problem?" and redirect Mary to talk directly with her dad, encouraging Mary's self-sufficiency and strengthening the father-daughter relationship. Instead, she creates a triangle: "O.K., I'll talk to him." An opportunity for intimacy between father and daughter is lost and Mary learns that she is not capable of solving her own problems.

5

The rest of this chapter is on the last two "ingredients" in nurturing: the special issues in accepting the obese child and some practical ways to give a child direct messages of acceptance.

STEP ONE. Accept him or her, limitations and all. In general, by the time your child reaches school age, what you see is what you get. You can expect your child to change somewhat—but not radically. Although, the more we change, the more our kids change. The first step in brushing up on nurturing skills is to come face-to-face with the ways in which your child does and does not measure up to your expectations.

Do I accept myself for who I am—imperfections and all? If I don't, my child won't accept herself and I won't accept my child either.

Start with positives. In which ways does your child measure up? You take pride in your child's accomplishments and good points. Some of these are more important to you than others. What are some of the good things about your child that set off good, warm feelings within you?

Confront negatives. In which ways does your child disappoint you? Think of the ways in which this child disappoints you, the characteristics that burn behind your eyes and grate on your nerves. List them all.

Let go of the negatives that aren't important. Yes, you're disappointed that she isn't more feminine and that he likes chess rather than football. You have a right to be disappointed. But that disappointment can add a layer to the bar-rier between you and your child. So if it isn't important, let it go. Work on burying it, mourning it and forgetting it.

It's so hard to give the affection I never got.

Determine which of the important negatives are open to change. Consider making changes. Which of the important negatives could possibly change? Now or later? Consider mapping out plans to help your child change them.

Work on accepting the important negatives that are unlikely to change. This means a loss. Accepting the loss doesn't happen overnight, if at all. It may help to consider whether it is better for you to hold on to those expectations and resent your child for not measuring up. What are the consequences to you and to your child of not coming to terms with your expectations? Is it better for you to give some thought to accepting that kid "as is?" Very difficult. Perhaps it is not the best path for you—or at all possible—but at least consider it.

Marie is a delightful child. She is a sweetheart through and through. It's just her weight that paralyzes me. She reminds me of my mother-in-law. She has my mother-in-law's body build. I feel like my own child has been invaded by this woman I can't bear. I don't know that I can ever accept how she looks.

Cary is one of these kids that everybody warms up to. She has a certain charm, particularly with adults. But her weight embarrasses me. I look at her and say to myself, "You are a bad mother." Those are such devastating feelings that some of it rubs off on my attitude toward her. I almost blame her for making me feel so bad. We're doing this weight group as a way of changing her weight and my feelings toward her.

If it doesn't work and the weight doesn't come off, then I'll have to sort through my feelings again.

Accepting your overweight child involves coming to terms with your own attitudes toward fat. In Western culture we have learned to equate fatness with being overindulgent, undisciplined, self-destructive and even immoral — that the laws of moderation and control have been violated. We are taught that there is something intrinsically wrong with fat people and that excessive body fat is ugly or repulsive. We are not taught the truth — that obesity is not a sickness, weakness or fault, but a condition that increases one's risk of certain chronic diseases — like diabetes and hypertension.

Keep in mind that attitudes toward weight are culture-bound. In some cultures fatness is revered. Fat tissue is viewed as fluffy, soft, nurturing, safe and curvaceous. Obese women are viewed as healthy and more womanly. Obese men are not "fat," they are big. They are more powerful because of their extra weight.

Can one hate the fat and still love the fat child?

Discrimination on account of weight is much like racism or sexism. It's based on fiction, not fact. Obese children have habits that are similar to normal weight kids' habits. Usually small differences in genetics, diet and exercise contribute to a child's weight.

Because societal prejudices are so pervasive it's likely that you have been the victim of discrimination, simply because your child is overfat. Reversing the trend, destigmatizing weight and separating an individual's value from the reading on the scale, start at home. Eliminating prejudicial attitudes helps you and it is very critical to your child's success with weight.

So put weight in its place. Weight is only one part of appearance and appearance is only one characteristic of an individual. Rather than buying into weightist attitudes, believe that your child's overfatness is not a sign of failure. See instead your child's cherubic smile, engaging manner, wit and kindness.

Obesity is a condition that elevates one's risk of getting other illnesses. You may not be sick if you're fat, but you are at increased risk.

Recognize that your child is okay regardless of weight and that you're an okay parent even though your child is overweight. Your child may be making progress with weight now and may soon become normal weight. On the other hand, his or her weight may never really stay at a normal level. Your child may be overweight for his or her entire life. That is a very real possibility.

So be realistic about the consequences of excessive weight. What does being overfat for a lifetime mean? Well, it means increased risk of certain diseases later and perhaps some social discrimination. From a purely objective standpoint, **that is all it means.**

Overweight may not be a catastrophe. However, it may be a loss for you, a loss of the dreams you had for your child. It may help to recognize that most parents have to give up dreams of perfection for their children. Most kids have at least one problem ranging from asthma to learning disabilities. Although your loss should not be minimized, it is often helpful to put it into the context of the losses experienced by other parents. In addition, you may want to re-examine the "perfect parents make perfect children" myth. If your kids aren't perfect it doesn't mean that you, your marriage and your family are not okay.

5

5

By recognizing that your child can be successful and worthy regardless of weight, and by freeing yourself from the fear that unless your child loses weight you are not a good parent, your attitudes change. You can be more accepting of your child without feeling that you must withhold approval to motivate him or her to lose weight. You can focus on the myriad of wonderful qualities your child possesses rather than overemphasizing weight.

I have one great kid. I don't know how I got so hung up on her weight.

STEP TWO. Give you child direct messages that you accept and value him or her. It's too important to be left to the indirect. *Of course I love her. I'm sure she knows.* But does she? Can you afford to chance it?

Many parents feel a great depth of love for their children, but they don't translate those life-giving feelings into a form that helps the child feel loved. You may feel lovingly toward your child, but your child may still not feel loved and accepted. For many parents, this is hard to fathom. Their emotional experience is so strong, that they feel that it must run over into their child's awareness. Sometimes yes. Sometimes no.

By giving your child direct messages of your love and appreciation for him or her, you set the nurturing cycle in motion. Your child begins to feel better about himself or herself and starts nurturing himself or herself and you in return. You feel better about your parenting and give your child more direct messages of your love.

TALKING

1. Tell your child that you value, appreciate and love him or her. Kids are little *warmth*

130

sponges. They hungrily soak up words that prompt them to conclude that they are loved and valued. This need for direct positive messages of love and acceptance is even more critical when your child has weight problems. The stigma attached to obesity means that your child fears or concludes that he or she is second rate in your eyes. The sense of loss and uncertainty that accompanies such a fear typically fuels the appetite.

So rule out the possibility that your child questions your acceptance of him or her. In your own way, tell you child this important idea:

I don't always like how you act, but I always love you.

Direct messages that you love and appreciate your child may feel uncomfortable to you. But they are music to your child's ears. With all the put-downs of the day, these direct messages soothe and reassure. The anxiety abates.

2. Praise your child often and effectively. Your lovely little boy has just cleaned out the cookie jar. You come home from work and he says he's not hungry for dinner. The baker's dozen chocolate chip cookies were enough. He looks very full and rather upset. What do you say?

——THE NURTURING CYCLE——

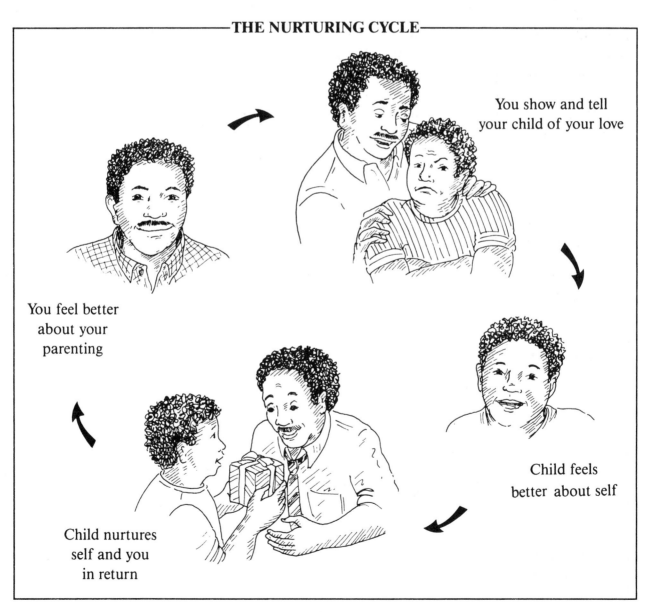

You show and tell your child of your love

Child feels better about self

Child nurtures self and you in return

You feel better about your parenting

5

If you keep eating cookies you'll never lose weight.

or

You stopped after the cookies. You could have easily gone on to eat the pizza or the crumb cake. But you stopped."

Which is more helpful? The second response. Why? Because it is positive. Positive reinforcement is what helps change behavior. Say what the youngster did right, not what he or she did wrong.

Make positive statements that describe but don't label. When you tell your child that she has a beautiful face or is a great artist, how does she respond? By denying it, by blushing. Your child is embarrassed and uncomfortable. Why? Because you are judging her; you are labeling her. And that is usually uncomfortable. If you say, "You always do perfectly on your math scores," you are also burdening him or her with an obligation to live up to, thus creating needless anxiety. "You did really well on your math test" avoids this pitfall.

Praising a child's **personality** or **characteristics** is not only anxiety-provoking but also does little to boost self-esteem. The child usually discounts the praise and often you for your poor judgment in making it.

Sometimes I feel like a cheer leader — or a whole squad of them embodied in one person. But I keep praising and congratulating Brian because he seems so much more confident and happy since I made the "squad."

Praise that describes **efforts** and **accomplishments** can be most helpful in boosting self-esteem. In this kind of praise parents describe what they see and how they feel. For instance, when Brian finishes weeding the vegetable garden: *"That garden looks like it is well taken care of. You made it go from a mass of weeds to something to be proud of. I feel good just looking at it."*

How does your description of his efforts and accomplishments improve Brian's feelings of

HELPFUL PRAISE	UNHELPFUL PRAISE
This salad you made is so crisp and tasty. I really enjoyed every bite of it.	You are a wonderful salad maker. You always make really crisp and tasty salads.
The note you sent me made me so happy.	You are always so thoughtful.
When you played that piano music I felt so relaxed.	You are a great piano player.
Thank you for picking up the cleaning for me. It made my afternoon easier.	You picked up the laundry! You are so helpful and generous.
I liked reading your poem, especially the part about sunset.	You are such a good poet, the best in the whole family.

5

worth? He draws his own conclusions from the statements about his worth. He infers from them that he is a positive and worthy individual. Brian actually does this praising. In other words, **you precipitate his praising himself.**

3. Reassure your child that he or she will be okay despite discomfort. Given that much of life is uncomfortable, children benefit from learning to reassure themselves. An internal dialog that is soothing and supportive lessens their anxiety and boosts their ability to cope with little and big difficulties.

This is even more important with obese kids because many are hypersensitive. Because of biologic factors or perhaps, indulgence, these children are extremely particular. Some only eat specific foods prepared in certain ways. Others aren't willing to experience the discomfort that most worthwhile pursuits require. Our job as parents is to help our kids learn to cope with a certain amount of discomfort.

Kids don't know how to label discomfort. When we reassure them that it's okay, we teach them to cope with it.

Children adopt this dialog from your direct statements. They internalize your comments and learn to interpret situations positively. Through your dialog with your children they learn to reassure themselves.

To reassure your child:

1. Acknowledge the difficulty of the situation or their feelings about it.

2. State that you believe it will be okay, that they can handle it.

133

I know you like potato salad better than green salad. Green salad doesn't taste as good as potato salad to me either. It is less fun to eat foods that aren't your favorites. But that's okay. It's something I do too. We will survive it.

You'd rather sit on the couch watching television than ride around the block on your bike. I know riding your bike is not what you want to do right now. Sometimes we have to do things we don't like. That's life. I know you can do it!

I know you really like potato chips in your lunch. I like potato chips, too. I know that it's hard for you to watch other kids eating chips when you don't have any. It is difficult. But there are worse things. I'm sure, eventually, you'll get used to having carrot sticks instead of chips.

Reassure your child often. Keep on acknowledging your child's discomfort and suggesting that a certain amount of unpleasantness is normal. Reassure him again and again. You will soon see him reassuring himself and you!

4. Give your child messages that he is more important than his weight. Some kids conclude from their parent's attention to their weight that their weight is the most important thing about them. They can conclude that if they don't get rid of the fat, you'll get rid of them, emotionally, if not physically. You need to reassure your child directly and indirectly that this is not the case. We'll talk more about this reassurance in Chapter 16. Taming the Monsters: Cravings and Secretive Eating. But for now, consider telling your child these things:

You are more important to me than your weight.

Other than FAMILY TIME, we won't talk about weight or diet. We have other important things to talk about, too.

This way you show and tell your child that weight has it's place, but that your greatest concern is your child's overall well-being. Although you need to make it clear that you won't give up and that you will keep working with your child to lose weight, your child needs to know that weight isn't everything.

So, other than FAMILY TIME, don't talk about food or weight. If the currency of family communications is "How did the diet go?" you accomplish several negative things. You reinforce the idea that weight is of paramount importance. You also give the message that weight is the way kids get attention in your family. These messages only cause trouble.

So cut the weight talk. When that inevitable question, "Oh, please can I have a cookie?" comes up, redirect your child, "You know what your snack choices are. After your snack let's go for a walk." If you child persists, use extinction. Pretend you do not hear the question. Just don't respond. Don't say a thing. It works. When you don't respond to the attention-getting diet chatter, they will stop it.

LISTENING

A child needs to feel listened to in order to feel valued and respected. When you give evidence that you are really listening to them, kids open up and let you in on their feelings, needs and opinions. You say good-by to the tight lipped "nothing" when you ask about their day. You put an end to the stoney silence at the dinner table that feels restrained rather than relaxed. When you don't listen they stop telling you how they feel and what is troubling them. They often interpret our not listening as not caring. Then the dialog stops.

Listen actively to your child. Active listening means listening to what your child says and saying back what you think he or she means. You

┌─────── **PARENT RESPONSE AFTER LISTENING TO THEIR CHILD:** ───────┐

LESS HELPFUL	MORE HELPFUL
If you would set the alarm you wouldn't have to complain about being late.	It sounds like you feel angry that you didn't set your alarm.
Don't blame your teacher for giving you that assignment. It's your responsibility to do your work.	You do have a lot of homework to finish by Friday.
You shouldn't be upset about the play. If you forget your lines no one will notice.	It is hard to remember all of those lines. You're really nervous about how it will go.
I'm tired of listening to you complain about being bored.	You're bored and feel like there is nothing to do.

└───┘

5

All feelings are acceptable. All behaviors are not.

take a jumble of thoughts and put them in order. It is clear evidence that you gave your child full attention. And it helps your child sort our his or her thoughts and feelings.

It sounds like you're worried about your homework.

You feel hurt that Kathy isn't playing with you this week.

TOUCHING

Most kids thrive on a goodly amount of parents' hugs, kisses, back rubs, holding hands, lapsitting and the like. Most of us like to touch and to be touched. Touching is one confirmation that the "I love you" has substance. It gives kids strong messages that they are worthy and good in mind, spirit and body.

Touching is often difficult for parents who were brought up with the "don't touch" dogma—

the keep-a-safe-distance rule. Some parents react to this early training by touching their kids a lot. Others continue to feel uncomfortable with physical closeness. If touching is difficult for you, think about getting some counseling on your own.

I don't know what I'd do if I couldn't hug and kiss Kathy. She's cuddly and loves to snuggle. So do I.

Charles always wants to poke, jab, embrace or otherwise touch me. I usually recoil. I just don't like it. I've told him that it's not him, it's that I hate to be touched. But I can tell he doesn't believe me. He thinks it's him.

I'm a real touching person. When I see someone I like, I want to hug 'em. I like to kiss and stroke the kids. Our first two kids felt the same way, but Alissa is different. She makes it clear that I'm invading her space. It has always perplexed—and hurt—me. I finally sat her down and told her how I felt. She reacted warmly, and gave me a tentative hug. I practically fell over.

135

Touching is difficult for kids when there is so much of it that it feels intrusive or when it comes at times when they don't want it. It also doesn't work when the physical expression doesn't match the parent's feelings or words. When you feel affectionate toward your child, touching is an appropriate extension of that feeling. When you feel angry, it is not.

DOING

Another concrete confirmation of your affection, respect, appreciation and approval is taking action. It's easy to live in a house with a kid for 18 years and never get all that involved. There's dinner table time and homework talk and the like, but you can do all that without getting into their world, learning about their interests and really getting involved.

Kids feel a lot more connected, loved and secure when we let go of our adult concerns for a few minutes and get right into their skins with them. When we show that we care about what they care about, they feel better and so do we. Getting involved in their interests and sharing our own interests with them in turn causes more closeness. It makes it easier to feel affection, talk warmly and listen actively to them.

After work I set aside the job hassles, get David and go out in the backyard and throw the football with him. It takes me away from my troubles and gets me into his world.

Sometimes Heather's "available" emotionally, and sometimes she's distant. I use drawing to connect with her. After half an hour of pastels, and getting "rainbow fingers," we both feel good.

PRIMING THE NURTURING CYCLE

Men's night out - Father and son have a regular night out alone for fun pursuits.

Shared kicks - Identifying a hobby to pursue together, like bowling, horses or miniatures.

Old-fashioned games - Monopoly, gin rummy, checkers, etc.

Walk-around-the block - Leaving family at home and the two of you getting away.

Get physical - A sport that physically vents aggressions like soccer or basketball.

Stand up for him or her - Go to bat on something that really matters to him or her, and is beyond their capabilities to handle, like a teacher who ridicules or a coach playing favorites.

Mutual indulgences - Do something to baby yourself and share it with your child - nobody else - taking turns in a scented bath, a manicure, or a back rub.

Little getaways - The two of you take off for an afternoon swim, a sled ride, a weeknight movie or a sporting event.

5

WRITING

Writing is healing. Writing your own journal of your struggles and frustrations can help you externalize your feelings and let go of them more easily. Some parents write little notes to their kids and drop them on their pillows or tuck them into a backpack. It can be a private, sweet connection.

Sometimes intense, negative feelings expressed verbally to your child can fuel an inferno. Taking a few minutes alone to write down your feelings can help you feel less stuck and help your feelings heal. A technique described by Dr. John Gray* called the LOVE LETTER is a structured way of working through your feelings and of sharing them with your child.

I write little notes to Rebecca. Usually just a dumb line or two. Then I find one from her under my pillow. It makes my day.

*("What You Feel, You Can Heal," $12.95 from Heart Publishing, 20 Sunnyside, Mill Valley, CA 94941)

My husband says to me, "I think you'd better write Kevin a LOVE LETTER. You'd feel better." He is usually right. It dissipates the anger and lets me feel sane and loving again.

Is there such a thing as overnurturing the child? When nurturing means overprotecting and overindulging, decidedly yes. Kids want to be seen for who they are - a child of a certain age, not a younger child. Some parents of obese kids overindulge and overprotect their kids, thinking that if a little bit is good a lot is better. Actually overindulged kids feel isolated and that sense of isolation usually fuels more and more outrageous, demanding behavior.

The building blocks of nurturing your child beautifully are within you. You may already be a skilled nurturer. If you are not, becoming one will lead to some personal growth that will enhance your own happiness, and self-nuturing, too.

THE LOVE LETTER TECHNIQUE

Unexpressed feelings pile up. They make mountains of anger. Peel back the anger and you'll notice hurt, sadness. Feel the sadness and then wait. You'll feel fear, then guilt and, finally, love.

Take a trowel to your piled up feelings and dig down to the love. You can do it through writing a LOVE LETTER, a powerful technique described by Dr. John Gray. It can help you get past some of the difficult feelings so you can experience and share the love you feel. The next time you feel angry with your child, write him or her a LOVE LETTER. Here are the rules:

Start with anger, then sadness, then fear, then guilt, then love. Write a few sentences on each feeling; keep each section the same size. After each section, pause and notice the next feeling coming up. Then write about that feeling. Do not stop your letter until you get to the love. Be patient until the love comes out. Sign your name at the end. Take a couple of minutes to think about what you need to hear from your child. Write it in a P.S.

Here is a sample LOVE LETTER to use as a guide for your use with your child or other close relationships.

Dear Marianne:

1) **anger** - I am so angry at you for being so lazy. I'm sick of nagging you to clean up your room. You just toss you things around like a complete slob. I feel disgusted by how sloppy you are.
2) **hurt** - I feel hurt that you don't respect me or our home more. I feel like you've slapped me in the face every time you throw your stuff around.
3) **fear** - I fear that you are going to grow up completely disorganized and confused because you can't find anything. I fear you don't love me.
4) **guilt** - I should have taught you to clean up better. I'm sloppy myself and I think it's catching.
5) **love** - I love you and just want the best for you. I understand that you are not in the habit of cleaning your room and that it is hard for you.

Love,

    Mom

P.S. I need to hear you love me.

Give it to your child and ask him or her to read it to you, role playing your feelings.

By working it through like this, this mother did not stuff her feelings or get stuck in only expressing her anger and chipping away at her daughter's sense of well-being. But wait, the room still isn't clean! However, cooling the anger and working it through to love blows away an emotional barrier to setting limits in a sane and effective way. Instead of lapsing into hollering or into swallowing her feelings and having them pop up in other ways, this woman can now set expectations, monitor behavior and follow through with consequences. The result? The mother feels better, the room gets cleaned up, and the child feels loved and safe.

SELF-ASSESSMENT

11. BUILDING YOUR CHILD'S SENSE OF WELL-BEING

This is a tough practice. If you are brave, work through this page which deals with accepting your child and the next on assessing yourself. You will identify your strengths and the areas that could benefit from your attention.

1. In which ways does your child measure up to your expectations? What about your child are you proud of?

_____

_____

In which ways does your child <u>not</u> measure up to your expectations? What about your child disappoints you?

_____

_____

Which of the things you just listed are not very important? Could you could let go of them?

_____

_____

Which of the important negatives are potentially changeable? When and how will you work on changing them?

_____

_____

Which of the important negatives are not changeable? Which of these will you work on accepting?

_____

_____

Describe your attitudes toward obesity in general and your feelings about your child's fatness.

_____

2. Now assess yourself. How often in the last week did you:

	rarely		sometimes		always
love and accept yourself	1	2	3	4	5
have a strong sense of who you were	1	2	3	4	5
feel in touch with your feelings	1	2	3	4	5
openly express your feelings	1	2	3	4	5
ask for what you needed	1	2	3	4	5
speak directly to people rather than use go-betweens	1	2	3	4	5
discriminate between your problems and those of other's	1	2	3	4	5
tell the absolute & complete truth in your close relationships	1	2	3	4	5
accept the ways your child is different from you	1	2	3	4	5
feel a loving bond with your child	1	2	3	4	5
encourage your child to express his or her feelings	1	2	3	4	5
teach your child to ask for what he or she needs	1	2	3	4	5
redirect your child when he or she used go-betweens	1	2	3	4	5
help your child discriminate between his or her problems and those of others	1	2	3	4	5
accept your child, limitations and all	1	2	3	4	5

give your child direct messages that he or she is accepted
and valued by using:

	rarely		sometimes		always
talking	1	2	3	4	5
listening	1	2	3	4	5
touching	1	2	3	4	5
doing	1	2	3	4	5
writing	1	2	3	4	5

5

3. In what ways do you nurture yourself?

_____

_____

4. How are you at asking for what you want in your close relationships?

_____

_____

5. List several areas in which you are doing particularly well already:

A._____

B._____

C._____

6. List a few areas in which are you not doing so well:

A._____

B._____

C._____

5

7. What changes will you make?

_____

_____

_____

_____

_____

12. EATING ON THE RUN

We all are "on the run." Our kids are rushed. Even our pets are hurried. When rushing is normal, any extra stress causes overload. In many families, overload triggers ordering out for pizza, tossing in the towel on exercise or stopping off for double cheeseburgers and fries.

I pick up Casey after his last class and take him to karate lessons. I usually end up leaving work 10 minutes late and rushing to meet him. We're both starving to death so we stop at the store for an ice cream or cookies on our way to the lesson.

I tell Rhonda to have breakfast, but she ends up late and doesn't have time. I'm calling to her *to brush her teeth two minutes before the bus arrives. What does she do? She gets a sweet roll during morning recess instead.*

Why are we in such a rush? Part of it is the competitiveness of our society. Our kids "need" to get ahead and so do we. We push them; we push ourselves: cramming more into a too-busy calendar, trying to make it all happen. We believe that they—and we—can do it all.

This rush also comes from the speed of change in our world. Technology has allowed us to go faster than we can go. Our "information society" has raised our awareness of our choices—and increased the complexity of our lives. As soon

5

as we've made choices and adapted, our environment changes again. We are almost constantly adapting to new realities.

So take it as a given that our days are well-packed. Do we have room left over for healthy habits? Does the rush of the day fuel our cravings for a slab of butter on that bread, a slow trail of fudge over the vanilla ice cream and a third beer?

There are many very busy people who have very healthy family lifestyles — and they are not magicians. Sure, a light diet and an active lifestyle require the same organization, consistency and follow-through as the most successful career. Perhaps more. Let's set up that organization so that you can stay healthy through fast times.

STEP 1. Deal with barriers to a healthy lifestyle. What are the barriers to healthy eating and exercise? You name it, it's a barrier. Here are a few:

Situations — Stressful events and situations take up your time and emotional energy. Healthy living takes a back seat. Sickness, school problems, work problems and the like take the wind out of the sails of healthy living.

Relationships — Troubles with relationships — a difficult marriage, a testy child, or outright sabotage by a grandparent can call a halt to even the most modest exercise plan. They can divert your attention enough when you're adding the salad dressing to pour on two glugs rather than a scant tablespoon.

Family structure — The family's way of operating needs to be in fine tune to support healthy habits. Some families benefit from a strong shot of organization, in other words, more structure. Others need less structure, to be more flexible and less rigid. Parents who are overprotective, over-involved and too close may not take a strong stand and get the family away form heavy foods. For others warmth, closeness and involvement in each other's lives have faded and so there's not the closeness that motivates us to do things — like healthy eating — for our kid's and family's benefit.

My job is a barrier. I don't know from one day to the next what my hours will be, so who can schedule exercise?

Priorities — Your career comes first. Your night out with your girl friend. Perhaps even your aerobics class. They are priorities. If getting low-fat food on the table at night and signing your child up for soccer class aren't happening, then perhaps it's because they are not high enough on your current priority list. Other things come first.

The most direct route to eating well and exercising consistently is to deal with the underlying barriers.

Yes, my work schedule is erratic and my career is extremely important to my feelings of self-worth. I'd be a screaming, shrieking, miserable parent without it. So the meals suffer. I know for sure that I need to make it more of a priority. And I want to get the kids to share the burden. The kids should stop acting like guests in the house and start helping with shopping, cooking and clean-up.

Jennifer and I know that our marriage troubles detract from keeping the meals healthy. We're worn out by the tension between us. We need to get into counseling and I think it's about time we do get going on that. But I also think that the tension would lessen if we could stop the frenzy and do something normal like go out for

5

a walk together or bump elbows over washing and chopping vegetables.

STEP 2. Organize the mechanics of a healthy family lifestyle. A little organization goes a long way toward making a healthy lifestyle happen, even on the most gruesome of days.

Have clear expectations about who plans meals, shops for food and cooks meals. If it isn't clear, or you are not pleased with how the responsibilities are divided up, take some time to re-think roles. Consider involving the children in planning and cooking meals. Share the burden.

Plan ahead light meals that the family enjoys. The responsibilities of family food are just as important as that financial statement or sales transaction. Put the same amount of pre-planning into your meals as you would into your work.

Give the same attention to preplanning meals that you give to scheduling your day's meetings.

Plan one choice at meals rather than fragmenting meals to please everyone. The family food preparer will only face exhaustion, despair and meal monotony by trying to please everybody. Prepare healthy food. If they don't like it, they can eat a little bit less. Avoid indulging tastes and overemphasizing the importance of having food that is perfectly palatable to everyone.

Avoid "burn-out" of the planner, shopper or preparer. If you want your efforts acknowledged, tell them. Have others do the dishes while you, the cook, take a break. Take care of yourself so you'll continue to have the motivation to fulfill your important responsibility.

QUICK CURES FOR NUTRITION WOES

See if any of these "eating on the run" scenarios fit you or your family:

BREAKFAST RUNNING OUT THE DOOR—That's right, your child gets up late once again.

Quick fix—Tell your child to grab a piece of fruit, slice of bread, cup of unsweetened cereal or a baggie of last night's leftovers as he or she leaves.

Solution—Tell your child that you expect him or her to eat breakfast before leaving for school. Define breakfast as at least a bowl of cereal or a piece of toast. Set up a consequence for not eating breakfast: doing the dinner dishes, taking out the trash, doing a chore rather than relaxing when he or she first comes home from school or the like. Once motivated, your child will usually think of solutions such as less dilly-dallying in the morning and setting the alarm earlier.

> **We solved the problem.
> Jenny makes her own lunches.
> I inspect them.**

BAG LUNCH IN A FLASH—Overslept, remembered lunch just as your child walks out the door.

Quick fix—Place two pieces of fruit, two slices of whole wheat bread and a non fat yogurt in a bag.

Solution—You or your child fix bag lunches the night before. Or plan ahead to fix lunches before the kids arise or while they eat their breakfast. Give yourself a break. Plan to purchase school lunches once each week.

GOOEY, YUMMY AFTER SCHOOL SNACKS—You have had a rough day and it feels good to feed your child chocolate chip cookies and milk, a round, sweet ice cream cone, or even (horrors!) twinkies and ho-hos. . . kids nurturant foods. It pleases and indulges us to feed the sticky, sweet fun foods to our kids. Certainly we should every once in a while. But obese kids will have a hard time losing weight with a steady diet of them. Indulging our own need to feed can spell failure at weight loss for our kids.

Quick cure—Feed them what you want, then fix them a very light dinner.

Solution—Consider why you are feeding them food that hurts them. Is it for them or for you? It's likely for you. What feelings does it bring up from your early years? What other way can you take care of those needs? When you feed them these foods, is it reassuring that you are a good, non-depriving parent? Is that an accurate assessment? Ask yourself some of these admittedly difficult questions.

HUNGRY AND CAUGHT IN TRAFFIC—You are hungry. The kids are restless. The car is stuffy. Your nerves are on edge and you spot a convenience store. A bag of chips and some sodas will perk up you and the kids.

> **I keep a bag of apples
> in the trunk. If it weren't
> for the apples, we'd be
> hitting the convenience store.
> No doubt about it.**

Quick fix—Choose low-fat, low-sugar foods at the store like pretzels, juice bars, and mineral water. Yes, if you look for them, you'll find a few light alternatives.

5

145

FAT IN FAST FOODS

Fat not only has more than twice the calories of carbohydrates and protein, it also is more likely to "go to fat." Whereas your body has to work very hard to make carbohydrate into fat, it easily makes food fat into body fat. Fat, quite simply, is fattening. Most fast food is drenched in fat. But some fast foods have less fat than others. Below are the teaspoons of fat you put in your body when you eat each of these fast foods. Some of these foods contain sugar, too.

PLACE	FOOD	TEASPOONS OF FAT
Wendy's	salad bar with no-fat dressing	0
several	orange juice	0
several	low-fat milk	1
McDonald's	soft-serve cone (4 teaspoons sugar)	1
McDonald's	hash brown potatoes	2
Jack-In-The-Box	regular taco	2
Carl's Jr.	milk shake (14 teaspoons sugar)	2
McDonald's	McLean Deluxe	3
Roy Rogers	hot fudge sundae (10 teaspoons sugar)	3
McDonald's	french fries	3
Burger King	apple pie (4 teaspoons sugar)	3
McDonald's	hamburger	3
McDonald's	cheeseburger	4
Wendy's	Danish (2 teaspoons sugar)	4
Kentucky Fried Chicken	extra crispy chicken thigh	5
Hardees	hot dog	5
McDonald's	Chicken McNuggets	5
Long John Silver	pecan pie (10 teaspoons sugar)	5
McDonald's	filet-o-fish sandwich	6
McDonald's	sausage McMuffin	6
Arby's	super roast beef sandwich	6
Wendy's	potato with cheese	8
Burger King	Whopper	8
McDonald's	Big Mac	8
Roy Rogers	eggs & biscuits with sausage	9
Jack-In-The-Box	sausage crescent	10
McDonald's	McDLT	10
Burger King	double beef Whopper with cheese	14
Wendy's	triple cheeseburger	15

5

Solution — Determine how to take better care of yourself so you don't end up hungry and irritable. Prevent hunger with a more substantial meal or a later snack. Subdue tensions by taking a few minutes to relax before taking on the traffic. Have light foods on hand in the car, such as fruit, crackers and juices, for times when you are hungry. In short, take care of yourself.

FAST FOOD SURVIVAL—Budget, fatigue and time point you straight to the fast food solution. There you are, ready to order, with kids hanging on your leg and a clerk chomping at the bit to process your order.

Quick fix—Order small. That's right. The small hamburger not the deluxe, multi-layered masterpiece. Choose juice or milk rather than sodas. Skip the fries. That's right, *skip the fries*. Use the salad bar selectively, skimping on dressing and anything else with mayonnaise or jello imbedded in it.

Solution—Keep handy a list of fast food places that can serve up light foods you and your family enjoy. Rather than using fast food places as last ditch efforts to make it through meal time, plan them into your week, if your lifestyle warrants it. But pre-plan the places and foods that are reasonably light.

DINNER FROM A BARE REFRIGERATOR—You open the refrigerator and see mustard, butter, and non-fat milk that has long since soured. It's time for dinner.

Quick fix—Check out the cupboard. Chances are you'll find a packaged rice mix. Cook it and add a can of water-packed tuna or scrambled eggs with every second yolk tossed out. Finish the meal with fruit. Better yet, grab a piece of fruit or a slice of plain whole wheat bread to quiet the hunger. Then make a quick trip to the grocery store.

Solution—Spread out the responsibility. The person responsible for planning, shopping and preparing food is overburdened or underacclaimed. Family food needs a different solution certainly in the short run—but perhaps in the long-term, too. If it isn't working, try a different solution, rather than sticking with the same plan.

Eating on the run can be good. Our lives are full. Food is not our primary gratifier. Our eating is sandwiched between activities that are meaningful, joyous or important to us. Or it can be bad. Our lives are rushed and empty. The pace and wear-and-tear of the day are "good" excuses to throw up our hands . . . and head for the junk food. By organizing our family's food, we can share the work and all reap the benefits of eating solutions that keep us both well and satisfied.

5

SELF-ASSESSMENT

12. EATING ON THE RUN

STEP 1. Deal with barriers to a healthy lifestyle. Reread the potential barriers described in this chapter. Think about the times when you end up feeling rushed and don't take time for family health.

What barriers occur in your family?

_____

_____

What will you do to lessen or get rid of these barriers?

_____

_____

STEP 2. Organize the mechanics of a healthy family lifestyle. Develop a plan for who will plan, shop, cook, and clean-up family food and meals.

Who will shop for the family food?

_____

Who will plan the family meals?

_____

Who will set the table?

Monday	_____	Friday	_____
Tuesday	_____	Saturday	_____
Wednesday	_____	Sunday	_____
Thursday	_____		

Who will cook the food?

Monday	_____	Friday	_____
Tuesday	_____	Saturday	_____
Wednesday	_____	Sunday	_____
Thursday	_____		

5

Who will clear the table?

Monday	_____	Friday	_____
Tuesday	_____	Saturday	_____
Wednesday	_____	Sunday	_____
Thursday	_____		

Who will do the dishes?

Monday	_____	Friday	_____
Tuesday	_____	Saturday	_____
Wednesday	_____	Sunday	_____
Thursday	_____		

Who will clean out the dishwasher or dry and put away the dishes?

Monday	_____	Friday	_____
Tuesday	_____	Saturday	_____
Wednesday	_____	Sunday	_____
Thursday	_____		

Name three restaurants or fast food places you can go to and eat healthfully:

1. _____

2. _____

3. _____

Name one "nutrition woe" that your family has. (Review common ones in this chapter.)

_____

_____

What "quick fix" or "solution" will you use for it?

_____

_____

5

QUIZ #5

TRUE OR FALSE

PRACTICE

_____ 1. Kids who have a bottomless appetite often need more nurturing.

_____ 2. If you do not accept and love yourself, it will be difficult to accept and love your child.

_____ 3. Kids get by fine without direct messages that their parents value them.

_____ 4. Being quiet yourself and simply listening to your child nurtures him or her.

_____ 5. Children need to know that they can express any feeling - even hating a sister or anger at their parent - and it is OK.

_____ 6. Each obese child should know that being honest with their parent is more important than being "good" on their diet.

_____ 7. A sandwich and milk is a standard brown bag lunch.

_____ 8. At McDonald's, there is less than twice as much fat in a Big Mac as in a hamburger.

FINAL

_____ 1. When kids feel empty and isolated, they often use food or television to fill the void.

_____ 2. Parents who haven't been well-nurtured, may have difficulty nurturing their children.

_____ 3. You can hold on to rejecting or resenting your child without showing it.

_____ 4. Kids need parents to set limits on how they act but not on how they feel.

_____ 5. Many obese children are indulged and need cues from their parents that they must cope with some discomfort.

_____ 6. Parents are better nurturers when they nurture themselves well.

_____ 7. There are two teaspoons of fat in a regular size order of french fries.

_____ 8. Milk that is served at school is a HEAVY FOOD.

SHAPEDOWN Family Contract #6

THE ACTIONS

Each of us agrees to the following this week:

1. Complete the readings, practices and quizzes for Section 6.

2. Record on my SUPPORT record each day.

3. Meet at least 4 of my 5 SUPPORT goals.

4. If overweight, lose weight: □ ½ + pound **OR** □ 1 + pounds.

THE REWARDS

If **we all** do all of these actions, then **we all** receive our rewards:

_____**'s reward:**_____
    child's name   provided by when?_____

_____**'s reward:**_____
    parent's name   provided by when?_____

_____**'s reward:**_____
    parent's name   provided by when?_____

6

When the family receives the rewards, _____ will be responsible for
                                             parent's name
rewarding the child. The child will be sure the parents have given themselves their reward.

_____   _____
   parent's signature   child's signature

_____   _____
   parent's signature   date

PARENT SUPPORT #6

	MON.	TUES.	WED.	THURS.	FRI.	SAT.	SUN.	TOTAL	MET MY GOAL?
We took FAMILY TIME each day to review these records and to praise each other.								___ days	YES NO
I watched no more than 0 2 4 6 or 8 hours of TV								___ hours	YES NO
I EXERCISED for 100 200 300 400 minutes or more.								___ minutes	YES NO
I correctly filled out MY FOOD! on 4 or more days.								___ days	YES NO
GOAL OF THE WEEK: I said the **Magic Words**[3] to my child on ___ or more days.								___ days	YES NO
TOTAL NUMBER OF GOALS MET ⇒									

3 "I feel . . . ", "I need . . . ", or "Would you please . . . "

6

152

MY FOOD!

Day _____

Time	Food or Drink	Amount	Free	Light	Heavy	Junk	Milk	Meat/Bns.	Veg.	Fruit	Grain

Ate mainly FREE & LIGHT Foods? yes no

Ate breakfast, lunch, dinner? yes no

Totals: - - - -

MY FOOD!

Day _____

Time	Food or Drink	Amount	Free	Light	Heavy	Junk	Milk	Meat/Bns.	Veg.	Fruit	Grain

Ate mainly FREE & LIGHT Foods? yes no

Ate breakfast, lunch, dinner? yes no

Totals: - - - -

6

Day _____

Time	Food or Drink	Amount	Free	Light	Heavy	Junk	Milk	Meat/Bns.	Veg.	Fruit	Grain

Ate mainly FREE & LIGHT Foods?   yes   no

Ate breakfast, lunch, dinner?   yes   no   Totals: −   −   −   −

Day _____

Time	Food or Drink	Amount	Free	Light	Heavy	Junk	Milk	Meat/Bns.	Veg.	Fruit	Grain

Ate mainly FREE & LIGHT Foods?   yes   no

Ate breakfast, lunch, dinner?   yes   no   Totals: −   −   −   −

6

154

13. HELPING KIDS TO SPEAK UP

Parent-child communication begins early. From day one, most parents strive to show and teach their kids to express their feelings, thoughts and needs.

Often kids with weight problems do not speak up. They keep their worries to themselves. They feel alone with them. Some children seem withdrawn and quiet. Others act very talkative. Almost boisterous. But when you listen carefully, you find that they stop short of really opening up about their feelings and needs.

How openly and effectively your child communicates bears directly on his or her weight. That's because obese kids often are very sensitive.

They collect worries and hurts. Or they truly have had a few tumbles in life, such as medical problems, family changes, or parents who have found it difficult to give unconditional love.

When kids feel really listened to the sixth cookie loses some of its appeal.

With all the bottled-up worries and sadnesses, kids escape into food. They comfort themselves with sweets. They stuff themselves with bread. They feel better when they eat. It takes their minds off of the uncomfortable feelings inside. For many children eating, sleeping and viewing

television are their only reliable escapes from distress.

Suzi is the sensitive one in the family. She shoulders everybody's problems and then keeps them inside. When I have a bad day at work, she picks up on it and you can see the tension. But she doesn't talk about it.

I often wonder what's on Alison's mind. She seems to be so careful about what she says to me and avoids talking to her dad. I have a really hard time approaching her, particularly about sensitive topics like weight.

Brian irritates me no end. I don't like to say that about my own son, but it's true. He doesn't have anything to say that isn't a whine or complaint. There is such tension between his sister and him that it spoils the whole mood at home. I really don't know why he acts this way or what's on his mind.

Teaching kids to communicate well is not easy. As a result, families vary widely in how freely members exchange ideas, information and concerns. In some families people hold it all in, in others they let it all out. In some there is crystal clear honesty, in others people shade the truth, give inconsistent messages or avoid talking about distressing feelings and situations. The tone of communication in the family may range, too, from positive and accepting to irritable, impatient and negative.

If a child does not speak up, it's usually because he has been taught not to. He doesn't speak un because no one listens to him. Or because his parents do not speak up themselves.

We don't purposely teach our kids not to speak up. It usually creeps up on us. The communication seems pretty good and then begins to go sour. Or we have some other responsibili-

ties to deal with and so we have less time and energy to talk. And too, normal personality and temperament differences make talking with some kids easier than with others.

If a child doesn't speak up, it's usually because no one listens to him or because his parents do not speak up, either.

So to help a child to speak up, a parent needs to assess his or her own communication skills. How is the communication with his or her co-parent? How is it with his or her child? Do family members encourage each other to talk about their thoughts, feelings and needs? Do they listen to each other? What did they learn about speaking up from their own parents? All these issues are central to a parent's ability to help his or her child speak up.

I don't get much from Tom. He feels that bringing home the paycheck is enough. He's not a talker.

My parents were yellers. My dad walked in the door from work and within two minutes we were all screaming. I don't want to repeat that in my own family. But maybe I've gone too far in the other direction.

My parents spoke politely to us. If they had any other disagreements or bad feelings, we didn't hear about them.

I'll tell you what I learned from my parents about talking: don't. It's not safe. You might get whapped or yelled at. When Lisa starts talking I completely tune out. I don't have the faintest idea why it is so difficult for me to listen to her.

I think we communicate pretty well, as a

6

family. We're talkative, even loud. But I know there are some buried truths that get skipped over.

In SHAPEDOWN, your children are learning that loving parents set limits with their behavior but want and need them to express their feelings and their needs. They are learning the magic words, "I feel . . .", "I need . . .", and "Would you please . . ."

The idea is that in their life with you, these are designated as **safe phrases**. They are welcome tools for children who need "a few good lines" to help them talk about what they feel and need and to ask for support. All of these are basic to making their lives and their relationships work.

"Would you please . . ." is particularly important. There is a strong relationship between obesity and not asking others for what one needs. Including "Would you please . . ." as magic words says its okay to have needs and to ask others to meet them.

The ground rules are clear. Both you and your child agree to listen to one another when either of you uses the magic words. But that's just the start of it. You also agree to acknowledge **the feelings** the other person is expressing. If your child says, "I feel angry at Dad!" you agree to turn off the stove, sit down and listen. Don't get caught up in the content - what Dad did, why he did it, etc. Focus on the feelings: "It sounds like you are angry," and then you listen some more.

The Magic Words

I feel . . .

I need . . .

Would you please . . .

In this chapter you'll go through a quick "tune up" on communication. This is not to say that everyone should communicate the same way. But there are some general ideas that you may want to adapt to your own personal style.

If you'd like to see your family communicate better, and you'd like to get some individual attention for it, talk to your SHAPEDOWN instructor for a referral to a counselor who specializes in family communication.

STEPS TO GREAT COMMUNICATION

STEP 1. Stimulate your child to speak up. As children get consistent messages that they will be listened to and that it is okay to speak up, they will more readily come out with their feelings, thoughts and needs. A handful of strategies can help that process along:

Ask them what they think. You want to know their opinion, proof positive that you care what they think. Sprinkle your conversation with, "What do you think? What is your opinion?"

Ask them how they feel. How do you encourage children to open up to you? Ask their feelings about things as they arise. By doing so you recognize that how they feel matters, and therefore, that they matter. By asking, you learn much about their day that discussions of spelling tests and peer gossip leave out. In addition, they will be more open to listening to you — when you really need them to — if you listen to them, and show them this degree of concern and interest.

So I asked Elizabeth how she felt. I got a groan. The next time I got a shrug and eyes rolled back. The third time the floodgates opened and she told me everything that's been going on during the last six months.

6

Ask them what they need. The best way to find out what kids need is to ask them. Although they are much more likely to tell you their physical or logistical needs—the ride, the pants, the spending money—even that is a good start. You get some important information and make them feel cared for.

Play fun-nice-know. Each family members says something that he or she did that day that was **fun**, something that was **kind or generous** and some information or a skill that they **learned**. This is a great dinner table ritual.

Play thumbs up—thumbs down. This game gives everybody a chance to practice using their thumbs! This variation on fun-nice-know means what went well today? (thumbs up) and what went not so well? (thumbs down).

Catch them at the right time. There is no perfect time to talk. But each child has times when opening up is easier. For some it's right when they get home from school. For others, it's bed time. Some children spontaneously open up when they are doing an activity with the parent—from washing dishes to playing softball.

My daughter is open almost all the time. She wants attention and is ready for it any time I can give it. But my son requires more. He's only open now and then, so if he starts talking, I put down everything and listen. If there's any pattern at all with him, it's at bed time. I listen to him read a book to me as a way of giving him a chance to talk every day.

When they are ready to talk, try to take the time. If you are not beat, and they really want to talk, try to listen, make comments, and ask questions. When the exuberance is bursting out of them, reinforce it by listening to them if you can.

If you cannot listen, tell them so. Nobody is receptive all the time. If the rice is boiling over and the aspirin didn't touch that pounding head, stop. *I would like to listen to you, but I can't now. I want to sit down and hear all about this as soon as I clean up this mess. It won't be more than five minutes.* Reassure them that you care what they have to say and set up a time when you can give them your full attention.

Tell them the times that you expect them not to talk to you unless it is a very dire emergency. A dire emergency is usually defined as an injury that draws blood. Part of being available to them is protecting yourself from burnout. Think about the times when you want them not to expect you to talk, for instance, when you are talking on the telephone, when you're in the bathroom, scanning the morning paper or dozing on Sunday mornings.

I don't tell Kathy the really heavy stuff, but I keep her informed about how I am. Otherwise I end up feeling more removed from her.

Open up to them. What they do will closely mirror what you do. Talk to them about your feelings, needs and thoughts. Stop short of unloading on them to the extent you would a best friend or spouse. They are kids, and do not benefit from taking on the full load of adult burdens. But do clue them in as to what you're feeling. If you're angry, they probably know it. Saying "I feel so angry," helps both of you.

The look on your face makes me think you may have some feelings going on inside you. How are you feeling?

You hate the divorce. It's so good for you to be talking about it.

It sounds like you feel upset about your homework.

You need some help with your math homework. I thought math was going great. I'm so glad you talk to me. I can help if you tell me what you need.

I know you hate exercising. Exercising to you is work. You seem to feel really strongly about it.

Fun-nice-know, let's see. Fun was roller skating, nice was getting the ice pack for Colin when he bumped his head and know . . . . we learned the 6 times tables.

No, you're not hungry. You just ate. You could be feeling bored, or sad. What are you feeling?

STEP 2. Motivate your child to keep the dialog going. You're half way there. They've started to talk. Now the challenge is to let them see that speaking up works. They are listened to and applauded, they feel better afterwards and their life goes better.

Repeat back what your child says to you. By summarizing what they say, we reassure them that we are listening to them. In addition, when we repeat it back they can let us know if we understood them correctly.

When you don't understand, ask questions. You know the problem. They talk and you have no idea what they're talking about. It's easy just to let it go and pretend you got it. Instead, try to follow what they say and ask questions to fill in the gaps. Getting involved actually makes the conversation more interesting for both of you.

When you don't like something about how they are communicating, tell them by using "I" messages. You probably won't last as a grade A listener if your child's talking irritates you. Shape his or her improved behavior by giving feedback.

I don't like it when you whine. Say how you

6

159

feel. If you don't like how Stephen is treating you say so, but whining isn't necessary.

I know you are excited about the experiment, but I don't like it when you interrupt me.

Use body language that suggests you are listening and interested. Take advantage of a variety of means of convincing your child that you really are listening and you really do care. Make eye contact with him or her. Lean forward in your chair. Walk over next to him or her.

Keep on listening actively. It is so effective. Listen to what your child says. Summarize it and say it back to him or her. When we feel listened to, we feel comforted.

When I see my daughter upset, I want to stop the hurt and tell her all the things I'll do to make it okay. But she really doesn't need that. What she needs is for me to listen to her.

All this stuff that I really don't want to hear is coming out of my son. He doesn't like school. He can't stand his little brother. It's all tumbling out of him, finally. As much as it hurts, I keep telling him that it's great that he's talking to me about how he feels. I tell him it hurts, but that I want to know what's bothering him so we can fix it.

I've been pulling feelings out of these children — and out of myself — for the last year. They're pretty good at saying that they're bored or angry or sad. Now I'm trying to balance it out by having them speak up when they feel positive feelings, like when they're excited about Christmas, happy about a new friendship or proud about a good grade.

Even when what they say hurts you, congratulate them for speaking up. It hurts deeply when our daughter says she's not getting enough hugs. It's just plain unpleasant to listen to your son tell you that the burned carrots taste *yucky*. To keep the dialog going, congratulate them for talking. *I hate the fact that I always burn the vegetables. You're right, they do taste yucky.*

Every so often, change your actions based on the feelings, needs or thoughts your child has expressed. Some kids don't feel listened to. They feel that no matter what they say we're going to do what we've already made up our minds to do. We're going to be rigid about it and say no. So once in a while, even when we really have our minds made up, we can consider their feelings enough to change our minds.

You know I really don't want to play basketball. It's not a sport I've ever liked. But you told me what you wanted. I like that. So this time I'll play.

Talk with your child about the risks and benefits of speaking up and opening up. The benefits are that they will feel less alone, and their problems and feelings will seem less overwhelming. They will learn about themselves, and their relationships will become closer. The risks are possible teasing or betrayal. If children open up slowly, they will gradually learn about how safe it is to talk to each individual.

Reassure your child that most meaningful communication, such as talks about hurts, jealousies and fears, is difficult. It's even difficult for big people.

SELF-ASSESSMENT

13. HELPING YOUR CHILD SPEAK UP

Assess your own communication.

How often do you:	never		sometimes		always
make requests of the other parent?	1	2	3	4	5
make requests of your child?	1	2	3	4	5
talk with the other parent about your needs?	1	2	3	4	5
talk with your child about your needs?	1	2	3	4	5
talk with the other parent about your feelings?	1	2	3	4	5
talk with your child about your feelings?	1	2	3	4	5
really listen to the other parent?	1	2	3	4	5
really listen to your child?	1	2	3	4	5

6

When you were growing up, what messages did your parents give you about speaking up?

When you spoke up, did they really listen to what you had to say?	YES	NO	NOT SURE
Were you encouraged to request help from your parents?	YES	NO	NOT SURE
Were you encouraged to speak up about your needs?	YES	NO	NOT SURE
Were you taught and shown how to open up about your feelings?	YES	NO	NOT SURE

This MAGIC WORDS Agreement is for you and your child. In it, you both promise to stop what you are doing and to listen to each other when the magic words are used. Moreover, you promise to acknowledge one another's feelings, such as saying, "It sounds like you are sad . . ." or "You feel hurt . . ". Please read this agreement with your child, changing it as necessary to fit your family's needs and views.

MAGIC WORDS AGREEMENT

I promise to stop what I am doing and to listen to you when you use these magic words:

I FEEL . . .

I NEED . . .

WOULD YOU PLEASE . . .

I promise to acknowledge your feelings (to say back to you what you said you were feeling).

Signed by parents and young person:

_____   _____

_____   _____

Date:_____

6

14. MAKING FAMILY ACTIVITIES PHYSICAL

We pursue work, housework, or school during the day and at night eat, watch television and do homework. On weekends we catch up on housework, go on errands, watch television, ask friends over and, you guessed it. . . . eat. Pretty inactive. Rather flat. Definitely food-focused.

We have little time as a family, so I try to make that time positive. The thing we most like to do together is enjoy a nice meal.

We have three children, all pretty far apart. So there is really nothing we can do together. For treats we go out for an ice cream cone or to McDonald's.

Our family life you can spell with two letters: T - V ! We watch an hour or two of sit-com's each night together. It's easy, comfortable and fun. Although the kids watch another couple of hours a day, which is probably too much.

Take a moment and think about your typical family week. Has the overstuffed armchair lifestyle gotten out of hand in your home? Here are the tell-tale signs:

6

6

TELL-TALE SIGNS
OF THE OVERSTUFFED
ARMCHAIR LIFESTYLE

- television viewed more than 1 hour per night

- no veggies at dinner more than one night per week

- no family sports on the weekend

- no attempts at family exercise during the week

Ready to unseat your overstuffed armchair lifestyle? Check out these steps:

1. Think about your own attitudes toward exercise. Does exercise mean work, pain, suffering, exhaustion, failure, embarrassment, no fun? Or is it physical creativity, play, relaxation, body fun, social time, private time? If your attitudes toward exercise are negative, you probably don't exercise. If they are negative, your child's perspective on exercise is likely to be negative, too. And your child is unlikely to exercise much.

My mother always told me how clumsy I was. So I generally avoided sports and went out for plays and clubs instead. I can't remember even one good experience with sports.

I am a very compulsive person. I can usually do what I set out to do except for exercise. Talking myself into jogging takes weeks or even months. Then I do it and feel elated. I'm so thrilled that I keep it up for a few weeks. Something happens and I stop. I just don't like to jog.

2. Pick a few kinds of exercise you like and begin doing them. The most effective way to prop up your attitudes toward exercise is to find some kinds of exercise you enjoy. There is not one best kind of exercise to do. Pick something that props up your mood, makes your body feel alive and clears your mind. Find something that gives you the lift you want. Plan to do it at a specific time of day, such as before breakfast or dinner, or after the dinner dishes are done.

I really like a morning walk when it's quiet out and the world is mine.

In general I dislike exercise, but I'm willing to try walking around the outside of the mall once each Saturday when I shop there.

I enjoy social sports: tennis, racquet ball and golf.

3. As a family, pick at least one short exercise break for weekday evenings. Kids who study do

WEEKDAY PLAY FOR FAMILIES

mini-trampoline while watching TV
after dinner walk around the neighborhood
jumping rope slowly
taking a slow family jog
turning on the radio and dancing
going out to an aerobics or dance class
neighborhood softball game
gentle wrestling with the kids
pillow fight
stationary bike while reading
slow jumping jacks
exercise videotape
driving a bit and taking a hike
frisbee throwing
basketball shooting in the back yard
family soccer or football

well to use activity breaks to revitalize their bodies and minds. Parents who push papers, people or machines all day can loosen up with a bit of evening exercise. Take a look at some possibilities other families have enjoyed.

Evening activities are apt to be with only two family members rather than the entire family. They range from ad hoc, spur of the moment getaways to nightly rituals. An after-dinner walk, in almost any weather, can be relaxing and set the stage for a peaceful evening.

Once you begin exercising on week nights, evenings change. You look forward to the evening's activities, not just the evening meal. Your energy level rises and you sleep better, too.

I am amazed by the changes in our evenings. Now we get up from the dinner table and everyone pitches in and cleans up. I get on my exer-cycle and Tim gets on the bouncer. Karen's been taking a tumbling class, and so starts doing somersaults on the carpet. The only drawback is that the lady downstairs keeps thinking it's an earthquake or something.

Now that we have our little walks after dinner, we eat less. We don't want to feel uncomfortable on the walk.

There's no question that playing football after dinner makes me voluntarily cut back on my after-work beers. If I have more than one can of light beer I simply can't catch the ball!

4. As a family, pick at least two kinds of exercise for weekends. There are errands to run, wash to do, friends to see. Not much time for family romps. Take the time. Kids talk differently to us when we sweat together. It's good to see pink cheeks and vigor in our kid's faces. Exercising

165

WEEKEND FAMILY FUN

go on a hike

go to an art show

spend a day at the park

browse in a bookstore

pick fruit at a fruit farm

run in a foot race

go bowling

visit a museum

play soccer

play softball

see a new movie

go to a concert

rent a sailboat

fly kites

bicycle in the country

wash the cars and bikes

window shop in the city

go swimming

buy a puppy and build its house

rent horses

---

together gives us a sense of family closeness and well-being. And it makes Sunday dinner taste that much better.

Consider family activities that center on something besides eating. If the activity spans a meal time, eat, but eat light foods. Focus on deriving pleasure and excitement from the activity, not just from eating.

Establishing new ways for your family to spend time together can move you from a pattern that has gone stale into a pattern that is healthier. This "leap" requires some real effort on your part. But once the change is made, most families find this more active lifestyle to be more gratifying for everyone.

6

SELF-ASSESSMENT

14. MAKING FAMILY ACTIVITY PHYSICAL

1. Describe your own attitudes toward exercise:

negative   1   2   3   4   5   positive

2. What kinds of exercise do you truly enjoy?

_____

_____

3. In which of these could you involve a family member?

_____

_____

4. Please list activities that other family members enjoy:

_____

_____

5. In which of these could you become involved?

_____

_____

6. Which activities will your family do on week days?

_____

7. Which activities will your family do on weekends?

_____

6

QUIZ #6

PRACTICE

1. Carol was feeling tired and overwhelmed and had just cut her thumb while slicing carrots for dinner. Her 12-year-old step-daughter, Allison, approached her and said, "I've got to talk with you. I'm feeling terrible." Which would be an appropriate response?
a. OK, tell me about it.
b. I'd love to listen, but not just this moment. I'd rather wait a few minutes until I can really listen.
c. How can I listen to you when I'm in the middle of all this? You expect too much of me.

2. Don was dissatisfied with his communication with his daughter, Karen. All their talk seemed rather superficial. Which strategies might be helpful?
a. for Don to begin talking more openly to Karen about his feelings.
b. for Don to tell Karen the details of his work problems.
c. for Don to ask Karen more often how she feels about things as they come up.

3. David says, "I don't know what I am going to do. Mrs. Jenkins gave me too much homework and I'll never finish. I know it'll be late." His father could respond with active listening by saying:
a. You can do it. It isn't so bad. Here, I'll help you organize it.
b. Sometimes she gives way too much homework.
c. You feel overwhelmed with the homework and afraid you can't finish it.

FINAL

1. Sophia listened to Barbara whine about her homework. It reminded her of her sister-in-law who had whined her entire life. Sophia should take and deep breath and then say:
a. nothing.
b. You're always whining just like your Aunt Susan. I wish you'd stop.
c. I hate it when you whine. I really drives me nuts. It's not a good habit. I want you right now to say exactly how you feel about your homework without whining.

2 . Karen says, "I can't stand Mr. Washington. He's a jerky teacher." Ben is listening actively to his daughter when he says:
a. I don't like him either.
b. You think Mr. Washington is a jerky teacher.
c. Why do you think he is a jerky teacher?

3. Rebecca didn't have nearly enough time with her 9-year-old son, Rudy, since she had started her full-time job for an accounting firm and he had seemed less open lately. Which strategies would be helpful for Rebecca to use to help her son open up?
a. tell him that she feels sad that they don't have as much time together.
b. make a practice of spending time with him at bed time, when he is more relaxed and open.
c. accept that relationships have to suffer if the mother works.

6

SHAPEDOWN Family Contract #7

THE ACTIONS

Each of us agrees to the following this week:

1. Complete the readings, practices and quizzes for Section 7.

2. Record on my SUPPORT record each day.

3. Meet at least 4 of my 5 SUPPORT goals.

4. If overweight, lose weight: ☐ ½ + pound   **OR**   ☐ 1 + pounds.

THE REWARDS

If **we all** do all of these actions, then **we all** receive our rewards:

_____'s reward:_____
　　child's name　　　　　　　provided by when?_____

_____'s reward:_____
　　parent's name　　　　　　　provided by when?_____

_____'s reward:_____
　　parent's name　　　　　　　provided by when?_____

When the family receives the rewards, _____ will be responsible for
　　　　　　　　　　　　　　　　　　parent's name
rewarding the child. The child will be sure the parents have given themselves their reward.

7

_____　　　　　_____
　　parent's signature　　　　　　　　　child's signature

_____　　　　　_____
　　parent's signature　　　　　　　　　　　date

PARENT SUPPORT #7

	MON.	TUES.	WED.	THURS.	FRI.	SAT.	SUN.	TOTAL	MET MY GOAL?
We took FAMILY TIME each day to review these records and to praise each other.								___ days	YES NO
I watched no more than 0 2 4 6 8 hours of TV								___ hours	YES NO
I EXERCISED for 150 200 250 300 400 minutes or more.								___ minutes	YES NO
I correctly filled out MY FOOD! on 4 or more days.								___ days	YES NO
GOAL OF THE WEEK: I told my child one thing I like about my body on ___ or more days.								___ days	YES NO

TOTAL NUMBER OF GOALS MET ⇒

HOW TO USE: MY FOOD!

Most of us eat when we aren't hungry some of the time, but if we do it a lot it is likely to bump up the scale. Since our energy needs vary a lot whether we're weekend athletes or women influenced by the menstrual cycle, the internal awareness of hunger and fullness is critical. It can give us the flexibility to respond to our body's needs, eating more when we need it and less when we don't, and keep the creeping pudgies at bay.

Starting to eat when you aren't hungry or stopping eating when you are long past satisfied can be a simple habit learned in childhood that requires some focused un-learning. Or it can be an eating disorder that usually calls for psychotherapy and other professional care. The hunger you perceive may not be purely biological. Mixing up the desire for food and the need for food is commonplace. However, a focus on our body and the hunger and fullness signals it sends us merits some attention.

This week we expand our food recording to include a HUNGER SCALE of your level of hunger and fullness when you start and stop eating. Whenever you start eating when you are not hungry, note what triggers you to begin eating. Whenever you stop eating when you are full or very full, observe what triggered you to continue past the point of being just satisfied but not full. Here is a list of common cues that railroad us into ignoring our own internal cues of hunger:

Moods - happy, sad, lonely, bored, deprived, miserable, elated - - you name it, it can trigger eating.

Times - eating because the clock tells you to; having a snack at your afternoon break whether you need it or not.

People - eating because people offer you food, cherishing pizzas out with a friend.

Foods - your favorites or your comfort foods, whatever they are from chocolate chip cookies to ice cream.

Situations - parties, office celebrations, business lunches, family celebrations.

Places - being in the kitchen, going to a restaurant, passing by the doughnut shop.

7

Some people say they avoid starting to eat because they can't stop. What are some common triggers to NOT stopping.

Habit - everyone in your family ate until they were stuffed - you learned to do it, too.

Deprivation - emotionally or physically, if you've deprive yourself of food, or forbid yourself treats, you'll tend to be sure to get enough.

Great food - foods you particularly like, favorite foods you don't get often, fantastic food you make a point of getting daily.

Feelings - feeling a void, an emptiness, isolation, loneliness, emotional neediness, boredom, anger, and so on.

Stimulation - a lively political discussion, arguing, watching television, all can distract you from your internal cues.

To manage these cues, you and your child can use strategies like these:

Blocking - Stop the cue before it reaches you. If you eat when you are bored, get active. If you eat in response to chocolate chip cookies, stop baking them.

Pausing - Instead of eating when you get a cue, stop and figure out your choices. Pause, think of all your choices (including eating), think about the positive and negative consequence of each and then decide on one of the choices

Delaying - Put it off. Wait ten minutes to eat, and then see if you still want to.

Eating style - The healthy family eating style you will learn about this week helps people stop eating before they are full.

... very hungry

... hungry

just... ...satisfied

full ...

very full...

7

172

MY FOOD!

Day _____

Time	Food or Drink	Amount	Free	Light	Heavy	Junk	Milk	Meat/Bns.	Veg.	Fruit	Grain	Hunger Score* Start	Stop

Ate mainly FREE & LIGHT Foods?   yes   no

Ate breakfast, lunch, dinner?   yes   no

Hungry when started eating?   yes   no

Totals: –   –   –   –

Stopped eating before full?   yes no

MY FOOD!

Day _____

Time	Food or Drink	Amount	Free	Light	Heavy	Junk	Milk	Meat/Bns.	Veg.	Fruit	Grain	Hunger Score* Start	Stop

Ate mainly FREE & LIGHT Foods?   yes   no

Ate breakfast, lunch, dinner?   yes   no

Hungry when started eating?   yes   no

Totals: –   –   –   –

Stopped eating before full?   yes no

7

* 1 = very hungry, 2 = hungry, 3 = just satisfied, 4 = full, 5 = very full

173

MY FOOD!

Day _____

Time	Food or Drink	Amount	Free	Light	Heavy	Junk	Milk	Meat/Bns.	Veg.	Fruit	Grain	Start	Stop

Hunger Score*

Ate mainly FREE & LIGHT Foods?   yes   no

Ate breakfast, lunch, dinner?   yes   no

Hungry when started eating?   yes   no

Totals: -   -   -   -

Stopped eating before full?   yes no

MY FOOD!

Day _____

Time	Food or Drink	Amount	Free	Light	Heavy	Junk	Milk	Meat/Bns.	Veg.	Fruit	Grain	Start	Stop

Hunger Score*

7

Ate mainly FREE & LIGHT Foods?   yes   no

Ate breakfast, lunch, dinner?   yes   no

Hungry when started eating?   yes   no

Totals: -   -   -   -

Stopped eating before full?   yes no

174

* 1 = very hungry, 2 = hungry, 3 = just satisfied, 4 = full, 5 = very full

Your family has a certain style of eating. You eat together or separately. The television is off or on. You rush through the meal, or savor it slowly. You cook and clean up together or separately. You nag the kids to eat their peas or you don't. Whatever pattern you've set up is your family's eating style.

The rush of the day and the evening news threaten a healthy family eating style. Yet most families agree it is important to establish a way of behaving around the evening meal that is calming and restoring. Eating together, breaking bread together restores the sanctity of the family. The distractions of the day fade beyond the imaginary line drawn around the family table.

The family feels whole again. Whether family members are feeling sad, joyful, bored, or angry, the feelings are shared. It is a time to be together.

The TV is blaring.
We are all tired and spaced out.
Is this any way to dine?

Unless we make it a priority, we are apt to adopt a style of eating that is chaotic and fails to restore. We eat separately, snacking rather than eating meals, heating up rather than cooking and listening to the television rather than to each other. Yet, if we make it a priority, we can put the soul back into dinner time. We can make it a

7

time of nurturing from the tone of the conversation to the care with which the food is prepared and the predictability of the dinner hour. This

nurturing provides a sense of well-being that used to be provided by excess calories.

HEALTHY FAMILY EATING STYLE

Parents and children eat together, at the same time and at the same table.

Mealtime is predictable. People know when to expect to eat.

The television is off; newspapers are out of sight.

Family members slowly savor their food, enjoying every bite.

Communication is open; family members talk freely and listen attentively.

Talk does not focus on weight, eating, exercise or nutrition.

Parents as well as children enjoy mealtime and their food.

Parents do not urge their children to eat or not to eat.

The parent is in charge of the timing of meals and snacks.

The parent is in charge of which foods are presented on the plate.

Children are in charge of whether and how much they eat of the food provided.

Children know what the eating rules are. They don't question their parents about what they have to eat.

Mealtime is over when the parents say so.

The television is almost always on while we eat. Talk is the last thing I want at the end of the day. The T.V. gives us each some space.

We usually have something quick like macaroni and cheese or soup and crackers during the week. On Sunday I cook and we have a nice meal.

We all make a point of being home by 6:30

for dinner. We eat and talk about our days, unless we're all too tired and then we just eat. But we are together then.

Sharon and I often don't know when we'll get off work. If a brief needs to go out or a customer calls late, we can be delayed as much as an hour or two. If we don't come home on time, the kids usually stick burritos into the microwave or fix sandwiches.

COMMON BARRIERS TO HEALTHY FAMILY EATING

Problems in the parental relationship — the child diverting attention by gaining weight, parents not getting support and cooperation from one another

Situational chaos — short term chaos related to specific situations such as a move or sickness

Chronic family chaos — not enough structure, order and routine

Drug or alcohol problem in one parent — co-alcoholic other parent who enables the alcoholic parent to continue his or her pattern

Parent's own weight or eating problem — dieting one week/feasting the next, keeping nothing but diet foods in the house

Parents not setting limits with the job — one parent has excessive work commitments/hours and other parent chooses not to confront him or her

Intergenerational family — parent unwilling to confront grandparent to make changes in mealtime

Family discord — parents dislike eating with their kids due to incompatibility, communication problems, or intergenerational differences

If you would like to see your current eating style improve, consider each of the aspects of a healthy family eating style. Pick one to change. Also examine the barriers to a healthy family eating style. Decide if you want to address any of those, too.

We decided that the television was depressing. We didn't need it. So we turned it off — all but Friday nights, when we have pizza and watch our favorite shows.

I'd like to put more energy into weekday meals. I don't want my daughter to grow up thinking dinner comes out of a tomato soup can. The only way I can make this happen is to get some cooperation. So we've divided up the planning, shopping and cooking. We each take one week night and leave Friday as a tomato soup can night.

Getting home at unpredictable hours worked well for Sharon's and my work, but it wasn't good for our family. Plus, the kids too often ate out of the freezer — and it wasn't vegetables! So we compromised and said we would be home by 6:30 Monday through Thursday nights and have dinner by 7:00. To improve the situation, we have begun to set limits with ourselves, getting up and leaving work when it isn't convenient, rather than working whatever hours we pleased.

FEEDING YOURSELF

Think about the role of food in your own life. Eating can be an intimate experience with one's self. Feeding ourselves, nourishing our bodies and spirits can be affirming and restoring, too. We can rely on food to make us feel alive and well.

Some people treat food like a pill they have to take. Others treat it like a deity.

7

Food can be a bologna sandwich—eaten but not tasted—to quiet hunger pangs and make the movie on time. It can be a way to pamper ourselves or to abuse ourselves. Our eating can be an expression of anger, frustration, boredom, loneliness, elation or depression. It can block out an unfriendly world or be a needed relief from the barrage of feelings of self-hate. The role of food in our lives is as individual as our thumbprints.

Food to me is a bother. I'd rather take a pill and forget it.

If it tastes good I'll eat it. Otherwise I'll wait until something comes along that's worth eating. The pleasure from the taste, texture and smell of food is extremely important to me. I could never understand people who didn't love to eat.

I'm pretty sane about food at least half the time. Then I go through a down time and I need it. I really have to have it. So it varies. When I'm down it's all I think about. When things are going pretty well, the day can go by without my thinking much about eating.

I've never really thought about it. I eat when I'm hungry. My diet's rather monotonous, actually.

I am addicted to it. My body is objectively scrawny, but food is my release. I'm always tearing out recipes and cooking up something. Half the time I don't eat it. But nonetheless I like being around food.

With so many central feelings wrapped up in eating, it's no wonder the idea of dieting is a downer or simply out of the question. In a face-off between weight loss and the soft, warm feelings involved in feeding and eating, weight loss is the loser. As you negotiate changes in your own eating and weight, take stock of the mean-ing of food for you, how you use food in your life. Consider alternatives.

I eat when I'm lonely and tense. I work all day then crash at night and eat like crazy. Perhaps I need more companionship at night, other than the kids. Or I've thought of playing the piano again. That might calm me down.

I've thought about getting addicted to jogging to substitute for my addiction to sweets, but my knees couldn't take it. Seriously though, my sweet tooth comes up mainly in the afternoon after I've had a diet lunch. So I've started eating an apple around then. It works.

I am an emotional overeater. Almost any emo-tion will trigger my appetite. I guess I'm ready to get some help for it. Not a diet, but a get-in-charge-of-your-life type approach.

FEEDING YOUR KIDS

In addition to family eating style, consider your own attitude toward feeding others. Feeding can be nothing more than a routine chore, or it can be imbued with layers of emotional over-tones. Even a father who eats only when restaurants or his wife feed him, can get in the act of feeding through food gifts and restaurant excursions.

To most people, feeding kids is fulfilling and fun. Providing food that sustains them feels nurturing. Watching a child eat, seeing a child "thrive," feels reassuring and life-affirming. The child will live and grow. Giving the child food that delights and pleases him or her is the easier form of indulgence. You experience certain feelings and give important messages through feeding your child. However, there are many other actions you can take that are calorie-free and will bring about similar feelings and messages.

7

Justine: *I feel a good deal of satisfaction that our family can get together at mealtime and feel good. When I was growing up, dinner was always tense. It was something to endure. So I make a point of fixing food that everybody likes and making the whole occasion relaxed and pleasurable.*

Marianne: *I am not aware of any particular feelings when I feed my daughter, but I have a strong reaction to denying her food. It makes me feel sad. She already has lots of disadvantages. She's not well-accepted at school. A few cookies make her happy. It's hard to deny her that.*

Bill: *Brian is concerned about his weight, but I just don't see it. He looks fine to me. When I see him eat I feel it's healthy, not sick. As a kid I was always the skinny one, always the one to get pushed around by bigger kids. I take a certain pride in Brian being good-sized.*

Think about experimenting with alternatives to feeding, alternatives that give similar messages to your child. Here are alternatives these parents chose:

Justine experimented with cutting back on fat and sugar in the food. The conviviality and pleasure at the table weren't affected. Meals were as satisfying as ever.

Marianne began indulging her daughter with things other than food. She signed her up for the horseback riding lessons her daughter had wanted and surprised her with new earrings. She also focused more directly on her daughter's unhappiness, talking with her about solutions to various problems.

Bill asked his son if he wanted karate lessons or weights to lift. Brian had no interest in karate lessons, but he did have an interest in free

7

179

weights. So they bought weights and made their basement into a gym.

YOUR FAMILY'S FOOD PHILOSOPHY

Whether or not you realize it, you do, in fact, have a family food philosophy. Your family food philosophy may be to "eat to live," "live to eat" or somewhere in between. Food may be everything to your family, or it may be nothing.

Eat to live families eat for health and energy. How the food tastes is of little importance. Fuss over preparing food is minimal. In these families people eat because they are hungry. They choose foods because they are easy to prepare and taste okay. They may eat pretty much the same thing day in and day out. In these families, if the stew burns it's no problem: they make peanut butter sandwiches.

We live to eat. My husband runs 5 miles a day so he can have a second plate of lasagne. Sarah and I don't run, but we do have seconds.

In **live to eat** families, food is a central theme of conversation. Meals are not thrown together; they are fussed and fretted over. And the food is so good! No monotony, just exciting, delicious and heart-warming foods. A good day is a fine dinner. **Live to eat** families use these luscious foods as the heart beat of family pleasure. In these families, when the stew burns the evening is through.

Which family philosophy is usually most helpful for obese kids? Neither. Somewhere in between is best.

If yours is an **eat to live** family you are missing out on one of life's important pleasures. Food is good and meant to be enjoyed. Food that has been prepared with care affirms us. Under emphasizing it can trigger kids' feelings of deprivation. Deprivation causes overeating.

What causes families to **eat to live**? Perhaps they consider getting pleasure from food to be weak or wrong. Or they clear the house of every food tastier than celery to cope with their own eating problem. By de-emphasizing eating and food because of their own struggles with eating and weight, they create a depriving food environment for their children.

On the other hand, **living to eat** is disastrous when it comes to losing weight. Overemphasizing food makes it impossible to cut back or lighten up. Something so dear is difficult to do without. What causes families to **live to eat**? Usually the parents have learned during their early years to rely heavily on food.

So attempts to lighten the diet are usually short-lived. Light foods don't taste a good as heavy foods. If your family's pleasure center is food, the family's mood can easily take a nosedive when meals lighten up. When the family is on the outs it's easy to give up on lightening meals.

Experiment with a new food philosophy. If you are an eat to live family, consider talking with each family member about the foods they enjoy and would like to eat more often. Buy them. Fix that delicious recipe. Take pleasure in eating.

If you keep a deprived food environment because of a family member's eating problem, think about addressing that problem. Now may be the time for that individual to get some help for his or her eating problem. Although some people resolve themselves to a life devoid of food enjoyment because once they start eating they don't stop, there is help. Most people with the

7

right support learn how to enjoy food and when to stop eating.

If you are a live to eat family, try shifting the focus away from food. Take the time to discover if it is possible for your family to get the feelings of love, pleasure, reassurance and family closeness from sources other than food. Do it for a specific period of time that you all agree on, perhaps for one month, perhaps for just a week.

During this time pinpoint the feelings that feeding and eating bring you. Then identify substitutes. See if you can broaden your range of sources of love, pleasure, reassurance and closeness until food pales as a central source. If this shift works for you, your family may choose to continue it.

SELF-ASSESSMENT

15. CREATING A HEALTHY FAMILY EATING STYLE

1. Rate your family's eating style. During the last seven days were your family meals like this:

	rarely		sometimes		always
Parents and children eat together, at the same time and at the same table.	1	2	3	4	5
Mealtime is predictable. People know when to expect to eat.	1	2	3	4	5
The television is off; newspapers are out of sight.	1	2	3	4	5
Family members slowly savor their food, enjoying every bite.	1	2	3	4	5
Communication is open; family members talk freely and listen attentively.	1	2	3	4	5
Talk does not focus on weight, eating, exercise or nutrition.	1	2	3	4	5
Parents as well as children enjoy mealtime and their food.	1	2	3	4	5
Parents do not urge their children to eat or not to eat.	1	2	3	4	5
The parent is in charge of the timing of meals and snacks.	1	2	3	4	5
The parent is in charge of which foods are presented on the plate.	1	2	3	4	5
Children are in charge of whether and how much they eat of the food provided.	1	2	3	4	5

7

Children know what the eating rules are. They don't question their parents about what they have to eat.　　1　2　3　4　5

Mealtime is over when the parents say so.　　1　2　3　4　5

Add up your score:

　　57 to 70 — terrific! a healthy family eating style
　　42 to 56 — very good! your eating style is quite good
　　29 to 41 — needs work! build on a healthy foundation
　　below 29 — extensive renovation of your family's eating style required!

2. Beyond nutrition, how important is food to you?

　　Not important　　1　2　3　4　5　　Extremely important

　　Describe the role of food in your life:_____

　　_____

　　_____

　　_____

3. How much do you rely on feeding as a means of expression?

　　Rely little　　1　2　3　4　5　　Rely a great deal

　　Describe what feeding your child means to you:_____

　　_____

　　_____

　　_____

4. What is your family's food philosophy?

　　Eat to live　　1　2　3　4　5　　Live to eat

　　What changes would you like to make in your family's food philosophy?

　　_____

　　_____

7

16. TAMING THE MONSTERS: CRAVINGS AND SECRETIVE EATING

There are everyday problems like traffic jams, unreasonable bosses and paying the bills. No fun. But manageable. Then there are the problems that pierce straight to the heart, that wound visibly and won't relent.

Take cravings, for instance:

Cindy talks of nothing but food. She marches through her days with a normal number of smiles and frowns, but when she speaks of food her face lights up. She glistens with excitement and pleasure. It's like she's anticipating a fix. I worry that she's addicted to food.

Bobby hounds me. Can't I pleeeeeease have a candy bar? Then he pouts, stomps around the

house and slams the door into his room. I'd be embarrassed if anybody saw him behave that way. He is fixated on getting that candy. He is driven, like he needs it on some deep, emotional level.

Or, try secretive eating:

Just ask Kevin, everything is fine with his diet. He loves the big salads we've been having for dinner. He doesn't complain about the pint-sized lunches I've been packing him. So I'm feeling pretty good about his weight and about him. Then I clean his room and find a box of chocolate chip cookies in his underwear drawer. My neighbor saw him with his friends eating dough-

nuts. Baker's dozen chocolate doughnuts. I felt furious. How could he lie to me? I'm doing all this work and he is sneaking. What kind of a kid does that?

These little monsters—the habits, that is— **have devastated even the most resilient parents.** First of all, your child is not a bad kid. There are probably some pretty coherent reasons why he or she is behaving this way. Let's take a moment and examine what might be going on when your child has cravings or eats secretly.

COMMON CAUSES OF CRAVINGS

GETTING ATTENTION

This is far and away the most common cause of cravings. If kids are not getting the nurturing they crave from their parents, they frequently try to get it from food instead. Their needs for nurturing are not being met. Do your best to stop the food talk. Use extinction. *I don't like it when you keep talking about cookies. If you continue I will not listen to you.* Ignore their comments. Don't say a word back to them when they bring up cookies. Then go on to give them the attention they need in other ways.

HUNGER

Check that you have made available healthy but not depriving foods regularly throughout the day. Caution: it's difficult to know if they are really hungry. Hunger is a complex process involving both the body and the mind. Also, kids can get used to eating a lot and feel hungry as they cut back, until their bodies adjust to less food.

DEPRIVATION

The food has been "too healthy" and they feel deprived. Reassure them that they can have a favorite food of their choice once a week. Or negotiate a trade-off. *What would you like to eat less of tomorrow so you can have that yogurt cone?*

ADJUSTING TO FOOD CHANGES

If eating cookies, candies, chips and the like is part of their normal pattern, a change will feel uncomfortable to them at first. Reassure them. *Lisa, I know this is a big change for you. It is for me, too. But I'm getting used to it. After a while you will, too.*

PUSHING YOUR BUTTON

The foods they crave are the ones their parent relies on, that is, the foods their parent uses for an emotional boost or loves to feed or hates to deny the child. They are foods that were important during the parent's early years. Of course they have a sixth sense about this "button." They push it every time. Your emotions take a nosedive and you give in. They keep it up because it works. Recognize how very difficult it is to change such a pattern. Also think about how difficult it is for your child to have an inconsistent parent, a parent who gives in repeatedly. It's scary for a child to have that much power. Set a limit and follow through consistently. That's what your child needs.

7

Lots of possibilities here. Consider the range of common causes of cravings.

Think through your child's most recent craving. What was really going on? Take a look at the above list and add some of your own causes. Figure out a strategy that matches the cause.

I thought Karen's cravings were to get attention. When she'd ask for a cookie I'd stop everything and respond to her. Honestly, there wasn't much else that I would stop dead in my tracks and answer her about. So I told Karen that I expected her not to talk about cookies, but that we would start taking ten minutes for "Karen time." Now I take that time to give her total, undivided attention. I listen to her read or work with her on her math homework. Lately I've been taking that time to help her learn embroidery. She gets me totally and reliably and that's seemed to squelch the cravings.

I think that with Stacy it was deprivation. I have my own struggles with food and with us being in SHAPEDOWN, I took the chance to take care of my own need to diet. So I relented a little bit. I said to Stacy, "OK, you want chips, you can have them some time this week. All you have to do is figure out a trade-off." She decided to have only half a sandwich on Friday and a small bag of chips. I wouldn't be for it every day, but once a week won't hurt.

I decided that this whole craving thing was just Jessica's way of getting to me. I love ice cream but we had been keeping it out of the house. She kept begging for ice cream. It's my weak spot because it's my "love food" and also because going to get an ice cream cone during my childhood was so ethereal and magical. The big tubs of ice cream and the sweet, round, drippy cones. I hate to deny Jessica those wonderful feelings. For me, it's best to not even entertain the topic of ice cream. No ice cream. That's it. Yogurt cones once a week. Ice cream, not at all.

What about secretive eating? Your child is eating food, especially the foods you don't want him or her to have. He or she is withholding that information from you, or blatantly lying about it. You are furious and hurt. What is going on?

Usually what is going on is that your child does not feel safe talking with you about his or her eating. Somehow the communication has broken down in this area. Your child needs that food emotionally, socially or physically and feels that if he tells you that, you will be angry and disappointed. If this common situation is going on in your family, take some immediate action:

1. Tell your child that you are hurt and disappointed in him and in yourself. You are hurt and disappointed in him because he didn't tell you about the food he was eating secretly. You are disappointed in yourself too. You did not make him feel comfortable about talking with you about his problem of wanting that additional food. What? His secretive eating is your fault, too? To some extent, yes. Obviously, with the love you pour on this kid he wouldn't go against your wishes lightly. He wants that love and approval. He's afraid that if he shares his desire for more food with you, you'll be angry or disappointed. He anticipates that you will not really listen to his problem and help him solve it.

2. Reassure your child that he or she is more important than weight. Sometimes our kids misinterpret our attention to their weight. They get confused and think we are putting their weight before them, that we are blowing their diet, exercise and weight patterns out of proportion. They really believe their weight has become so important to us that if they don't appear to eat right, we will disapprove of them, even reject them. Sound outlandish? Check it out with your child. Chances are, these ideas have more than crossed

7

his or her mind.

We need to reassure them. *I care about all the things in your life, not just weight. I am helping you lose weight because I care about you. I'm going to stick with you and keep on working on weight, but even if you were to be heavy forever that wouldn't make me love you less.*

3. Tell your child that honesty between the two of you is more important to you than weight. His eating candy upsets you, but knowing that he couldn't tell you about his problem upsets you even more. Your child should know that your trust is more important than any cookie binge. He needs to know that he can come to you with any problem in his diet or exercise and you will not love him any less. You will be happy that your child felt comfortable enough to be honest with you about it.

4. Tell your child that when he tells you about times he's "blown it" you will help him solve the problem so it won't be so hard next time. By keeping the communication lines open, you can teach your child how to handle various situations. You can give your child ideas to draw upon the next time the situation arises.

Okay, you've set up new rules. Now picture this. While you are getting chicken fat under your fingernails from separating the skin from the chicken and cutting your right thumb chopping the broccoli for dinner, your child is finishing off his second candy bar—the ones with peanuts and nougat and melty chocolate—with his friend, Andrew. He comes to you to talk about it. How would you handle it?

Mom, I really blew it. I ate two candy bars in my room. Two of those giant sized ones that are supposed to be a whole meal. I can't believe I did it.

It's so good you're talking to me about it, Jeremy. I'm really proud of you for opening up to me. How do you feel about it?

Sad, ashamed.

What will the consequences be of eating two giant-sized candy bars?

I'll probably gain a pound this week.

Maybe, maybe not. It's not terrific that you had that candy. But it's not the worse thing in the world. Besides you've been eating light lately. Remember when you said no to seconds at the Barlow's house?

Yeh.

You can learn something from having eaten that candy. What did you learn from it, Jeremy?

I learned that I have a hard time saying no candy when I go with Andrew to the store.

Good thinking, Jeremy. Now, what could you do differently next time?

I don't know.

I think you do. Tell me one thing you could do differently.

I could stay home and never see Andrew again.

Would that be good for you?

No, I'd rather just tell him that I'm not hungry when he wants to get a snack.

That's right. Or you could go with him and have something else.

Our relationship— being truthful with each other—is more important than whether or not you had cookies.

I could have a diet soda. And they have some apples there, but they're usually mushy ones.

I think we did learn a lot from talking about it. I'm so pleased that you felt comfortable talking to me about this. There are going to be lots of ups and downs and we need to talk them through.

- Reassure your child that the incident was not catastrophic.

- Point out some of the good things he has done.

- Tell him that you both can learn from it.

- Discuss other choices he has for next time.

- Congratulate your child again for talking with you.

TALKING TO YOUR CHILD ABOUT SLIP-UPS

Congratulate your child for telling you when he or she overeats or under-exercises.

Ask how he or she feels about what happened. This is another opportunity to help your child recognize his or her feelings.

Ask what he or she feels the consequences will be. Help your child make a connection between diet or exercise behavior and weight and body fat.

Reassure your child that the incident is a problem but that it is not a catastrophe. Put the incident in perspective. Of course, it's not terrific, but it isn't the end of the world, either.

Point out some of the good things he or she has done. Support a self-concept in your child

7

187

that says he's successful at losing weight. Mention the positive actions he has taken recently.

Tell him or her that when you talk about what happened you both learn from it. Reframe the overeating as a learning experience. You and your child can problem-solve and come up with ways of handling that situation in the future.

Discuss other choices he or she has for next time. What triggered the overeating? What were his choices—throwing the candy out, not buying it to begin with, coming to you before eating the candy and talking about it, taking a walk, calling a friend, and so on. Help him decide on some alternatives for next time.

Congratulate your child again for talking with you. Reassure him or her that by talking about it he and the entire family can be successful in managing weight, diet and exercise.

Do what you can to help your child see slip-ups as learning experiences, not as failures. Slip-ups happen to everyone. It could always have been worse. There are a lot of good things you've done, too. If your child learns to view slip-ups as learning experiences, he or she will get back on track sooner.

These techniques should work. Put them into practice. Expect to see steady improvement in your child's cravings and secretive eating. If you don't, it's probably because your child or family is unusually stressed. If so, the quickest route to taming the cravings and banishing the secretive eating is to get some more support. Consider family, marital or individual counseling. Caring for weight problems has a way of surfacing other, underlying problems. That's fortunate. If you can recognize a problem early and get the right kind of support, you're more likely to solve it or improve it. Even though it hurts to recognize problems and take some steps to deal with them, doing so is a loving gift to our kids and to ourselves. We want to set them up for the happiest, healthiest life possible.

7

SELF-ASSESSMENT

16. TAMING THE MONSTERS: CRAVINGS AND SECRETIVE EATING

1. My child has cravings: YES   NO   NOT SURE

   I believe that my child has cravings because he or she: (check all that apply)

   ☐ wants more attention

   ☐ is hungry

   ☐ feels deprived

   ☐ is adjusting to eating healthier foods

   ☐ is pushing my buttons

2. My child secretly eats: YES   NO   NOT SURE

   I talked to my child about his or her secretive eating, using these steps: (check all that apply)

   ☐ I told him that I was hurt and disappointed in him.

   ☐ I told him that I was disappointed in myself.

   ☐ I reassured him that he was more important than weight.

   ☐ I told him that our being honest with one another is more important than weight.

   ☐ I told him to tell me when he has slipped up and that we'll talk about it and work on solutions for the next time.

   Things I will do to decrease my child's cravings:

   _____

   _____

7

3. I talked to my child about slip-ups. I: (check all that apply)

☐ congratulated him for telling me about it.

☐ asked how he felt about what happened.

☐ asked what he feels the effects will be (on weight).

☐ reassured him that it was a problem, but not a catastrophe.

☐ pointed out some of the good things he has done.

☐ told him that we both can learn from it.

☐ discussed other choices he has for the next time.

☐ congratulated him again for talking with me.

7

QUIZ #7

TRUE OR FALSE

PRACTICE

____ 1. Parents and children should eat dinner together most of the time.

____ 2. It is OK to watch TV nightly while eating if it is a program everybody likes.

____ 3. If a child doesn't eat something, the parent should urge him or her to eat it.

____ 4. Everybody should eat the foods they like, even if it means family members all eating different food.

____ 5. When the child eats secretively, there has been a communication breakdown between parent and child.

____ 6. Talking about food cravings can be a way for the child to get parental attention.

____ 7. When a child tells a parent about a slip up, the parent should congratulate the child for opening up.

FINAL

____ 1. Meal time should be predictable.

____ 2. Nutrition and diet should be discussed at dinner.

____ 3. If a child wants a snack, he or she should be able to have one without checking with the parent.

____ 4. During dinner, children should not question their parents about what they have to eat.

____ 5. Empty candy wrappers stashed in the bedroom infuriate parents but mean that the child does not feel safe talking about his or her needs.

____ 6. Cravings can be caused by hunger.

____ 7. Slip ups are learning experiences, not failures.

7

Practice Quiz Answers: 1.T 2.F 3.F 4.F 5.T 6.T 7.T

THE ACTIONS

Each of us agrees to the following this week:

1. Complete the readings, practices and quizzes for Section 8.

2. Record on my SUPPORT record each day.

3. Meet at least 4 of my 5 SUPPORT goals.

4. If overweight, lose weight: □ ½ + pound **OR** □ 1 + pounds.

THE REWARDS

If **we all** do all of these actions, then **we all** receive our rewards:

_____'s reward:_____
child's name   provided by when?_____

_____'s reward:_____
parent's name   provided by when?_____

_____'s reward:_____
parent's name   provided by when?_____

When the family receives the rewards, _____ will be responsible for
               parent's name
rewarding the child. The child will be sure the parents have given themselves their reward.

8

_____   _____
     parent's signature   child's signature

_____   _____
     parent's signature   date

PARENT SUPPORT #8

	MON.	TUES.	WED.	THURS.	FRI.	SAT.	SUN.	TOTAL	MET MY GOAL?
We took **FAMILY TIME** each day to review these records and to praise each other.								___ days	YES NO
I watched no more than 0 2 4 6 8 hours of TV								___ hours	YES NO
I EXERCISED for 150 200 250 300 400 minutes or more.								___ minutes	YES NO
I correctly filled out **MY FOOD!** on 2 or more days.								___ days	YES NO
GOAL OF THE WEEK: Our family did chores together on ___ or more days.								___ days	YES NO

TOTAL NUMBER OF GOALS MET ⇒

193

8

Day _____

Time	Food or Drink	Amount	Free	Light	Heavy	Junk	Milk	Meat/Bns.	Veg.	Fruit	Grain	Start	Stop

Ate mainly FREE & LIGHT Foods?   yes   no

Ate breakfast, lunch, dinner?   yes   no

Hungry when started eating?   yes   no

Totals: –   –   –   –

Stopped eating before full?   yes   no

━━━━━━━━━━ MY FOOD! ━━━━━━━━━━ Hunger Score*

Day _____

Time	Food or Drink	Amount	Free	Light	Heavy	Junk	Milk	Meat/Bns.	Veg.	Fruit	Grain	Start	Stop

8

Ate mainly FREE & LIGHT Foods?   yes   no

Ate breakfast, lunch, dinner?   yes   no

Hungry when started eating?   yes   no

Totals: –   –   –   –

Stopped eating before full?   yes   no

* 1 = very hungry, 2 = hungry, 3 = just satisfied, 4 = full, 5 = very full

17. ENCOURAGING AN ACTIVE LIFESTYLE

Consider a typical day in the life of this child: Gets up. (Late) Dresses and leaves home. Sits in class all morning. Has lunch with schoolmates. The boy next to her taunts her with candy. She's the last child to finish the run around the field in P.E. class. School is out. Goes home to homework and a note to take out the trash. Doesn't do either. Watches TV. Has a couple of bowls of cereal. Then a fruit roll-up and three cookies. Puts off the math. Finally takes out the trash. Mom comes home at 6:00 p.m. after a grueling day. They eat dinner—pepperoni pizza—and watch television. She does her math homework after mom prods the third time. Lights out at 9:00.

What are the qualities of this child's lifestyle that encourage fatness?

Sedentary—She barely moves. Her metabolic rate diminishes and so she uses very few calories to keep her body functioning. What's more, she expends few exercise calories. This adds up to an energy output that would make all but the most Spartan eater gain weight.

Bored—What is a common mood that triggers overeating in children? Boredom. Eating is recreational, something to do. The busy, engaged child has little time to ponder how another snack would taste. The idle child counts the minutes

until the next meal. On a field trip at school a child can go all day without eating, whereas on a Saturday at home he or she is "starving" all day long. With chronic inactivity a child develops a passive stance on life, feeling little internal control. This usually leads to eating more.

Turning off the television is a bold act.

Few gratifiers — Food helps gratify basic human needs for feeling alive, stimulated, comforted and pleasured. When there are few gratifiers, your child relies more on food. By getting those satisfiers from sources other than food, your child simply needs food less. Food pales in comparison to the excitement of living.

Little growth and development — Being active and engaged develops personal competencies, social skills and knowledge. It sets children up for an orientation toward the world that is active and engaged. Without the sense of competence that comes with trying out and learning from new situations, children may regress and withdraw. Food is typically a safe companion when a child is staving off growth.

Michael has no interests. He never seems to want to do anything. I got our town's recreation department catalog and went through every class they offered. He wasn't interested in any of them. He loves watching television. Other than that nothing moves him.

Erica and my new husband have never really hit it off. To some extent it's him. She is left over from my other life, a reminder of it. But she's hostile to him at times and I feel caught in the middle. So when we're having adult time, she sulks and watches television. Erica's life would be more active if this war would come to an end.

If I didn't push Becky every step of the way she wouldn't do anything. It's just been that way the last year or so. It may be that her weight is bothering her and she just feels too embarrassed to get out and do things.

I really love my work, but I know both my daughter and I would be better off if we had more time together. By the time I get home at night there's not much left of me. We try to talk, but often I'm just too tired. I don't have the patience it takes to draw her out, discover activities she likes and make arrangements for her to do them.

SUPPORTING AN ACTIVE LIFESTYLE

From a parent's perspective, allowing your child to be inactive is a piece of cake. It's much easier. When we are dog-tired from the workday, fussing with our spouse, dealing with family illnesses, worried about eating or drinking too much, used up emotionally, or busy with our own interests, the television is God's gift to parents. It keeps children happy without requiring much from us. Let them fill up their hours with television, homework and free play. It's what we resort to when our resources are stretched too thin. New activities usually draw heavily on our time, attention and money. That's why it's as easy as slicing butter to drift into a pattern in which kids are inactive and disengaged from the breadth of life's possibilities.

Kids get active and they blossom right before our eyes. The eye twinkles, the smile is whimsical. They stand straighter.

Thinking of bolstering the activity and enriching your child's lifestyle? Take a look at these possibilities:

8

196

Limit television viewing. Do you believe that television viewing causes obesity in kids? One national study found that the more kids viewed television, the greater the chance that they were overweight. Most children watch 20 to 25 hours of television a week, not to mention the time they spend playing video and computer games.

And what do kids do to keep their hands and mouths busy while watching television? Munch on chips, of course. And to make matters even worse, commercials bombard the kids with food messages for candy cereals, sodas, doughnuts and fast foods. More than 80 percent of the food commercials are for junk foods. Television commercials are our kids' major source of nutrition information! With toy based programming, the commercials are even more lethal.

What's more, television is a passive activity — viewers receive but don't give. Kids listen without being listened to. It's sedentary, too. In fact, children become so lethargic during television viewing that their metabolic rate can approach a near comatose state!

We limit television to one hour per day, after the homework and exercise are done.

My husband really enjoys relaxing with television and so do I. We watch as much as we can of it. The only change is that Cynthia can't watch until her homework is done, and the first half hour we each watch we have to bounce on the mini-trampoline.

We were so fixated on the television that the house felt odd without the constant background noise. We decided to go "cold turkey" and take it out of the house for a month. Now we don't miss it at all. We play music more and are busier doing things, not vegetating on the couch.

Consider setting limits with the family's tele-vision viewing. Some families decide to store their television in the garage; others settle on limiting television time to an hour per day. When television time is limited or eliminated, there is more time in the evening — time for family activities or for individual pursuits, hobbies and projects that are active and enriching.

Require your child to walk or bike rather than ride in the car or bus. Say "no" more often to driving your child. In most neighborhoods children can walk or bike to and from school — or to and from a distant bus stop or car pool meeting place. You are not neglecting your child when you say "no" to driving. You are helping your child become more self-sufficient, responsible and physically fit.

AN ACTIVE DAILY PATTERN FOR KIDS	
exercise	1 hour
chores	½ hour
enriching activities	½ hour
television	≤ 1 hour

Require your child to do household duties that are active or interesting. Yes, that's it. Chores. There is a lot to learn and many calories to expend through household duties. Doing the wash, folding and putting away clothes, vacuuming the carpets, washing the dishes, sweeping the porch and walkway, pulling weeds, planting flowers, washing windows and cleaning out the garage all expend calories and boost confidence.

Chores give your child a physical sign of family closeness, a sense of responsibility and increased competence. To complement mopping

8

the floor, also entertain your child's interests around the house. If he moans about the color of the room, get him to help you paint it. If she wants to make a swing in the back yard or refinish the chipped patio furniture, encourage her to help you do it. Stimulate your child to pursue activities around the house that excite and fulfill him.

I realized that part of my resentment of Aaron was that I was acting like his servant, always picking up after him. Now he cleans his own room and his bathroom every week and has the table set when I get home at night.

Of all the housework jobs, I hate washing dishes most. After all these years of hating the dishes it finally occurred to me that Becky loves water and at 8 is certainly old enough to wash dishes. What a relief. She actually enjoys doing the dishes! I just cook, eat and then watch the news in quiet.

CHORES FOR KIDS

AGE	CHORE	CHORE
6 - 8	make his own bed	take out the trash
	clean up his room	get the mail
	fold his own laundry and put it away	feed the dog/cat
	set the table/clear the table	groom the dog/cat
	wipe off counters/dust tabletops	sweep the garage
	help make fruit or veggie salads for dinner	pull weeds/water plants
9 - 13	all of the above plus:	wash/rinse dishes
	sort laundry and put it in washer and dryer	clean out dishwasher or dry/put away dishes
	clean bathroom sink and bathtub	sweep and mop the floors
	buy a few things at the convenience store	vacuum
	fix simple dinners	bathe the dog
		walk the dog/cat

Require your child to try new interests and activities. This comes under the theme, "Weight loss requires parents to feel comfortable making their children uncomfortable." Your child will probably disdain tennis lessons, craft classes, play practice, soccer teams and the like. Fine. Give your child choices. "It is important for you to have at least two interests. Here are some possibilities. Choose two of them." Find out about interests from your school, park and recreation department, church and other parents. Use the telephone book. Extend your tentacles and find a wide array of possibilities.

Find structured activities. You plan to kick a soccer ball around the field on Saturday mornings, but then its too cold or you're too busy. Soccer doesn't happen. Instead, enroll your child in soccer classes those same mornings. Your child is more likely to make soccer a habit when there are social pressures and structured expectations.

Include after school activities. Right after school there's a low point for most kids. They're

8

restless and tired from a long day of the same routine. Inactivity in the afternoon is a sure-fire set up for non-stop eating. Setting up after school activities is essential. When play practice or piano lessons make the afternoon fly by, they head off trips to the refrigerator.

Support friendships with other children who are active. Kids want to do what their friends do. So invite over schoolmates who immediately bring out the soccer ball or jump rope. These children will encourage your child to be active. Discourage friendships with kids whose only interests are passive playing.

Check out your own activity. Active parents have active kids. Stimulate your child's activity by getting busy and engaged yourself. Once the television is off, there is lots of time. Use it for things you enjoy on your own as well as for family activities.

HEALTHY AFTER SCHOOL SCHEDULES

Kids Who Come Home

Arrive home—Your child has walked or biked home. Perhaps ridden home. It's time to share what's left of the day.

Transition time—A few minutes of rest, listening to music, a chat with Mom or Dad, listening to one video on MTV or time alone in their rooms are all reasonably healthy ways to let down from the day. All of these activities are better alternatives than eating those three bowls of cornflakes. Expect your child to need a little time to shake off the pace of the school day.

Snack—Post the list of okay snacks on the refrigerator door.

Physical Activity time—No, it's not time to

8

199

study. The studying will get done, but kids have been pent up all day, and, if they're fit, they're probably restless. Time for exercise.

Homework — Kids complain about having so much homework, but most — if they don't dawdle — can do it all in one to two hours. Have them settle down and get it done.

Chores and Enriching activities — Time for piano practicing, brownies, tennis lessons, doing the morning dishes, sweeping the front steps and the like.

When parents are not at home — Most children need structure and nurturing. Leave a note welcoming them home. Write out exactly what you expect them to do. That's right, a schedule. It's very reassuring to kids. It's a message that you care. If your work permits, call them when they arrive home to help warm their transition time.

HEALTHY AFTER SCHOOL SCHEDULES

Kids in After School Day Care

Transition time — After school programs handle it with aplomb. They take roll, have quiet time or read a story. They have transition time down pat.

Snack — Talk with the program director about their snack policy. Do they serve the children healthy snacks in moderate amounts? If so, do not single out your child. If not, talk to them about establishing better policies for the benefit of all children. If their policy is outright awful, request just fruit or vegetables for your child, or have your child bring his or her own snack. In addition, put pressure on the program to change its nutrition policy. Ask to have a sign-up of other parents who want their children to have healthy food after school. Don't be fooled. Peanut butter graham crackers and grape juice is not a very nutritious snack. Where's the fruit and veggies?

Physical Activity — Be directive about your child's activity after school, also. Playing in the playground is easy for the teachers, but not the best for your child. Some kids do get sufficient physical activity on their own. But others don't. Most obese kids are among the latter. Talk with the program director. Tell him or her that you want structured exercise, at least an hour of it. Ask to bring your child's bike and roller skates to school. Suggest that they offer organized activities like soccer and dance. Most after-school directors will respond to your requests. And if they do, when you arrive home at night a good portion of your child's physical activity will be done — a terrific reward for your efforts.

Homework — Ask your child to get a start on his or her homework at the after-school program. This frees up more of the evening time for activities together.

Arrive home — You pick them up. Time for the evening together.

Transition time — Transition time again. Expect your child to take a few minutes of transition time to talk with you, listen to music, sit on his or her bed or even watch a few minutes of television. Let him take that time.

Chores and Enriching activities — Time to help with dinner, set the table, practice the piano and the like. Your child may have had some enriching experiences during his or her after school program, but some family time, piano practicing, woodworking, paper-folding, drawing, singing and the like add considerably to the evening.

ENRICHING ACTIVITIES

Planting a Garden
Playing Guitar
Drawing People
Scouts & Youth Groups
Writing Poems
Making Gifts
Getting a Pen Pal
Taking Care of Animals
Learning Photography
Being in a School Play
Starting a Recycling Service
Learning to Knit
Crafts Projects
Collecting Stamps
Hiking & Exploring
Repairing a Sink
Building a Model
Joining a Sports Team
Sewing a Skirt
Painting Their Room
Singing in a Choir
Writing to Relatives
Working with Wood
Taking Karate Lessons
Camping Out
Skiing & Ice Skating
Exploring the City
Taking Dance Lessons
Riding Horses
Learning to Cook
Being in a Walk-a-thon
Making Food for a Food Bank
Starting a Business
Church Groups & Classes
Volunteering in a Day Care Center
Learning the Computer
Biking

MOTIVATING YOUR CHILD TO BE ACTIVE

Reassure your child – Let your child know that it is okay if an activity is not fun the first time.

He is learning something, just like he learns math from doing math homework. Usually in time, the tennis ball stops always going over the fence and tennis becomes more fun. Kids need to know that you expect them to cope with a certain amount of discomfort. They need your reassurance that though they might be uncomfortable, they'll survive it.

I told Angela, "Sure, it's difficult to learn the piano. It's normal to be uncomfortable with it at first, maybe a little scared. All your life you'll try new things and be excited or uncomfortable about them. That's normal. That's how we learn and grow."

Let your child choose two or more interests. Take advantage of the motivational technique of letting them choose among the choices you give them. Present your child with a laundry list of activities. Ask him or her to add some activities to it. Tell your child that you expect him or her to choose a particular number of activities — usually 2 — and that at least one of them should involve physical activity.

Becky was really uncomfortable with the idea of taking on new things. So I listed the possibilities: ballet, jazz dance, gymnastics, piano, art class or karate. I told her that I expected her to pick two and that at least one of those had to be some kind of exercise.

Set limits on the kinds of activities your child can choose. Okay, now you've set up your child to choose activities, and what does he select? Horseback riding (at $15 per hour) and Yamaha piano lessons ($40 per month and six hours weekly of your time). This active lifestyle may lead to your own exhaustion and financial ruin! If it's too much, say so. Have your child choose something else.

8

Set clear expectations for how your child participates. Our kids know just how to get back at us. Sure, they'll be active. Of course they will moan, complain and whine before, during and after the activity.

So tell your child what quality of participation you expect. For instance, if she chooses piano lessons, you expect her to attend the lessons and practice without complaining or being reminded. If he signs up for soccer, you expect him to play hard and do the best he can for the entire eight weeks. Next time he can choose whether he prefers soccer or another sport.

Of course, keep an attentive parental eye to your child's participation, in case the class or kids are terribly unsuited to him or her. If so, intervene. Otherwise, just encourage. Turn a deaf ear to his negative remarks.

Michael played soccer and just drifted around the field, not really trying. It drove me crazy. So when we got home after the third week of this I sat him down and said, "People who don't try stay in bed without toys or books all day." That did it. He runs around and really plays now.

Praise your child repeatedly. He shows up at softball and misses the ball every time it comes to him. You say, "It's so great to see you try so hard." She goes to ballet class and strains to touch her calves while the other girls make themselves into pretzels. You say, "Sweetheart, you are looking more like a ballerina every day."

I am so impressed with what's happened with my son Mark. Two years ago when his dad and I were divorced he couldn't even keep his toys straight. I had to wade through the room. It was so depressing. Now he's seven and he cleans up his room every morning before breakfast—the rule is that he can't come downstairs until his room is clean, bed is made, teeth are brushed, hair is combed and he's dressed. With everything done, he comes downstairs for breakfast and then leaves for school.

I thought all this would be a battle, but now that Kelly has more activities and does more chores around the house, she even carries herself differently. I can just see what it's done for her self-esteem. She really sparkles. People comment on it.

These kids are stuck in an inactive spiral. They are aware of their shortcomings and need your compassionate praise to get them through the rough times. This requires you to be understanding of their limitations and patient with their progress. It's only natural to see your child struggling and feel sad, frustrated and guilty. Turn those feelings into positive reactions and heap on the praise—praise your child for trying, and yourself for changing your child's direction.

8

SELF-ASSESSMENT

17. ENCOURAGING AN ACTIVE LIFESTYLE

	I expect my child to:		**I expect myself to:**	
	Recommended	What I expect:	Recommended	What I expect:
exercise	1 hour or more	_____ hour	1 hour or more	_____ hour
chores	½ hour or more	_____ hour	½ hour or more	_____ hour
interests/activities	½ hour or more	_____ hour	½ hour or more	_____ hour
television	1 hour or less	_____ hour	1 hour or less	_____ hour

Changes I expect my child to make in his or her lifestyle:

exercise

_____

_____

chores

_____

_____

interests/activities

_____

_____

television

_____

_____

8

Changes I will make in my lifestyle:

exercise

_____

_____

chores

_____

_____

interests/activities

_____

_____

television

_____

_____

8

There is always a special occasion. Start with birthdays, add Christmas, Easter, Hanukkah, Valentine's Day and the Fourth of July, and you have a roller coaster of special occasions, each a golden opportunity to pop pounds of fat and sugar onto our waiting tongues. Yes, we do fear gaining weight on holidays. But it's a fragile fear, one that doesn't pale our outright glee. We have a sanctioned time to overindulge. Splendid! After all, everyone feasts on special occasions. Or do they?

Many people enjoy parties, events and holidays and still lose weight. These people are not Spartans or recluses. They go to the parties and have the fun. But they don't overdo it. They keep

trade-offs in mind. Some people actually accelerate their weight loss during the holidays. They are busy having fun and don't have time to stuff.

Special occasions only become problems when they're extremely food-focused, or when they cause weight loss to stop for more than one week.

Before you think about how to lighten holiday meals, first decide if you want to lighten them. You may want to indulge on special occasions and make up for it before or after. It's easier and you don't take the risk of having your child feel

deprived. There are disadvantages though, too. Focusing a holiday entirely around food gives a contradictory message to your child: healthy food tastes good but we prefer unhealthy foods when we celebrate. In addition, if it lasts for several days or weeks, your child will probably gain weight. Gaining weight is very hard on children. They become disappointed and discouraged. It's not easy making do with fewer Christmas cookies, but it's even harder on them to gain back the weight they had lost.

Keep in mind that depriving your family of holiday foods is not the goal. Birthdays call for birthday cakes, Christmas for pumpkin pie and Halloween for candy treats. Deprivation doesn't work. It's perfectly okay to plan to overeat for the fun of it every once in a while. Reassure yourself that eating for the fun of it on special occasions only becomes a problem when it's extreme enough to center the holiday around eating, or prolonged enough to cause your child to stop losing weight for more than one week.

Think about the causes of your reluctance to make special occasion food lighter. Your memories of holiday eating as a child were extremely happy. You want that for your child. You like to overeat on holidays, and don't want to deprive your child while you overindulge. You feel guilty about how much time you spend with your child and see this as a way of counterbalancing it. There are endless possibilities.

There's no denying it. I feed her because it make me feel happy. It's bad for her but it's good for me.

Guilt, pure and simple. She's teased a lot and I'm at work long hours. I feel sorry for her, and candy and cookies make her feel better. They also soothe my guilt.

My happiest Christmas memory was eating

chocolates, one after another, right from the box. Seeing my daughter do the same thing brings back the little girl in me. I never had a weight problem as a child. I just got a lot of cavities.

The questions to ask yourself are difficult ones. *Is this really good for my child? Am I doing this for me or for my child?* They are worth asking even though they may hurt.

Already you've made giant strides toward healthy eating on special occasions. You're focusing less on food. That alone is bound to change special occasions. Food is no longer what special occasions are all about.

For most families, it's a relief to de-emphasize food on special occasions. No swollen tummies or need to down antacids. The tension about *Will I blow it?* is diminished. The holidays give us lots of different kinds of pleasure, not just food pleasure.

If you think people can keep from gaining weight during holidays, you've never met our family. Food is the holiday, plain and simple. Christmas is cookies, candy, plum pudding, egg nog, and pumpkin pies. Easter is chocolate bunnies, candy eggs and jelly beans, and those cute little marshmallow chickens . . . should I go on?

If you do want to temper the eating on special occasions, experiment with a few strategies. Other families have found these tips helpful while they lightened up their special occasion eating:

It can hurt when we ask, "Is eating like this good for my child or am I doing it because it's good for me?"

8

206

Plan activities rather than meals. The feast of Christmas Day can be surrounded with events such as dropping off small gifts to neighbors, sledding, seeing a movie or going ice skating. Avoid being trapped inside the house all day, cooking and eating. Go for a hike, take a walk, play touch football, fly a kite, or go sledding. Satisfy your child and yourself with entertainment rather than with food.

Share your time with people you enjoy — Because people are the heart of special occasion pleasure, pay special attention to whom you choose to include. If you don't enjoy the people you normally get together with, reconsider inviting them, or add several people whom you really enjoy to your list. Ask a special friend over for your child — and for you. If the holiday meal is already set, plan a family outing in the morning, like a movie or morning hike. Share the day with people who bring out feelings of warmth and joy.

Lighten the food — de-fat it! You know how to do it! Adding a salad and vegetables with dip to the traditional chicken barbecue on the Fourth of July doesn't detract. Nor does cutting down fat in some of your favorites, like using low-fat rather than regular evaporated milk in the pumpkin pie, and skipping the butter in the stuffing.

Ask your child to pick the one holiday food that is most important to him or her. Find out which food your child really values. Include it in the meal. You may be making whipped cream for the pumpkin pie because you would miss it, whereas to your child the turkey gravy may be the most important food.

Give gifts that are not food. It may be a family tradition to give candy hearts on Valentine's Day and Easter baskets on Easter. Reexamine whether it is a tradition worth hanging on to. The alternatives are many, ranging from flowers to books to baseball tickets.

EATING OUT

Whether it's at McDonald's or a fancy Italian restaurant, eating out is a treat that most families look forward to. It is a time to eat and enjoy without hassle, fuss or, thank God, dishes.

Jenny is our only child and we've been able to keep our careers on track and enjoy her largely by getting help any way we can. By the time Jenny was four she could order off of any fast food menu in town.

When we go to McDonald's it costs us at least $12, sometimes $15 by the time we get two Big Mac's, 2 large fries, 2 sodas and 2 Happy Meals. It's expensive but it's a habit. Plus, when the kids are screaming and we're all hungry, it's fast. It keeps us civil when the hunger monster attacks.

There is no reason to give up eating out. Even though the family is eating lighter and is more active, there is still room for eating out. First, however, judge how vulnerable you are to the restaurant's primary goal: persuading you to eat too much.

Restaurants clearly coax us to overeat. There we are captive in a chair. They pass before us baskets of bread, plates of butter, huge servings, appetizers, soup and salad in addition to entrees suited to lumber jacks. The reason? The more they serve the more they can charge without dispute.

How does the meal they try to sell you compare to the meal your family needs to satisfy hunger? Below are some examples of the calories provided in meals that restaurants sell, compared to the calories of meals that most people need to feel just satisfied, but not full.

8

──MEAL THE RESTAURANT SELLS── ──MEAL TO STOP FEELING HUNGRY──

Fast Food Meal

large cheeseburger	small hamburger
large fries	
large soda	small soda

950 calories **350 calories**

Italian Dinner

minestrone soup	minestrone soup
salad with dressing	
bread, ¼ basket	bread, 1 slice
butter, 4 pats	butter, 1 pat
half chicken	quarter chicken
rice, 1/2 cup	rice, 1/2 cup
peas, 1/2 cup	peas, 1/2 cup
milk, regular, 8 ounces	
chocolate sundae, 1 scoop	

1655 calories **640 calories**

Pancake Breakfast

pancakes, 6	pancakes, 2
whipped butter, 4 tablespoons	whipped butter, 1 tablespoon
syrup, 4 tablespoons	syrup, 2 tablespoons
eggs, scrambled, 3 large	egg, scrambled, 1 large
sausages, link, 4	
orange juice, 6 ounces	orange juice, 6 ounces

1480 calories **570 calories**

8

There is nothing intrinsically wrong with eating at restaurants. It's just how we react to their enticing us to buy and eat too much food. Talk with your child and other family members and agree on a plan for restaurant eating.

If we act assertively, eating in restaurants won't conflict with healthy family eating. Speaking up in restaurants takes some doing. It means asking your server to give it to you your way. Ask your server to:

- remove from the table any foods which you do not want to eat (e.g., bread, crackers, butter, salt).

- tell you exactly how the food is prepared and what comes with it on the plate

- have the food prepared and served with no butter, oil, mayonnaise or buttery, greasy, sticky sweet sauces

- take back to the kitchen all of the food that doesn't come the way you ordered it

- remove your plate as soon as you are finished eating

There is no halfway with our family. We agreed that we don't want to go to McDonald's unless we can all have Big Mac's, fries, sodas and shakes. So we're going to cut out fast-food places.

We're going to stop going out for pancake breakfasts, but not restaurant dinners. We can order for ourselves and decide what we want.

TIPS ON EATING OUT

Don't look at the menu — Most restaurants serve standard foods. Menus present you with an abundance of temptations. So, if possible, decide what you want and order it without gazing at the menu's display of fountain favorites and luscious desserts.

Ask exactly what food is served — The fish on the dinner may be broiled at 200 calories or breaded, deep-fried and sauced at 1,000 calories. Avoid surprises by asking up front how the food is prepared and what comes on the plate with it.

Speak up and request substitutions — If the hamburger comes with fries and you don't want fries, request lighter alternatives like sliced tomatoes or a green salad. If you want your food fixed without oil or butter, tell your server. You are the customer and deserve to be accommodated.

Order all dressings, sauces and butter on the side — Because a ladle of salad dressing adds 300 calories to that skinny salad, don't rely on the cook or waitress to decide on the amount of

8

RULES OF THUMB FOR ORDERING FAST FOOD

Order small	a small hamburger, not a double cheese supreme
No fried foods	no fries, no fried chicken, no fried fish
Watch the sauces	leave off the special mayonnaise sauce, ask for more mustard, ketchup, lettuce, and tomatoes instead
Choose no sugar drinks	ask for diet soda, non-fat milk or water
Bring along lighter foods	keep a bag of apples in the trunk to add to your meal
Enjoy light salads	head for the salad bar but choose the veggies not the jello, limit dressing to one tablespoon

---

dressing that suits you. Ask for it on the side so that you have complete control over the amount you eat.

Avoid restaurants that are nutritional disasters —You can easily order LIGHT FOODS at almost every restaurant. However, some restaurants are complete nutritional disasters. For instance, fast food chicken restaurants deep fat fry their chicken under pressure so fat is squeezed into every morsel. To accompany this fat-infused food there are fatty french fries, puffy white rolls, and greasy shaving-foam pies.

Check out light meals —Many diet plates are concocted to be high protein and low carbohydrate. Because most high protein foods are high in fat, it's no wonder that high protein meals often have a high caloric density and a lot of calories. Don't be cajoled by "high protein" hype into thinking that a light meal is necessarily low in calories.

After you eat, get away —As soon as you fin-

ish, get your body away from the table. Go to the bathroom, ask the server to remove your plate, take a walk, but get away from food! You are "just satisfied." Nibbling at cold crumbs of food will push you into feeling "very full."

Valentine's Day —This day for lovers is for little sweethearts, too. Most children receive valentines of some sort, often edible.

Strategies to try —Give your little sweetheart a frilly valentine, a single red rose or a *date* for a horseback ride or movie.

Easter —The chocolate bunnies, marshmallow chickens, jelly beans, where would we be without them?

Strategies to try —Have a real Easter egg hunt with decorated hard-boiled eggs. Give an Easter basket full of straw, little toy bunnies and chicks and a special new book. Treat your child to flowers—cut or in a pot—decorated with a stuffed bunny.

8

Halloween — Halloween is purely a kid's holiday. It's their day to make their fantasies come to life. Halloween is candy. Or is it? Dressing up, trick or treating and going to Halloween parties and festivals are great fun, in and of themselves.

Strategies to try — Tell the child to pick out 10 pieces of candy. Throw the rest away. Exchange the candy for a five dollar bill. Let them eat all they want that night. Do away with the rest the next day.

Hanukkah — Many Jewish people celebrate only Hanukkah. Others are involved in some festivities related to Christmas. Kids who celebrate both have that many more holidays to contend with.

Strategies to try — Hanukkah and other Jewish holidays center around food. Although often the foods served for these holiday meals could be lightened up a bit by skimming off the fat and choosing foods lower in sugar and fat, the kind of food is not typically the problem. Instead, the emotional importance of food and the emphasis placed on eating enough — that is, eating a lot — gets in the way of weight loss for kids. Some Jewish families strive to retain the family's orientation toward food yet expect their child to lose weight. It usually doesn't work. The entire family needs to question their attitudes toward overeating, overfeeding and overemphasizing food and make changes that to do not interfere with cultural and religious practices.

Christmas — Gingerbread houses, butter cookies, fudge, candy canes, egg nog, chocolate candy, Christmas parties, Christmas eve, Christmas breakfast, Christmas dinner, News Years eve, New Years dinner. Football games. Chips, dip and sodas. Difficult to escape.

Strategies to try — Serve large quantities of food, but make them light. Present platters of crisp veggies and dip to reach for during the game. Make crafts projects instead of baking Christmas cookies, or bake the cookies and give all but a few away immediately. Make your most lavish dinners. Leave salt and sugar the same, yet cut back on fat. Give away all candy gifts, or let your child take a bite of two — so that it isn't forbidden — and then get rid of it.

BIRTHDAY PARTIES

Now that we've handled the easy stuff, let's get to the clincher: birthday parties. Birthday parties are part of being a kid, and eating like the others creates a sense of well-being and fitting in. Your child should go to birthday parties and eat the foods served. This is a time when cutting back almost always feels depriving. Besides, it's hard to believe that a 2″ by 2″ cube of cake caused that two-pound weight gain.

Okay, but some kids go to lots of birthday parties — add to them cookies at school and candy at Grandma's and the weight skyrockets. What can we do? When an occasion such as a birthday party comes up, try these steps:

STEP 1. Reassure your child. Say, "We have two birthday parties this week. I want you to enjoy the parties. There's no reason why you can't eat the foods they serve."

STEP 2. Require your child to make a trade-off. If you eat the party food and don't change your food or exercise the rest of the week you probably won't lose weight. So if you go to the party you need to make a trade-off. You need to eat less or eat lighter or exercise more other times during the week.

STEP 3. Give your child two choices for a trade-off. Say "Trade-offs I can think of are walking home from school each day, or eating veggies rather than other snacks after school all

8

211

week. Can you think of other trade-offs?"

STEP 4. Let your child to choose a trade-off. Decrease your little one's resentment and support his or her sense of effectiveness. Let your child come up with the trade-off he or she will use.

The most common birthday party problem is when the child goes "hog wild" and eats three of everything. You end up disappointed in your child. The likely culprit is too much deprivation. Or not feeling comfortable confiding in the parents about his or her desire for food. In either case we need to recognize that the child is not a bad kid. And the child is not totally to blame. We usually have a hand in it, either by depriving or not openly communicating. So we need to talk intimately with our child and do some problem-solving. **What caused the overeating? How will he or she do next time?** When the next birthday party comes along, talk with your child about it that day.

Tell your child what you expect him or her to eat. *I expect you to have no more than one serving of each food.*

After the party, ask him or her how it went. *What did you like best about the party? I told you that I expected you to have no more than one serving of each food? Your being honest with me is more important than whether you had three servings or not. Let's talk about what you ate.*

If your child did what you expected, congratu-late him or her. If not, problem solve. *You ate just the way you planned to eat. Congratulations. I feel very proud of how responsible you were.* **or** *I expected you to eat one serving and you had two of everything. It's good that you told me. I'm proud of you for that. I do not like it that you overate. We're working together as a family to get healthy. It's important that we all do our own part. Let's talk about how you could do things differently next time.*

Kids' special occasions are also our own. We are excited and stressed. Our expectations are high. Great food is everywhere and so we eat too much. Our kids' eating mirrors our own.

Taking care of our child's weight means taking care, too, of our own. To pay attention to our weight we have to set aside time for rest and relaxation, in other words, do less and pay more attention to our bodies and feelings. When we take an extra long bath or a boys' night out, we are supporting our child's weight loss.

When special occasions cause slip-ups, don't magnify them. Help your child see bouts of overeating or skipping exercise as learning experiences, not failures. From every binge or feast there is plenty to learn that will help your child later. There is always something that your child did during those days that was good. Stress the positive. Even if your child gains a bundle during the holidays, it doesn't mean you're a bad parent or your child is out of control. There is always January.

8

SELF-ASSESSMENT

18. ENJOYING SPECIAL OCCASION EATING

What are the special occasions in your life? On which occasions is overeating a problem? Chart out the entire year and all the special occasions there are. Develop some plans for managing these occasions so that they don't interfere with your family's habit changes.

How I will change eating and activities on:

Valentine's Day _____

_____

Easter/Passover _____

_____

Halloween _____

_____

Christmas/Hanukkah _____

_____

Birthdays _____

_____

Restaurants _____

_____

Fast Food Places _____

_____

Other _____

_____

8

QUIZ #8

PRACTICE

1. Nine-year-old Lisa has never liked group activities. She is a "loner". What response could her father use to prompt her to join a group activity?

   a. sign her up for volleyball even though she hates it.
   b. don't, rather, let Lisa be Lisa and let go of wanting her to be a "joiner".
   c. require Lisa to participate in one group activity of her choice each season.

2. The Goldman's live almost a mile from 10-year-old Kenny's school in a suburban area. Although it is flat, there are several intersections between home and the school. Should Kenny take the bus to school?

   a. Yes, it's not worth risking an injury.
   b. No, with training he should walk or bike safely. Without gradually gaining independence

   c. It is an individual matter, one that parents must weigh carefully.

3. A 7-year-old (with instruction and parental non-perfectionism) is capable of successfully:

   a. making his or her own bed
   b. keeping all toys and clothes off the floor
   c. setting and clearing the table at meal time
   d. making macaroni and cheese alone
   e. taking out the trash
   f. feeding the dog
   g. sweeping the garage
   h. folding the laundry and putting it away

4. Which of these fast food meals is a light meal?

   a. a small hamburger, fries and low fat (2%) milk
   b. a fish sandwich and orange juice
   c. a small hamburger and a diet soda
   d. a broccoli and cheese stuffed potato

8

5. How could Martha talk to 10-year-old Tami about the two birthday parties in one weekend?

   a. Ask her to think of three ways she could handle it.
   b. Tell her to go to the parties and eat the food served.
   c. Suggest that she skip one of the parties.

QUIZ #8 (Continued)

FINAL

1. At 11, Megan has not done well in interests she has tried. She was clumsy at tennis and whimpy at soccer. What strategies should her mother try?

   a. Try other sports at which she might excel, such as power walking or hiking.
   b. Focus on enjoyment, not achievement. Help her find something she enjoys, perhaps dance or aerobics.
   c. Try non-sports, non-competitive interests, like starting a weekly stamp club with a couple of friends.
   d. Reassure her that she doesn't have to love or be great at every interest immediately.

2. In Mary's culture, men do not do household chores. She feels uncomfortable asking her son John to do them. How could she get past this barrier?

   a. Think about the life John will lead. Will someone pick up after him in the future?
   b. Look at chores as games, something to keep the children active and busy.
   c. Assign him only traditional male chores to do.

3. An 11 year-old (with instruction and parental non-perfectionism) is capable of successfully:
   a. vacuuming the carpet
   b. scouring the bath tub
   c. ironing shirts
   d. folding and putting away the family's wash
   e. making a healthy bag lunch
   f. straightening the kitchen cupboards
   g. making tuna sandwiches and a fruit salad for dinner
   h. sorting, washing and drying the laundry

4. Which of these fast food meals is a light meal?

   a. fried chicken and a green salad, no dressing
   b. a double cheeseburger and a diet soda
   c. the salad bar: lettuce, macaroni salad, sliced egg, jello salad, carrots and cheese
   d. chicken salad (1 teaspoon of dressing) and diet soda

8

5. You dine at an Italian restaurant that serves complete, wonderful five-course meals. Which of these meals is reasonably healthful and you can finish and be just satisfied, not full?

   a. the minestrone soup, a piece of bread and a salad with dressing on the side
   b. a salad with dressing on the side and an entree of spaghetti and marinara sauce
   c. baked chicken with mushrooms, rice and peas
   d. the entire five course meal, eating 1/3 of each course

Practice Quiz Answers: 1.C 2. B,C 3.ALL 4.C 5.A

THE ACTIONS

Each of us agrees to the following this week:

1. Complete the readings, practices and quizzes for Section 9.

2. Record on my SUPPORT record each day.

3. Meet at least 4 of my 5 SUPPORT goals.

4. If overweight, lose weight: ☐ ¼ + pound **OR** ☐ 1 + pounds.

THE REWARDS

If **we all** do all of these actions, then **we all** receive our rewards:

_____'s reward:_____
child's name   provided by when?_____

_____'s reward:_____
parent's name   provided by when?_____

_____'s reward:_____
parent's name   provided by when?_____

When the family receives the rewards, _____ will be responsible for
                                         parent's name
rewarding the child. The child will be sure the parents have given themselves their reward.

_____   _____
parent's signature   child's signature

_____   _____
parent's signature   date

9

PARENT SUPPORT #9

	MON.	TUES.	WED.	THURS.	FRI.	SAT.	SUN.	TOTAL	MET MY GOAL?
We took FAMILY TIME each day to review these records and to praise each other.								___ days	YES NO
I watched no more than 0 2 4 6 8 hours of TV								___ hours	YES NO
I EXERCISED for 150 200 250 300 400 minutes or more.								___ minutes	YES NO
I correctly filled out MY FOOD! on 2 or more days.								___ days	YES NO
GOAL OF THE WEEK: Our family ate dinner together on ___ or more days.								___ days	YES NO

TOTAL NUMBER OF GOALS MET ⇒

217

9

MY FOOD!

Day _____

Time	Food or Drink	Amount	Free	Light	Heavy	Junk	Milk	Meat/Bns.	Veg.	Fruit	Grain	Hunger Score* Start	Stop

Ate mainly FREE & LIGHT Foods?   yes   no

Ate breakfast, lunch, dinner?   yes   no

Hungry when started eating?   yes   no

Totals: -   -   -   -

Stopped eating before full?   yes no

MY FOOD!

Day _____

Time	Food or Drink	Amount	Free	Light	Heavy	Junk	Milk	Meat/Bns.	Veg.	Fruit	Grain	Hunger Score* Start	Stop

9

Ate mainly FREE & LIGHT Foods?   yes   no

Ate breakfast, lunch, dinner?   yes   no

Hungry when started eating?   yes   no

Totals: -   -   -   -

Stopped eating before full?   yes no

* 1 = very hungry, 2 = hungry, 3 = just satisfied, 4 = full, 5 = very full

19. ASSESSING YOUR PROGRESS

You have now completed SHAPEDOWN. You have finished but you are not done. Just the way SHAPEDOWN meant you never had to go on a diet, it also means never going off one. That's right, the lifestyle changes you have made need your continued attention.

During the coming months you'll fine tune the changes you've made. You will need to make substantial alterations each season and each time your family changes—in other words, almost continuously. What works in June for exercise falls flat on its face in December. When your family can no longer bear the neighborhood walks, you'll stop them and perhaps stop exercising altogether unless you find a substitute. If you stop problem solving, the problems mount up and chip away at your healthier lifestyle. Then you're back to square one—and even worse, you've tried and failed. Your child has tried and failed.

Right now let's take time to take stock of what you have accomplished so far. In the next chapter you will set goals and decide on the support you'll need to keep your focus on weight and to lift you over the rough spots.

SELF ASSESSMENT

19. ASSESSING YOUR PROGRESS

To assess your family, please read each of the sentences below. Choose the one response for each question that best describes what you or your child did or felt **during the last week**. Afterwards you will score this questionnaire.

FAMILY HABIT INVENTORY

Example:

My child snacked on fruit, vegetables or other low fat, low sugar foods.

_____	always	4
_____	often	3
_____	sometimes	2
✓	rarely	1
_____	never	0

My child snacked on fruit, vegetables or other low fat, low sugar foods.

_____	always	4
_____	often	3
_____	sometimes	2
_____	rarely	1
_____	never	0

My child had fried or fatty foods like fried chicken, bacon, eggs, fries, chips or ice cream.

_____	always	0
_____	often	1
_____	sometimes	2
_____	rarely	3
_____	never	4

My child ate at least one cup of vegetables a day.

_____	always	4
_____	often	3
_____	sometimes	2
_____	rarely	1
_____	never	0

1. The foods my child eats.　　　　　　　　　Total _____

9

My child had second helpings of food.

	always	0
_____	often	1
_____	sometimes	2
_____	rarely	3
_____	never	4

My child ate a lot when he or she snacked.

	always	0
_____	often	1
_____	sometimes	2
_____	rarely	3
_____	never	4

My child ate small amounts at dinner.

	always	4
_____	often	3
_____	sometimes	2
_____	rarely	1
_____	never	0

2. How much my child eats.   Total _____

My child skipped breakfast.

	always	0
_____	often	1
_____	sometimes	2
_____	rarely	3
_____	never	4

My child ate at least four times a day.

	always	4
_____	often	3
_____	sometimes	2
_____	rarely	1
_____	never	0

My child ate regular meals.

	always	4
_____	often	3
_____	sometimes	2
_____	rarely	1
_____	never	0

3. How often my child eats.   Total _____

9

The meals at home consisted mainly of low fat and low sugar foods.

_____	always	4
_____	often	3
_____	sometimes	2
_____	rarely	1
_____	never	0

At home, there were cakes, pies, cookies, candy, ice cream or chips.

_____	always	0
_____	often	1
_____	sometimes	2
_____	rarely	3
_____	never	4

There was a bowl of cut-up, ready-to-eat vegetables in the refrigerator.

_____	always	4
_____	often	3
_____	sometimes	2
_____	rarely	1
_____	never	0

4. Light family food.   Total _____

We watched television while we ate dinner.

_____	always	0
_____	often	1
_____	sometimes	2
_____	rarely	3
_____	never	4

The family ate dinner together.

_____	always	4
_____	often	3
_____	sometimes	2
_____	rarely	1
_____	never	0

We enjoyed our food, eating slowly and savoring every bite.

_____	always	4
_____	often	3
_____	sometimes	2
_____	rarely	1
_____	never	0

5. Family eating style.   Total _____

9

My child exercised hard for an hour or more on school days.

_____	always	4
_____	often	3
_____	sometimes	2
_____	rarely	1
_____	never	0

My child had no time all day to exercise.

_____	always	0
_____	often	1
_____	sometimes	2
_____	rarely	3
_____	never	4

My child exercised for at least two hours on the weekend.

_____	always	4
_____	often	3
_____	sometimes	2
_____	rarely	1
_____	never	0

6. How much my child exercises.

Total _____

My child watched an hour or less of television per day.

_____	always	4
_____	often	3
_____	sometimes	2
_____	rarely	1
_____	never	0

My child seemed bored or idle.

_____	always	0
_____	often	1
_____	sometimes	2
_____	rarely	3
_____	never	4

My child had nothing, other than homework, to do after school.

_____	always	0
_____	often	1
_____	sometimes	2
_____	rarely	3
_____	never	4

7. My child's active lifestyle.

Total _____

9

My child was excited about learning new things.

_____	always	4
_____	often	3
_____	sometimes	2
_____	rarely	1
_____	never	0

My child did household chores.

_____	always	4
_____	often	3
_____	sometimes	2
_____	rarely	1
_____	never	0

My child had interests and activities that he or she really enjoyed.

_____	always	4
_____	often	3
_____	sometimes	2
_____	rarely	1
_____	never	0

8. My child's enriching lifestyle.

Total _____

On the weekends we took a walk, played sports or exercised together.

_____	always	4
_____	often	3
_____	sometimes	2
_____	rarely	1
_____	never	0

Our family time included exercising together.

_____	always	4
_____	often	3
_____	sometimes	2
_____	rarely	1
_____	never	0

All we did together as a family was talk, eat or watch television.

_____	always	0
_____	often	1
_____	sometimes	2
_____	rarely	3
_____	never	4

9. Active family time.

Total _____

9

I felt guilty, sad or fearful about my child's weight or eating.

_____	always	0
_____	often	1
_____	sometimes	2
_____	rarely	3
_____	never	4

I felt angry or resentful about my child's weight or eating.

_____	always	0
_____	often	1
_____	sometimes	2
_____	rarely	3
_____	never	4

I accepted completely the body build my child inherited.

_____	always	4
_____	often	3
_____	sometimes	2
_____	rarely	1
_____	never	0

10. Feelings about my child's weight.   Total_____

I told myself that my child really isn't that heavy.

_____	always	0
_____	often	1
_____	sometimes	2
_____	rarely	3
_____	never	4

I thought that my child would grow into his weight.

_____	always	0
_____	often	1
_____	sometimes	2
_____	rarely	3
_____	never	4

I believed that the weight problem would take care of itself.

_____	always	0
_____	often	1
_____	sometimes	2
_____	rarely	3
_____	never	4

11. Facing my child's weight problem.   Total_____

9

My child kept asking for food again and again until I gave in.

_____	always	0
_____	often	1
_____	sometimes	2
_____	rarely	3
_____	never	4

I felt that I could not make my child exercise.

_____	always	0
_____	often	1
_____	sometimes	2
_____	rarely	3
_____	never	4

I found it difficult to say "no" to my child and make it stick.

_____	always	0
_____	often	1
_____	sometimes	2
_____	rarely	3
_____	never	4

12.   Setting limits and following through.   Total _____

When my child overate I lectured or scolded him or her.

_____	always	0
_____	often	1
_____	sometimes	2
_____	rarely	3
_____	never	4

When I wanted to reward or treat my child I gave him or her food.

_____	always	0
_____	often	1
_____	sometimes	2
_____	rarely	3
_____	never	4

I complimented my child on exercising or eating.

_____	always	4
_____	often	3
_____	sometimes	2
_____	rarely	1
_____	never	0

13.   Rewarding my child positively.   Total _____

9

I asked my child about his or her feelings and needs.

_____	always	4
_____	often	3
_____	sometimes	2
_____	rarely	1
_____	never	0

I listened attentively to my child.

_____	always	4
_____	often	3
_____	sometimes	2
_____	rarely	1
_____	never	0

When I asked questions, I got honest answers from my child.

_____	always	4
_____	often	3
_____	sometimes	2
_____	rarely	1
_____	never	0

14. Communicating with my child.

Total _____

I reassured my child that despite discomfort he or she would be OK.

_____	always	4
_____	often	3
_____	sometimes	2
_____	rarely	1
_____	never	0

I praised my child.

_____	always	4
_____	often	3
_____	sometimes	2
_____	rarely	1
_____	never	0

I gave my child direct messages that I accept and value him or her.

_____	always	4
_____	often	3
_____	sometimes	2
_____	rarely	1
_____	never	0

15. Building on my child's well-being.

Total _____

9

We parent(s) exercised for at least 60 minutes three or more times.	_____ always	4
	_____ often	3
	_____ sometimes	2
	_____ rarely	1
	_____ never	0
We parent(s) were normal weight or slowly losing weight.	_____ always	4
	_____ often	3
	_____ sometimes	2
	_____ rarely	1
	_____ never	0
We parent(s) ate mainly low fat and low sugar foods.	_____ always	4
	_____ often	3
	_____ sometimes	2
	_____ rarely	1
	_____ never	0
16. Role model for exercise, food and weight.	Total _____	

Now go back and score each group of three questions. Total each group of scores. Record the total scores on the Family Habit Inventory Summary on the next page.

9

FAMILY HABIT INVENTORY SUMMARY

BEHAVIOR OR FEELING	SCORE
Food	
1. The foods my child eats	_____
2. How much my child eats	_____
3. How often my child eats	_____
4. Light family food	_____
5. Family eating style	_____
Activity	
6. How much my child exercises	_____
7. My child's active lifestyle	_____
8. My child's enriching lifestyle	_____
9. Active family time	_____
Parenting	
10. Feelings about my child's weight	_____
11. Facing the weight problem	_____
12. Setting limits and following through	_____
13. Rewarding my child positively	_____
14. Communicating with my child	_____
15. Building on my child's well-being	_____
16. Role model for exercise, food and weight	_____
TOTAL SCORE	_____

Scores for each area range from 0 to 12. Total scores range from 0 to 192. Higher scores indicate behaviors and attitudes associated with successful weight management in children.

9

Look back at your FAMILY HABIT INVENTORY SUMMARY and compare it to the SUMMARY you completed at the end of Chapter 2. List the areas that have improved the most during SHAPEDOWN. Also list the areas you wish to improve.

Improved during SHAPEDOWN:
(Lower scores in Chapter 2 are now higher)

_____

_____

_____

_____

_____

_____

_____

Areas to improve:
(Scores still low)

_____

_____

_____

_____

_____

_____

_____

9

In the short weeks that you have experienced SHAPEDOWN, your family has changed, but studies show that permanent change takes longer, usually two years or more. We suggest that you continue with SHAPEDOWN, either with frequent contact with your instructor (monthly visits) or by enrolling in ADVANCED SHAPEDOWN or the TEEN SHAPEDOWN program.

ADVANCED SHAPEDOWN

If your child is 12 or younger, we recommend ADVANCED SHAPEDOWN. Only families that have completed the entire SHAPEDOWN program are eligible for ADVANCED SHAPEDOWN. This program is designed to give families a more secure transition into permanent lifestyle changes.

TEEN SHAPEDOWN

If your child is 13 or older, we recommend TEEN SHAPEDOWN. In this program, your teen will be with other adolescents and receive peer support to improve his or her weight. The activities of the group program and the readings and practices in the TEEN SHAPEDOWN book reinforce the SHAPEDOWN training he or she just completed. It deepens their understandings of themselves and of their food, activity and weight and strengthens their weight management skills. In addition, the separate parent sessions will help you shift responsibility for weight to your teen and gain support from other parents who are guiding their child through the roller coaster of adolescence.

9

231

A unique feature of ADVANCED SHAPEDOWN is that it assists you in anticipating the changes your child will experience in adolescence and lays out clear strategies for dealing effectively with everything from group eating binges to declarations of vegetarianism to uncertainty about what a teen truly requires nutritionally. It is full of ideas, support and stimulation to help keep you and your child on track through the roller coaster of adolescence.

We suggest that you continue with ADVANCED SHAPEDOWN if any of these conditions are present in your child or family:

family obesity
child is still obese
child is not exercising for 60 + minutes daily
child's diet is still poor quality
child emotionally overeats
child is having peer difficulties
child is not actively pursuing interests
child watches more than 1 hour of TV daily
child doesn't communicate openly/effectively

OTHER HELP

One of the major reasons SHAPEDOWN is only delivered by teams of health professionals is that in the course of caring for a child's weight problem, families often find other issues that benefit from professional care. If medical problems, marital stress, parental emotional difficulties or family communication have come up for you and you want some assistance in resolving them, be sure to get several referrals from your SHAPEDOWN instructor.

NO HELP

If you go it alone, watch for red flags indicating you need support. Let's say you prefer not to schedule regular visits with your SHAPEDOWN instructor. You're planning on weighing weekly and taking FAMILY TIME, but that's all. Great. But watch for signs that your child isn't getting enough support. The idea is to nip the problems in the bud. If you see these warning signs, we strongly recommend that you pick up the phone and call your SHAPEDOWN instructor. Get some support to turn things around.

RED FLAGS
CONTACT YOUR SHAPEDOWN INSTRUCTOR FOR MORE SUPPORT

WEIGHT GAIN OF MORE THAN FIVE POUNDS

STOPS EATING WITH FAMILY

STOPS EXERCISING FOR MORE THAN TWO WEEKS

USES DIURETICS, DIET PILLS, OR LAXATIVES TO CONTROL WEIGHT

BINGE EATS

VOMITS TO CONTROL WEIGHT

WITHDRAWS FROM FRIENDS OR FAMILY

SIGNIFICANT CHANGE IN MOOD OR ATTITUDES

SCHOOL PERFORMANCE DECLINES SIGNIFICANTLY

9

After all this introspection, it's time to plan your own goals and actions. In addition, if you have thoughts or comments about SHAPE-DOWN please be sure to contact your instructor or write us at Balboa Publishing.

We appreciate your openness in letting us into your family and hope that your experience with SHAPEDOWN has been stimulating and rewarding. If yours is like most families, your child's weight has triggered the entire family to shift a bit here and there. May you take that subtle shift and coax it to blossom into more vitality and harmony within your family.

9

20. AFTER SHAPEDOWN

GOALS

Changes my child will make in the next three months:

eating habits: _____

activity patterns: _____

weight: _____

feelings: _____

other goals: _____

Changes our family will make in the next three months:

family food: _____

family exercise: _____

family communication: _____

parental feelings: _____

parental habits or weight: _____

other goals: _____

ACTION PLAN

We will:

_____ begin ADVANCED SHAPEDOWN

_____ begin TEEN SHAPEDOWN

_____ visit our SHAPEDOWN instructor

_____ get referrals for other kinds of help

_____ go it alone

Other actions we will take:

_____

_____

9

QUIZ #9

PRACTICE

1. In addition to the contact you will have with your SHAPEDOWN instructor in ADVANCED SHAPEDOWN, which of these are "red flags", that is, signs to schedule an additional visit with your SHAPEDOWN instructor?

   a. an observable increase in body fatness in the child
   b. a slight increase in fatness in girls during puberty
   c. use of diuretics, diet pills or laxative to lose weight
   d. puberty
   e. major change in school performance

2. It is particularly important to continue with ADVANCED SHAPEDOWN if the young person:

   a. has a triceps skinfold of greater than the 85th %tile
   b. is exercising less than one hour daily
   c. is not eating in a healthy way
   d. emotionally overeats
   e. is not involved with peers and active in interests
   f. watches more than one hour of television per day
   g. does not communicate openly and effectively with family members

FINAL

1. Which of the following are "red flags", that is signs to schedule a visit with your SHAPEDOWN instructor?

   a. an increase in body fatness in the parent
   b. a rapid weight loss in the adolescent
   c. curiosity and worries about body in early adolescence
   d. a major change in mood in the child
   e. binge eating or vomiting in the child or adolescent

2. It is particularly important to continue with ADVANCED SHAPEDOWN if the parent:

   a. wants to know more about helping an adolescent manage weight
   b. wants more group support for managing family weight problems
   c. wants the child to receive more training and support for managing his or her weight
   d. is depressed
   e. is concerned about mental difficulties
   f. wants to improve his or her limit-setting skills.

9

Practice Quiz Answers: 1.A,C,E 2. ALL

FOOD SUMMARY

FREE FOODS			
artichokes	dill pickles	mineral water	soy sauce
asparagus	eggplant	mushrooms	spices
bamboo shoots	flavorings	mustard	sprouts
broccoli	garlic	onion powder	summer squash
broth	green beans	onions	tabasco sauce
brussels sprouts	green onions	peppers	tea
cabbage	greens	popcorn, plain	tomatoes
carrots	herbs	radishes	tomato juice
cauliflower	horseradish	salad dressing, no oil	vegetable juice
celery	jicama	sauerkraut	vinegar
cinnamon	lemons	soda, diet	water
coffee	lettuce	soda water	water chestnuts
cucumbers	limes	sour pickles	zucchini

LIGHT FOODS			
apples	cereal, unsweetened	hamburger buns	rice
applesauce, canned	cheese, reduced fat	hominy grits	rice cakes
without sugar	cherries	lentils	spaghetti, plain
apricots	chicken, light	meat, lean red,	split peas
bananas	meat, no skin	all fat removes	strawberries
bagel (plain)	clear soups	milk, non-fat	sweet potatoes
blackberries	cottage cheese	milk, low fat (1%)	tangerines
black-eyed peas	low-fat	nectarines	tortillas
beans, dried	crackers, low-fat	oranges	tuna, canned
beans, refried	english muffins	papaya	in water
biscuits	fish	peaches	turkey, light
bran	fruit, canned	peas	meat, no skin
bread	in water	pineapple	vegetable soups
bread sticks	fruit, canned	plums	watermelons
bulgar	in juice	potatoes	winter squash
buttermilk	grapefruit	prunes	yogurt, plain
cantaloupe	grapes	raisins	low-fat

HEAVY FOODS			
almonds	cottage cheese,	macaroni &	potato salad
applesauce,	creamed	cheese	pudding
sweetened	crackers, high-fat	macaroni salad	stuffing
avocado	cream soups	meat, red	sunflower seeds
cereal, sweetened	eggs	milk, chocolate	taco shells
cheese	fish, fried	milk, ice	tofu
chicken, fried	fish sticks	milk, low-fat (2%)	tuna, pack in
chicken or turkey	french toast	milk, whole	oil
dark meat	fries	muffins	turkey hot dogs
chicken or turkey	fruit, canned	pancakes	vegetables in sauce
with skin	in syrup	peanut butter	waffles
chili	fruit rolls	peanuts	yogurt, flavored
coconut	granola	pizza	yogurt, low-fat
corn bread	hash browns	popcorn, buttered	frozen

JUNK FOODS			
bacon	doughnuts	kool-aid	salt
beer	fruit drinks	lard	salt pork
butter	granola candy	liquor	sausage
candy	bars	margarine	shakes
candy cereal	gravy	marmalade	sherbet
cakes	gum	mayonnaise	sodas, regular
chips	half and half	oil	sour cream
chocolate	honey	olives	sugar
chocolate topping	hot dogs	pastries	sweet pickles
cookies	ice cream	pies	syrup
cream cheese	jam	popsicles	tartar sauce
cream sauce	jello	salad dressing	whipped cream
croissants	jelly	salami	wine

MY WEIGHT RECORD

Write down your starting weight. This weight corresponds to the "0" at the black dot under week 1. Compare your weight each week with your starting weight. For example, if your starting weight was 162 pounds and your weight at week 2 was 161 pounds, you should put a dot at -1 under week 2. Then connect the two dots. Continue plotting like this each week.

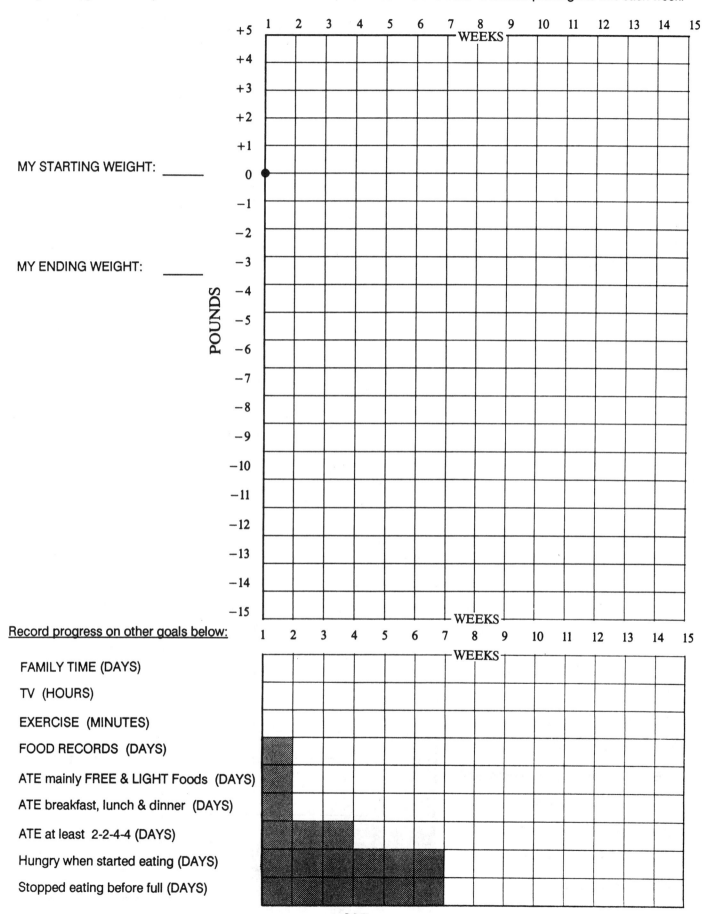

MY STARTING WEIGHT: _____

MY ENDING WEIGHT: _____

POUNDS

Record progress on other goals below:

FAMILY TIME (DAYS)

TV (HOURS)

EXERCISE (MINUTES)

FOOD RECORDS (DAYS)

ATE mainly FREE & LIGHT Foods (DAYS)

ATE breakfast, lunch & dinner (DAYS)

ATE at least 2-2-4-4 (DAYS)

Hungry when started eating (DAYS)

Stopped eating before full (DAYS)

237

MY WEIGHT RECORD

Write down your starting weight. This weight corresponds to the "0" at the black dot under week 1. Compare your weight each week with your starting weight. For example, if your starting weight was 162 pounds and your weight at week 2 was 161 pounds, you should put a dot at -1 under week 2. Then connect the two dots. Continue plotting like this each week.

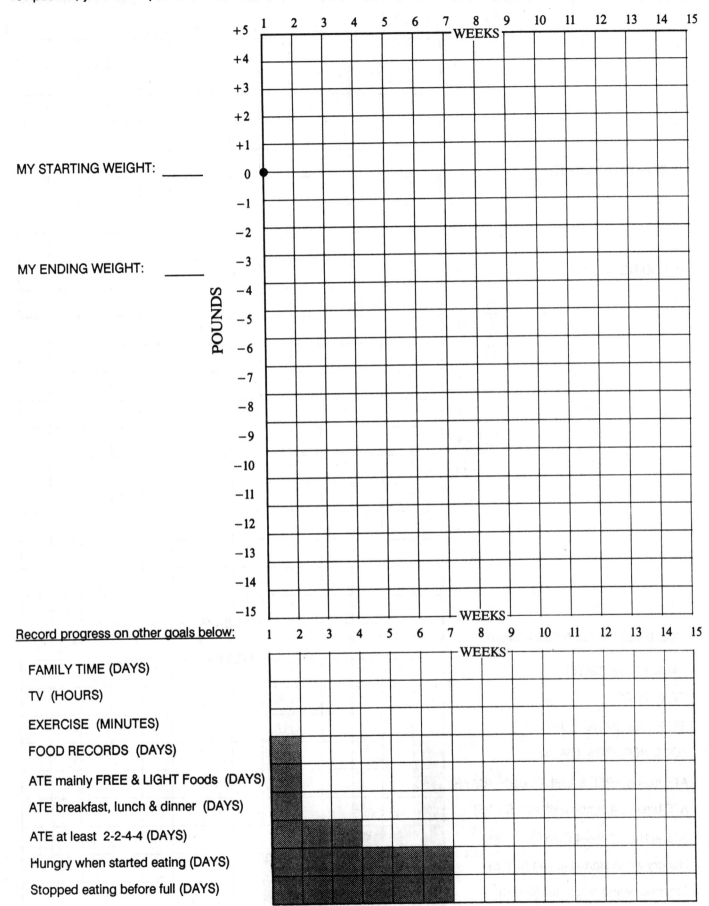

MY STARTING WEIGHT: _____

MY ENDING WEIGHT: _____

POUNDS

WEEKS

Record progress on other goals below:

FAMILY TIME (DAYS)

TV (HOURS)

EXERCISE (MINUTES)

FOOD RECORDS (DAYS)

ATE mainly FREE & LIGHT Foods (DAYS)

ATE breakfast, lunch & dinner (DAYS)

ATE at least 2-2-4-4 (DAYS)

Hungry when started eating (DAYS)

Stopped eating before full (DAYS)

238

MY BODY

	Date ___/___/___	Date ___/___/___	Date ___/___/___
Weight (pounds)			
Height (inches)			
Body Mass Index (BMI)			
Waist circumference (inches)			
Hip circumference (inches)			
Waist: hip ratio			
Blood Pressure	___/___	___/___	___/___
Strength: curl-ups (# in 1 min.)			
Flexibility: sit and reach (inches)			
Endurance: step test (min./sec. up to 3/0)	___/___	___/___	___/___
step test (1 min. heart rate)			

MY BODY

	Date ___/___/___	Date ___/___/___	Date ___/___/___
Weight (pounds)			
Height (inches)			
Body Mass Index (BMI)			
Waist circumference (inches)			
Hip circumference (inches)			
Waist: hip ratio	___/___	___/___	___/___
Blood Pressure			
Strength: curl-ups (# in 1 min.)			
Flexibility: sit and reach (inches)			
Endurance: step test (min./sec. up to 3/0)	___/___	___/___	___/___
step test (1 min. heart rate)			

MY FOOD!

Day _____

Time	Food or Drink	Amount	Food Type			
			Free	Light	Heavy	Junk

Ate mainly FREE & LIGHT Foods?   yes   no   Ate breakfast, lunch & dinner?   yes   no

MY FOOD!

Day _____

Time	Food or Drink	Amount	Food Type			
			Free	Light	Heavy	Junk

Ate mainly FREE & LIGHT Foods?   yes   no   Ate breakfast, lunch & dinner?   yes   no

MY FOOD!

Day _____

Time	Food or Drink	Amount	Free	Light	Heavy	Junk	Milk	Meat/Bns.	Veg.	Fruit	Grain

Ate mainly FREE & LIGHT Foods?　yes　no

Ate breakfast, lunch, dinner?　yes　no

Totals:　–　–　–　–

MY FOOD!

Day _____

Time	Food or Drink	Amount	Free	Light	Heavy	Junk	Milk	Meat/Bns.	Veg.	Fruit	Grain

Ate mainly FREE & LIGHT Foods?　yes　no

Ate breakfast, lunch, dinner?　yes　no

Totals:　–　–　–　–

MY FOOD!

Day _____

Time	Food or Drink	Amount	Free	Light	Heavy	Junk	Milk	Meat/Bns.	Veg.	Fruit	Grain	Hunger Score* Start	Stop

Ate mainly **FREE & LIGHT** Foods? yes no

Ate breakfast, lunch, dinner? yes no

Hungry when started eating? yes no

Totals: – – – –

Stopped eating before full? yes no

MY FOOD!

Day _____

Time	Food or Drink	Amount	Free	Light	Heavy	Junk	Milk	Meat/Bns.	Veg.	Fruit	Grain	Hunger Score* Start	Stop

Ate mainly **FREE & LIGHT** Foods? yes no

Ate breakfast, lunch, dinner? yes no

Hungry when started eating? yes no

Totals: – – – –

Stopped eating before full? yes no

* 1 = very hungry, 2 = hungry, 3 = just satisfied, 4 = full, 5 = very full

FOOD RECORD

Day_____   Name_____

	TIME	FOOD	AMOUNT
Morning			
Afternoon			
Evening			

T-31.0

The Food Guide Pyramid
A Guide to Daily Food Choices

MyPyramid
STEPS TO A HEALTHIER YOU
MyPyramid.gov

GRAINS	VEGETABLES	FRUITS	MILK	MEAT & BEANS
Make half your grains whole	Vary your veggies	Focus on fruits	Get your calcium-rich foods	Go lean with protein

GRAINS	VEGETABLES	FRUITS	MILK	MEAT & BEANS
Eat at least 3 oz. of whole-grain cereals, breads, crackers, rice, or pasta every day 1 oz. is about 1 slice of bread, about 1 cup of breakfast cereal, or ½ cup of cooked rice, cereal, or pasta	Eat more dark-green veggies like broccoli, spinach, and other dark leafy greens Eat more orange vegetables like carrots and sweetpotatoes Eat more dry beans and peas like pinto beans, kidney beans, and lentils	Eat a variety of fruit Choose fresh, frozen, canned, or dried fruit Go easy on fruit juices	Go low-fat or fat-free when you choose milk, yogurt, and other milk products If you don't or can't consume milk, choose lactose-free products or other calcium sources such as fortified foods and beverages	Choose low-fat or lean meats and poultry Bake it, broil it, or grill it Vary your protein routine — choose more fish, beans, peas, nuts, and seeds

For a 2,000-calorie diet, you need the amounts below from each food group. To find the amounts that are right for you, go to MyPyramid.gov.

Eat 6 oz. every day	Eat 2½ cups every day	Eat 2 cups every day	Get 3 cups every day; for kids aged 2 to 8, it's 2	Eat 5½ oz. every day

Find your balance between food and physical activity

Be sure to stay within your daily calorie needs.

Be physically active for at least 30 minutes most days of the week.

About 60 minutes a day of physical activity may be needed to prevent weight gain.

For sustaining weight loss, at least 60 to 90 minutes a day of physical activity may be required.

Children and teenagers should be physically active for 60 minutes every day, or most days.

Know the limits on fats, sugars, and salt (sodium)

Make most of your fat sources from fish, nuts, and vegetable oils.

Limit solid fats like butter, stick margarine, shortening, and lard, as well as foods that contain these.

Check the Nutrition Facts label to keep saturated fats, *trans* fats, and sodium low.

Choose food and beverages low in added sugars. Added sugars contribute calories with few, if any, nutrients.

MyPyramid.gov
STEPS TO A HEALTHIER YOU

245

U.S. Department of Agriculture
Center for Nutrition Policy and Promotion

USDA

EXERCISE INVENTORY

Aerobic Exercise — Keep track of how many minutes you exercise, aerobically, that is, when your heart rate after exercise is 12 to 15 beats in 6 seconds. Mark an "X" in each of the boxes below for each 10 minutes of aerobic exercise you do.

Day	Minutes of Exercise	Type of Exercise

Minutes of Exercise scale: 0 10 20 30 40 50 60 70 80 90

Day											Type of Exercise
MON											_____
TUE											_____
WED											_____
THU											_____
FRI											_____
SAT											_____
SUN											_____

Flexibility Exercise — Circle the days you stretched, danced or did other forms of movement that improved your flexibility.

MON   TUE   WED   THU   FRI   SAT   SUN

What did you do?_____

Strength Exercise — Circle the days you lifted weights, did calisthenics or other forms of exercise that improved your strength.

MON   TUE   WED   THU   FRI   SAT   SUN

What did you do?_____

MY TARGET HABIT:_____ Name_____

MY GOAL:
    WHAT I WILL DO:_____
    HOW MANY DAYS: ☐ 1   ☐ 2   ☐ 3   ☐ 4   ☐ 5   ☐ 6   ☐ 7

CHANGED MY HABIT?

	YES	NO	WHAT I DID:
MONDAY	☐	☐	_____
			_____
TUESDAY	☐	☐	_____
			_____
WEDNESDAY	☐	☐	_____
			_____
THURSDAY	☐	☐	_____
			_____
FRIDAY	☐	☐	_____
			_____
SATURDAY	☐	☐	_____
			_____
SUNDAY	☐	☐	_____
			_____

REACHED MY GOAL?   ☐ YES   ☐ ALMOST   ☐ NO

MY FEELINGS ABOUT MY PROGRESS:

_____

_____

The one change I will make this week:

_____

Strategies I will use to make this change happen:

1. _____

2. _____

3. _____

P-1.0

© SHAPEDOWN

✂ —

ACTION PLAN

The one change I will make this week:

_____

Strategies I will use to make this change happen:

1. _____

2. _____

3. _____

P-1.0

© SHAPEDOWN

Directions: Please read each sentence below and answer either true, false or not sure.

1. Overweight people usually eat more than normal weight people do.   true   false   unsure

2. A healthy weight loss is three pounds per week.   true   false   unsure

3. There are two types of fitness: endurance and strength.   true   false   unsure

4. Fruit-flavored yogurt is a low-calorie food.   true   false   unsure

5. Overweight people usually exercise as much as normal weight people do.   true   false   unsure

6. Weight lifting is aerobic exercise.   true   false   unsure

7. Eating noodles, bread or potatoes is fattening.   true   false   unsure

8. Doing sit-ups takes fat off of your stomach.   true   false   unsure

9. Skipping breakfast helps you lose weight.   true   false   unsure

10. If you exercise 20 minutes each day you will lose weight.   true   false   unsure

11. Thin people should eat a diet low in fat and sugar.   true   false   unsure

12. About 75 percent of the calories from cheese is fat.   true   false   unsure

13. Exercise is aerobic if your heart rate afterward is 10 to 15 beats in 6 seconds.   true   false   unsure

14. To lose weight, do not read or watch television while you eat.   true   false   unsure

15. Talking about your feelings helps you lose weight.   true   false   unsure

16. To lose weight, stop eating when you are barely satisfied.   true   false   unsure

17. You can go to parties often and still lose weight.   true   false   unsure

18. Eating at salad bars can be fattening.   true   false   unsure

19. What you think controls how you feel.   true   false   unsure

20. To lose weight you must change your habits all seven days of the week.   true   false   unsure

21. Playing baseball is aerobic exercise.   true   false   unsure

22. When you diet you are good; and when you binge, you are bad.   true   false   unsure
       true   false   unsure

23. Red meat is always higher in fat than chicken.   true   false   unsure

24. Bananas are fattening.   true   false   unsure

25. You will find out how much fat you've gained or lost by weighing yourself often.   true   false   unsure

KNOW Correct responses are listed below . Count one point for each correct response. Range is 0 to 25. Score the response "unsure" as 0.

1.	false
2.	false
3.	false
4.	false
5.	false
6.	false
7.	false
8.	false
9.	false
10.	false
11.	true
12.	true
13.	true
14.	true
15.	true
16.	true
17.	true
18.	true
19.	true
20.	false
21.	false
22.	false
23.	false
24.	false
25.	false

HABIT INVENTORY

Think about the last seven days. How often did you:

	never				always
exercise for one hour	1	2	3	4	5
exercise for endurance	1	2	3	4	5
exercise for strength	1	2	3	4	5
exercise for flexibility	1	2	3	4	5
eat mainly FREE FOODS and LIGHT FOODS	1	2	3	4	5
eat three to five times a day	1	2	3	4	5
eat small or average amounts	1	2	3	4	5
use a thin eating style	1	2	3	4	5
have a thin eating environment	1	2	3	4	5
eat when you were hungry	1	2	3	4	5
stop eating when you were just satisfied	1	2	3	4	5
manage my non-hunger cues	1	2	3	4	5
keep active, not bored	1	2	3	4	5
speak up, ask for what you want, say what you think	1	2	3	4	5
open up, talk about your feelings	1	2	3	4	5
manage special occasion eating	1	2	3	4	5
manage binge eating	1	2	3	4	5
have a role for your family in managing your weight	1	2	3	4	5
have a role for your friends in managing your weight	1	2	3	4	5

T-35.0

I want to share SHAPEDOWN with the person named below. Please:

____ send this person the SHAPEDOWN parent guide and child'or teen workbook I've ordered below and the names and addresses of the three SHAPEDOWN programs nearest to him or her. (Complete order form below.)

____ send this person complete SHAPEDOWN information and the names and addresses of the three SHAPEDOWN programs nearest to him or her.

———————————— CONSIDER ADVANCED SHAPEDOWN ————————————

____ send me a copy of ADVANCED SHAPEDOWN.

ADVANCED SHAPEDOWN is for all SHAPEDOWN families to support the changes made in SHAPEDOWN in becoming permanent. The guide is a helping hand that stimulates you to keep on track, further sharpen your skills in food, exercise and communication and prepares you for the changing needs of the adolescent. For your copy of the ADVANCED SHAPEDOWN Guide, check with your SHAPEDOWN instructor or use this form to order directly from the publisher.

———————————————————— ORDER FORM ————————————————————

Quantity	Item #	Description	Cost	Amount
_____	451	SHAPEDOWN - Level 1 Workbook (Ages 6 to 8)	24.95	_____
_____	452	SHAPEDOWN - Level 2 Workbook (Ages 9 or 10)	24.95	_____
_____	454	SHAPEDOWN - Level 3 Workbook (Ages 11 or 12)	24.95	_____
_____	453	SHAPEDOWN Parent's Guide To Supporting Your Child	24.95	_____
_____	457	ADVANCED SHAPEDOWN Children's Workbook	24.95	_____
_____	459	ADVANCED SHAPEDOWN Child's Parent Guide	24.95	_____
_____	401	SHAPEDOWN Just For Teens! Workbook (ages 12-20)	24.95	_____
_____	402	SHAPEDOWN Parent's Guide To Supporting Your Teen	24.95	_____
		Shipping per book	4.00	_____
			TOTAL	_____

Payment method: ☐ Visa/Mastercard #_____ Exp. ___/___

☐ Check (payable to BALBOA PUBLISHING)

SHIP TO:

Name _____

Address _____

City _____ State _____ Zip _____

Please mail your order to:

BALBOA PUBLISHING
1323 San Anselmo Avenue
San Anselmo, CA 94960

Or you may order on the Internet: **www.shapedown.com**

Or phone (415-453-8886), fax (415-453-8888), or email (shapedown@aol.com)your order.